O9-AIE-390

vegan under pressure

PERFECT VEGAN MEALS
MADE QUICK AND EASY
IN YOUR PRESSURE COOKER

By Jill Nussinow, MS, RDN

Houghton Mifflin Harcourt

Boston   New York

Copyright © 2016 by Jill Nussinow, MS, RDN

Photography © 2016 by Lauren Volo
Illustrations by Olivia de Salve Villedieu
Book design by Alissa Faden

All rights reserved.

PLEASE MAKE SURE WHEN USING A PRESSURE COOKER TO FOLLOW THE
MANUFACTURER'S INSTRUCTIONS FOR SAFE USE. THE PUBLISHER AND
THE AUTHOR DISCLAIM RESPONSIBILITY FOR ANY ADVERSE EFFECTS
RESULTING DIRECTLY OR INDIRECTLY FROM INFORMATION CONTAINED IN
THIS BOOK, INCLUDING BUT NOT LIMITED TO THOSE RESULTING FROM THE
USE OF A PRESSURE COOKER.

For information about permission to reproduce selections from this book, write
to trade.permissions@hmhco.com or to Permissions, Houghton Mifflin Harcourt
Publishing Company, 3 Park Avenue, 19th Floor, New York, New York 10016.

www.hmhco.com

Names: Nussinow, Jill, author.
Title: Vegan under pressure : perfect vegan meals made quick and easy in your
   pressure cooker / by Jill Nussinow.
Description: Boston : Houghton Mifflin Harcourt, 2016.
Identifiers: LCCN 2015038039| ISBN 9780544464025 (paperback) | ISBN
   9780544464032 (ebook)
Subjects: LCSH: Vegan cooking. | Pressure cooking. | Quick and easy cooking.
   | BISAC: COOKING / Vegetarian & Vegan. | COOKING / Methods / Special
   Appliances. | COOKING / Methods / Quick & Easy. | LCGFT: Cookbooks.
Classification: LCC TX837 .N8846 2016 | DDC 641.5/636--dc23
LC record available at http://lccn.loc.gov/2015038039

Printed in the United States of America

DOC 10 9 8

4500694048

Some base recipes and reference information have been previously published
in slightly different form in *The New Fast Food* by Jill Nussinow.

CONTENTS

INTRODUCTION

I've always cared about my food, what I ate, what it tasted like, and also how healthy it was for me. That's why I became a Registered Dietitian. Food is an integral part of my personal and professional life. I have also followed a vegetarian diet, and then a vegan diet, since I was a teenager. When I first took meat off the menu and moved to a plant-based diet, I'd spend hours cooking whole grains and dried beans. I didn't have enough time in my busy life to invest in cooking the way that I wanted to eat. Almost twenty years ago I rediscovered the age-old method of pressure cooking. It had been there right under my nose all the time—in my mother's kitchen.

My mother used a pressure cooker for standbys like pot roast, coq au vin, and lentils. As a kid, I feared the hissing pot with the scary jiggler on top. I avoided the kitchen when it was in use. Mom's cooker actually blew its top once, resulting in food everywhere, including the ceiling. I swore off the idea of using a pressure cooker until my growing love of beans and grains cooked from scratch coincided with the advent of the safer, modern, spring-valve cookers in the early 1990s, providing the impetus for me to join the pressure cooking crowd.

At the time few were extolling the device's virtues. But Lorna Sass, "the queen of pressure cooking" and my mentor, had just written her book *Cooking Under Pressure* in 1989 and begun her one-woman crusade. When I saw Lorna in action, I realized that I needed to hop on the bandwagon and learn everything I could about the art of pressure cooking.

When I got my hands on a modern, sleek, and shiny stainless steel pressure cooker in 1995, I started experimenting and quickly was able to produce amazing results—dishes full of intense flavor in a matter of minutes. Shortly thereafter, I began teaching classes to educate others about the virtues of pressure cooking. Becoming a vegan pressure cooking expert has taken time and experimentation to refine my techniques and build my recipe repertoire.

Using a pressure cooker has changed my cooking life and my health. Time and energy spent in the kitchen has decreased while my energy level and diet of fabulous healthy food has improved. Gone are the excuses for not eating better-tasting whole foods. I can cook flavorful beans, vegetables, soups, stews, fillings, sauces, and so much more in an hour or less—and now you can too.

Pressure cooking is not foolproof, and it's not difficult: Using a pressure cooker is a skill that you can learn with expert guidance and attentiveness. It differs from traditional stovetop cooking or what I learned in nutrition school. In spite of the old wives' tales and even the story of my mom's pressure cooking mayhem, the modern pressure cooker is extremely safe when the instructions are followed.

First and foremost: pay attention—to the food you are cooking, the size and type of your cooker, the heat source, altitude, and amount of liquid (both in the food itself and additional liquid). Just like when you learned to drive a car, ride a bicycle, or any other new skill, practice and focus leads to success.

Start with the basics: Get to know your cooker. Read the manufacturer's instructions carefully. The biggest variable will be the food. One batch of dried beans may be very different from the next. The new potatoes picked yesterday cook faster than regular supermarket potatoes. The reason? Moisture content in freshly picked fruits and vegetables is higher than the moisture in produce that has been sitting on the shelves, or traveling, for days.

Take notes as you use these recipes, and adjust time and liquid for your pressure cooker, ingredients, preferences, and environment. Remember that the best part of cooking with the pressure cooker is that even if the result is overcooked food, you can almost always use it. Well-cooked beans, grains, and vegetables can easily become dips, spreads, soups, or burgers.

Do you live at higher altitudes? You probably know that it takes longer to cook. The pressure cooker will make seemingly impossible-to-cook dishes, such as dried beans, possible. You can even use your pressure cooker to boil water more quickly.

Many people are so excited to get their pressure cooker and can't wait to start cooking. But the first recipe that I suggest you try is the water test (page 17), which will not result in anything to eat or drink, as the water is at almost 250°F—too hot to even make a good cup of tea. However, you will learn how your cooker works and what to expect from it when it reaches pressure.

While I generally encourage creative cooking, when you are learning to use a pressure cooker, it's not the time for experimentation. Wait until you have some practice, hone your pressure cooking technique, and then let your creative juices flow.

6 Pressure Cooking Rules

Follow these rules carefully to prevent potential problems and you will quickly love the results you achieve with your cooker:

1. Read the manufacturer's instructions that come with your pressure cooker.

2. Always add the amount of liquid to the pressure cooker that the recipe specifies.

3. Never attempt to fry in the cooker.

4. Don't overfill the cooker: half full for beans or grains or foods that expand, two-thirds full for all else.

5. Don't leave the house while using a stovetop pressure cooker.

6. Read through this book and experiment with these and your own recipes for the best results.

Most people limit their vegan pressure cooking to artichokes or legumes. They are missing the full extent of what the pressure cooker can do. Grains cook in half the time of stovetop cooking. Cooking lovely legumes takes minutes, not hours, from either dried or soaked beans. Green vegetables cook quickly, in just a minute or two, and have enhanced flavor; winter vegetables such as squash, beets, celery root, and potato pieces are tender in just a few minutes; and fruit turns into tasty compotes in just a couple of minutes. Your pressure cooker will serve you well from breakfast through dessert. My goal is to teach and share with you my experience and love of pressure cooking. I use my pressure cooker daily. It has become the most important appliance that I own and I hope it will become yours too.

Yours in health,
Jill Nussinow, MS, RDN

ONE

Introduction *to* Pressure Cooking

Using a pressure cooker is not new. In fact, you might remember your mother or grandmother using one. Perhaps you remember pressure cooked food tasting wonderful (or, unfortunately, maybe eating vegetables "cooked to death" in one). The pressure cooker never went away, but with the arrival of more convenience foods and more mothers working, pressure cooker use waned. But it came back in the 1990s when my mentor and colleague, Lorna Sass, wrote the first truly modern pressure cooker cookbook: *Cooking Under Pressure*. She has been helping people use the pressure cooker ever since.

Those of us who follow a vegan (plant-based) diet know the importance of legumes and whole grains, as well as vegetables and fruit. How nice it is that pressure cooking is one of the best and easiest ways to cook beans and grains at home in no time at all, and also a terrific way to simply cook all manner of vegetables.

What the Pressure Cooker Can Do for You

Pressure cookers are making a comeback because they are a green, energy-efficient way to cook healthy food with less nutrient loss than other methods. Home cooks also appreciate that a pressure cooker saves money and cooks great-tasting food quickly.

Conventional vegan cooking can be time consuming. But a pressure cooker makes it quick and easy—most foods cook 50 to 70 percent faster than with other cooking methods, making the "not enough time to cook" excuses slip away. Consider the foundations of a healthy, plant-based diet: legumes, whole grains, and vegetables. The pressure cooker reduces cooking time for most beans from 1 hour on the stove to only 4 to 8 minutes at pressure. Whole grain cooking time, from fast-cooking quinoa to long-cooking wild rice, is cut in half. Many vegetables can cook in just a minute. The speed of pressure cooking can change your outlook on getting dinner on the table on a busy weeknight. And the pressure cooker makes cooking one-pot meals (such as chilis, stews, and curries) fast, with greatly improved flavor.

You don't have to adjust cooking times when you double or triple a recipe; the cooker takes care of that for you. Larger recipes do take longer to reach pressure, but that is before timing starts.

The cooker also uses less energy, both yours and that from your energy provider. In fact, the lower fuel consumption is one reason that pressure cookers are used extensively in home kitchens around the world, especially in Europe, India, and South America. (In 2005, in order to save fuel and keep people eating well during fuel shortages, the Cuban government sold everyone a Chinese-made pressure cooker for $5.50, payable in monthly installments. As a result, the pressure cooker is essential in Cuban kitchens and used several times a day to cook otherwise time- and fuel-intensive foods like dried beans and rice along with yucca and sweet potatoes—all fantastic parts of a vegan diet!)

You will likely find that once you start using your pressure cooker, it will become one of your most used kitchen tools, simplifying making vegan meals.

The Pressure Cooker and Your Health

If you are looking to cut back on calories and fat, most pressure cookers allow you to dry sauté foods without any oil (see page 20), which drastically cuts down on excess fat. Because pressure cooking intensifies flavors, you won't find the same loss of flavor when you sauté without oil.

In addition, many foods cooked in a pressure cooker retain the nutrient-rich cooking liquid, so you are not throwing away any nutrients. In fact, a few studies from Europe show that pressure cooking preserves more nutrients than other cooking methods, such as stovetop and microwave cooking. This is due to cooking in a sealed environment without air. Vitamin C, one of the nutrients studied, is volatile and destroyed by air.

Pressure Cooking On the Road—or Water

If you have a boat or RV, a pressure cooker might be your new best friend. Cooking in boats or RVs means limited storage space, limited fuel, and—not incidentally—needing to have a lid that stays in place on a pot! A pressure cooker addresses these concerns, along with providing the ability to cook many great meals from just a few ingredients.

A cabin or other small living space with limited access to fuel is also perfect for pressure cooking. If you are living off the grid without direct electricity or natural gas, a small pressure cooker cooks food much faster and more efficiently than any other method.

And for those concerned about potential health problems from cans and their BPA (bisphenol-A) linings, the ability to cook dried beans in just 12 minutes in the pressure cooker means that we only need to keep cans of beans around for emergencies. And there's the cost savings too: Buying organic dried beans and cooking them under pressure lets you eat organic for the cost of conventional.

Why Use a Pressure Cooker Instead of a Slow Cooker?

People love slow cookers because they can put the ingredients in before they leave for work and come home to a nice one-pot meal or crock of beans. And the slow cooker does these well—except that the ingredients tend to all blend together, resulting in a mushy product with no distinct colors, flavors, textures, or tastes. (Although beans do come out great.) However, the biggest disadvantage of the slow cooker is that you need to plan ahead and prep dinner in the morning, or more likely the night before.

If you're like me, and find yourself wondering at 3 in the afternoon or, more honestly, at 5 pm, "What am I going to make for dinner?"—then the pressure cooker is *the* kitchen tool for you. Even at that late hour, you can get a great meal on the table by 6 pm, if you have the ingredients on hand. With a well-stocked pantry, (including fridge and freezer staples) and a little fresh produce you can cook well every night. Since pressure cooking is so fast, it's easy to pre-cook big batches of beans and grains to stash in the freezer, which will simplify your cooking life. I often pull previously cooked food out of the freezer and pretend that someone cooked for me. It works every time and I thank myself for having thought ahead.

How the Pressure Cooker Works

Boiling water on the stovetop takes place at 212°F (at sea level). But if you lock a lid on a pressure cooker and let the boiling water and steam build up pressure in the pot, when the pressure reaches 15 psi (pounds per square inch), the temperature inside the cooker climbs to about 250°F. This intense, hot steam cooks the food much more quickly and causes more flavor infusion than stovetop or oven cooking.

Early pressure cookers had a "jiggler" on the top that would turn and hiss when the heat was on and it was under pressure. The jiggler in these models is the pressure valve, and consistent heat must be maintained to keep it at pressure. If you have one of these older-style jiggler cookers and like it, by all means continue using it, but be careful as some vegan foods, such as beans and grains, foam and can cause the vent to get blocked and the pot to build up too much pressure.

I prefer the modern stovetop pressure cooker that has a spring valve instead of a jiggler. Usually it is a stainless steel pot with a triple-ply bottom that works well as both a pressure-cooker pot and as a large pot for conventional stovetop cooking, so you can sauté foods before cooking under pressure. These cookers usually have at least four pressure release safety valves, compared to just a couple on the older jiggler top models, so the lid is unlikely to blow off.

In addition to the stovetop cookers, there are modern electric pressure cookers that work in the same way as the stovetop cookers but are freestanding appliances that sit on the counter. Their advantage is that you do not have to make any adjustments in heat level, as it is automatic. Although you can't place the cooking pot on the stovetop to sauté like with a stovetop cooker, most electric cookers have a sauté mode. You then switch the mode to pressure, lock on the lid, set the timer and the cooker will make heat adjustments and do all the timing.

Some electric pressure cookers also allow you to preset a start or end time so that you can have steaming hot steel-cut oats ready for you when you awaken in the morning.

Choosing a Pressure Cooker, or Two

When it comes to modern pressure cookers, you have two choices: stovetop or electric.

Stovetop Pressure Cookers

A stovetop pressure cooker is a heavy pot that cooks on your stovetop. It has a locking lid, a pressure valve, and frequently a mechanism that allows you to release the pressure. Often a steamer or pasta cooking basket is included with the cooker. Remember that your stovetop pressure cooker can also be simply used on the stove as a great heavy-bottomed pot with the glass lid, and for steaming.

The best stovetop pressure cookers are made of stainless steel. Most are made in Europe or manufactured from European designs and made in China or India. There are still some American-made pressure cookers on the market, including Presto, Mirro, and WearEver. The leading brands of European cookers include Fagor, Fissler, Kuhn Rikon, Magefesa, and WMF. Other cookers include Manttra and Futura by Hawkins from India.

When purchasing a pressure cooker, consider the cost, size, shape, materials, features, and place of manufacture. Some of these factors might be more important to you than others.

Expect to pay upwards of $50 and most often around $100 or more for a quality stainless-steel, modern stovetop pressure cooker with a triple-ply bottom from a reputable manufacturer.

To cook well, the cooker should be able to reach 15 psi (pounds per square inch) of pressure on the stovetop. Many of the newer models offer both low and high pressure settings, and some even have variable pressure settings between low and high. The lower pressure setting works well with quick-cooking vegetables, but other than that, I use it infrequently. In addition, having two pressure settings often makes for a smoother and quieter quick release, but it's not necessary.

A Bit of Pressure Cooker History

While the pressure cooker has been in existence since the late 1600s, its use in home kitchens, especially in America, is much more recent.

The National Pressure Cooker Company, the maker of Presto, was the first U.S. company to make a 4-quart pressure cooker in the 1940s, when the government was encouraging people to be self-sufficient by canning foods and planting victory gardens. The War Production Board encouraged the manufacturing and use of pressure cookers and it worked. In 1941, there were just 11 pressure cooker manufacturers. By 1945, there were more than 85. But many cookers were made of inferior metal and lacked sufficient safety features, which gave all pressure cookers a bad name.

Europeans didn't have the same metal and manufacturing issues and so had better quality cookers, making the pressure cooker a European kitchen staple. To this day, the sturdiest and most well designed pressure cookers mainly come from European manufacturers.

From the 1940s through the '60s, North Americans had very little incentive to check out pressure cookers for time-saving reasons because there were so many other available time-saving "conveniences," including microwave ovens, frozen foods, and fast food outlets.

In recent years, with the growing number of people concerned about the origins and healthfulness of their food, but still wanting to cook it quickly, it was the perfect time to take another look at the pressure cooker and see what it could do to change personal and planetary health by cooking food quickly, safely, and deliciously.

Jiggle-Top Pressure Cooker   *Electric Pressure Cooker*   *Stovetop Pressure Cooker*

A number of manufacturers offer pressure cooker sets. They usually include two pots, one pressure lid, and one glass lid. The idea is that you can cook your brown rice in one pot, remove the pressure lid, and then put on the glass lid to keep the food hot. You then use the second pot with the pressure lid to cook your curry or stew (or other main course). The cookers are more affordable this way and if you are serious about pressure cooking, you might find this dual pot combo highly efficient. Alternatively, you can buy two different sized pots, each of which comes with a pressure lid, or choose to buy one stovetop and one electric, to enjoy the benefits of both.

I have used many of the U.S. and European cookers mentioned, and they all get the job done. The biggest difference is style and features, which I explain to my classes as the difference between driving a Honda or Toyota versus driving a BMW or Mercedes. They'll all get you to your destination, but with different levels of comfort and control.

The two most important features to consider are: 1) how easily the lid locks on, some do it automatically and others need to be locked with a button; and 2) how easy it is to see when the pressure valve has popped up to indicate a cooker is at pressure. A visual indication of the pressure is important to know when your pot has reached pressure, and as a means of checking once in a while to be sure that it has maintained pressure. Most pots have a red or yellow button, or metal rod that rises. Some are easier to see than others. I like to have a stem that I can easily spot, either by height or by color, as I walk by the stove.

Old Jiggle-Top Pressure Cookers

The old jiggle-top pressure cookers required that you pay more attention and take more care when releasing pressure. You either had to wait for the pressure to release naturally or carry the hot, heavy pot to the sink and run water over it until the pressure dropped. Sometimes people got impatient and used special tactics to release the pressure, resulting in explosions and major kitchen messes. Other times pieces of food got stuck in the vent and clogged it, causing the pressure to build, the lid to blow off, and, often, the hot contents to spew. These mishaps were the exceptions, but like other bad experiences, the horror stories lingered and caused great fear and trepidation among would-be pressure cooker users.

In addition, the old jiggle-top cookers were often made of aluminum, which is reason enough to toss the one that you might currently own (even if it was your grandmother's favorite pot). Although aluminum is a good heat conductor, there's the potential for it to seep into your food, which makes its safety questionable. However, if you have a jiggle-top cooker that you love using and find that it works well for you, then feel free to continue using it with caution.

Most lids have handles, some short and some long, and some manufacturers are now making those handles detachable so that the pot lid can be cleaned more easily.

YOUR HEAT SOURCE

Most stovetop cookers will work on electric, gas, glass top, induction, butane, propane, and any other heat source. (In India, sometimes they use pressure cookers over open fire, fueled from many sources.) As long as your cooker has a triple-ply bottom, you won't have a problem with your heat (although cooking over fire is inadvisable due to the possibility of melting the handles). If you have an older, or even newer, aluminum cooker, it won't work on a glass top or induction burner, which is just one more reason to avoid aluminum.

If your burners take a while to get hot or cool down, as with most electric, glass top, and induction cook tops, you might want to use two burners at different heat levels to even out the heat: You can bring your cooker to pressure over the high heat, then move the cooker to the lower heat so that you can maintain pressure. You'll discover this with experience.

Do You Know How to Drive?

Think back to when you learned to drive. You might recall that your first driving lesson was a bit scary. There was so much to do and keep track of, and so many things that could go wrong. I remember trying to keep my hands on the wheel while looking in the mirrors, assessing traffic, and keeping centered in my lane—it all seemed like more than what was possible, in addition to trying to keep calm while my father sat nervously next to me, hoping that I would do everything perfectly. Still, I learned to drive and have done so for thousands and thousands of miles.

Learning to cook with a pressure cooker is similar to learning to drive—but you won't have an accident with another vehicle. With a multitude of safety features in modern pressure cookers, accidents are completely avoidable. You can still have problems with overcooked food, but course corrections are possible so that you will still be able to put food on the table.

Fear not…the modern pressure cooker is easy to use. But just like with any other skill, the more you practice, the better you will get. Before you know it, you will have gained confidence and will be trying new recipes.

A quick release will seem like an easy lane change on a two lane road, not a six-lane freeway. Opening the cooker to add additional ingredients will be easier than adjusting the radio with one hand on the wheel.

As for style, most pressure cookers do the same thing, so you don't necessarily need the luxury model with the high-end dashboard to get your food cooked. These are preferences.

I often equate the stovetop pressure cooker to driving a stick shift car, while the electric cooker is like driving a standard car with an automatic transmission. The stick shift provides great handling on winding roads and the autobahn, but doesn't perform nearly as well in the hills of San Francisco. Both kinds of vehicles will get you to your destination.

Many people are intimidated by the pressure cooker because they can't see what is happening inside the pot. Trust me; I have not seen the inner workings of the pot either. But I do lend you my years of pressure cooking experience to teach you to relax and enjoy the ride. Just remember to obey the "rules of the road"—and the rules of the cooker.

Electric Presure Cookers

An electric pressure cooker sits on the counter. It has a locking lid, and housing that holds and heats an insert that holds the food. The insert, which may be made of stainless steel, nonstick, or ceramic coating, can easily be removed for cleaning. Most of the new electric models are digital and have flat buttons that you push to set the time or adjust pressure. Some offer a number of cook settings, from brown and sauté, to slow cooker, to two levels of pressure cooking, and some also have a yogurt function. They often look similar to digital slow cookers except for the pressure valve on the top of the lid. They generally cost $100 to $150. Their popularity is increasing rapidly, but they don't have a long track record so you'll have to choose based on the features you are seeking rather than reputation.

When I wrote my last book I stated that I was not a fan of the electric pressure cooker. That was true—then. I now own a number of electric cookers and I see how they can be effective in the kitchen. Many of them are multifunctional, which means that one can replace some other kitchen appliances such as a steamer, slow cooker, or rice cooker, and maybe even your yogurt maker.

A colleague explained the biggest benefit of the electric cooker to me this way: "I can put the brown rice on to cook, take the dog for a walk, and come back and my rice is done. It's on the 'keep warm' setting." (But please note that not all electric pressure cookers have a "keep warm setting.")

Choosing the right electric cooker is like choosing any other appliance: Get what suits your needs. Features and options to consider include the amount of pressure achieved (most only get to 11 psi and work just fine); a sauté or browning function; the option of two pressure settings; a delayed start time, and a "keep warm" setting.

What I consider to be a drawback to the electric pressure cooker is that the maximum pressure achieved by most electric cookers falls below the American standard of 15 psi used for stovetop cookers, with most electric cookers

> A well-stocked kitchen must include a pressure cooker or two. Recently, I heard a statement on the Food Network show *The Next Iron Chef.* Alton Brown said, "You can't be an Iron Chef without knowing how to use a pressure cooker." I will amend that statement by saying, "It's hard to be a great vegan cook without using a pressure cooker."

topping out under 13 psi. However, this seems to have less of an impact than one would think, due to the second reason: The pots are well insulated, as they should be. The insulated pot, along with the lower pressure setting, causes the pot to take longer to get to pressure and longer for the pressure to release than a stovetop cooker. That additional time balances out the lower pressure so that all the recipes in this book will cook in the same time at pressure in both electric and stovetop cookers, but they will take longer to get to pressure and to release in electric models.

Once at pressure, the pot does the timing, according to the time that you set. It seems that even though the pressure is up, there is a short delay before the timer starts counting down. This is fine for longer-cooking ingredients, but detrimental when cooking tender vegetables. Some cookers allow for a timing setting of 0, which is just over 1 minute at pressure, which is good for quick-cooking vegetables.

Where things get tricky with the electric cooker is waiting for the pressure to come down naturally. Because of the insulation of the pot, it might take 20 to 30 minutes for the pressure to release instead of 10 minutes for the same

Stovetop vs. Electric Pressure Cookers

	Stovetop	Electric
PSI High pressure	13 to 15	9 to 13
PSI Low pressure	8 to 10	7 to 8
Sizes	4 quart to 10 quart	4 quart to 8 quart
Can it Sauté?	Always	Some models can
Timing	Set your own timer	Automated Timer
	Can cook for portions of a minute	1-minute intervals only
Material	Stainless steel, aluminum, nonstick	Stainless steel, nonstick, ceramic

food in a stovetop pressure cooker. The food will often be "ready" well before the pressure is released. To rectify that issue, you can quick-release the pressure (if the pot is less than half full with liquid) after 15 minutes of waiting for the pressure release. I use this method when cooking beans and grains, and it can also be used for a half-full pot of soup, stew, chili, or curry. But do not do this with a more than half-full pot of any dish with a lot of liquid.

For me, a sauté (or browning) function is essential in an electric pressure cooker since most of my recipes start by sautéing aromatics. (Although I know that many people just put all the food into the pot and hit start.) The heat of the sauté function is often hotter than medium heat on the stovetop, so food might cook faster. I also prefer a cooker with a stainless steel (rather than nonstick) insert, which eliminates any issues about the nonstick interior chipping off.

I also think it's important that an electric pressure cooker have two pressure settings (many do not), as I often use the low pressure setting for fast-cooking vegetables.

Another feature to look for is a delay start time, which allows you to set the cooker to start at a later time. Vegan food doesn't have the same food safety issues that animal products do. I prefer cooking beans and grains as needed, but this function works well if you are out all day and want to come home to hot food.

One feature that can be a negative or positive is the "keep warm" feature on many electric pots: After the time is up and the pot would be cooling down, "keep warm" automatically turns on. If you do not turn it off, it will take a bit longer for the pressure to release, which can result in overcooked food, especially if you are not home when your food has finished pressure cooking. Of course, if you are at home and hear the timer beep to signal the end of cooking, be sure to hit the off button.

One of the nice features of electric cookers is the ability to purchase an extra insert so that you can cook one batch of food immediately after you take out the first insert. Some people like to store their food in the refrigerator in the inner pot.

There's a lot to like about an electric pressure cooker. If I had 2 cookers, one would be electric and one would be a sleek stovetop model that has performance handling, in a different size than the 5- or 6-quart electric models.

If I could only have one pressure cooker, I would likely choose a stovetop model since it provides great control. And if the power goes out, I can still cook food on my gas, butane, or propane stove.

Choosing the Right Size

As I tell my students, when it comes to pressure cookers, size matters. I once met a woman who lives in Colorado, at a high altitude, and mentioned that pressure cooking might be helpful for her. She said, "Of course we don't want a pressure cooker, there are only two of us." I told her that you don't need a big family to use a pressure cooker. I do plenty of cooking for myself and it works out quite well.

In fact, you can cook 1 cup of rice in any size cooker, although it's not as efficient to do so in a larger 8- or 10-quart cooker. If you have a larger cooker, you'll want to cook 2 cups of rice, then tuck the extra into the freezer for another meal.

Stovetop cookers come in sizes from 2 quarts (good for cooking vegetables) to 12 quarts (for big batches of vegetable stock). Most people purchase a medium-size (6- to 10-quart) cooker.

If you plan on cooking large amounts of food, buy the largest cooker that you can easily store and use. If you are cooking only for the two of you, or a family of four or five, a 6- or 8-quart cooker will likely be large enough. I suggest buying a 10-quart cooker only if you're cooking for a large family, or if you want to do any pressure canning (which is not covered in this book), as I find a 10-quart cooker a bit unwieldy for everyday use—not the case with a well-made 8-quart model.

Remember that in order for a pressure cooker to work, you can only fill it half to two-thirds full, so cooking more than 2 to 3 quarts of food isn't possible in a 4-quart cooker. To help you with the math, this means that you can cook 8 cups of beans, which is less than 4 cups dried beans. A 4-quart cooker can be perfect for a family of two, yet less than ideal if you have a family of four. Of course, if you like to cook a lot at one time and enjoy leftovers, or freeze items for later, you'll want to choose a larger cooker.

A 12-quart pressure cooker is used most often in a commercial kitchen since it is expensive and a space hog in most home kitchens.

Size of Family	Recommended Size of Cooker
1 to 2	3- to 4-quart or larger
2 to 3	4- to 6-quart or larger
4 to 5	6- to 8-quart or larger
6 or more	8- or 10-quart

The heights of cookers vary and can be a factor if you have limited kitchen storage. Or, you can do what I do, and let one cooker live on the stovetop so that it gets used often. If you are looking for something for your RV or boat, a small or wide and shallow model might work best. There are pressure cooker sets that have one interchangeable lid for two pots of the same diameter but hold different volumes of food.

The diameter of your stove burner might be a factor, although I've found that a well-made cooker will heat up on a burner of any size as long as the pot is not smaller than the burner. A pot that's too small for a burner can end up with the flame going up the sides of the pot, leading to possible handle damage and a discolored exterior.

I usually have at least one of my pressure cookers on my stove at all times, just waiting for me to use it. I don't have a place to store all my cookers easily and keeping one out reminds me to use it more often. This is a working piece of equipment, meant for daily, or almost daily, use.

TWO

Pressure Cooking Basics

Here's how pressure cooking works, at its simplest: You add liquid and food to a metal pot with a special locking lid that has a gasket. Then apply high heat, causing the liquid to boil, which turns into steam and makes the pressure rise. The pressure pushes up the pressure valve, which seals the pot and prevents the pot from being opened. The super-heated steam—250°F versus 212°F for boiling water—cooks the food quickly and efficiently in less than half the time of traditional stovetop cooking.

Older pressure cookers, called first generation, have a jiggler on top, which regulates pressure, while newer second and third generation cookers usually have a spring valve, a little button, which pops up when the pot is under pressure. There is also an in-between version, a modified jiggle-top, which emits some steam from a non-removable jiggler.

With modern cookers, the gaskets, which are generally essential for sealing the pot, are usually made of silicone, rather than rubber or other material. The modern cookers, both stovetop and electric, have more pressure release valves and often have special lid-locking mechanisms, both of which make the cookers safer and easier to use. As long as you don't leave your stovetop cooker pot under pressure over high heat and walk away without setting a timer, or even worse, leave the house, stovetop pressure cooking safety issues will likely be nonexistent.

Using Your
Stovetop Pressure Cooker

If you are used to doing stovetop cooking in a pan, then switching to a stovetop pressure cooker will be easy. The main difference is that the pressure cooker has a couple more parts, such as the gasket, which fits inside the pot lid, and a pressure valve, which most often is attached to the pot but can be removed for cleaning. (Keep track of it, as it is most important.)

The basic technique for using a stovetop pressure cooker is to add all the ingredients to the pot (if you like, you can first sauté the ingredients, then add the liquid), lock on the lid, and turn up the heat to bring the cooker to pressure. As soon as the pot reaches pressure (when the valve pops up), set your timer, **lower the heat to maintain pressure**, and wait for the timer to beep. You will then either quick release the pressure manually at the stove if you have a modern cooker (a major improvement over older models) or run it under cold water to bring down the pressure if you are using a jiggle-top cooker. Alternatively, if the recipe calls for a natural pressure release, simply remove the cooker from the heat and let it sit, which allows the pressure to gradually release—this takes from 5 to 10 or more minutes, depending on how much food is in the pot.

Stovetop Pressure Cooker

The stovetop pressure cooker lid from the top and bottom. Note the important features.

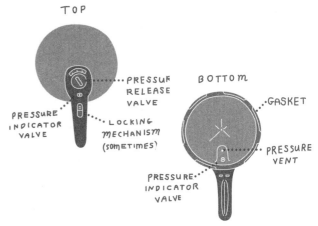

Be aware that the food is still cooking during the natural pressure release—which can be desirable, especially with recipes containing whole grains or beans. When the pressure is released, remove the lid, always carefully tilting it away from you to avoid getting burned by the steam.

How a Pressure Cooker Works

To bring the stovetop pressure cooker to pressure, you need high heat to create steam.

When the steam builds up sufficiently to cause the pressure indicator to rise, lower the heat to maintain pressure.

When you are ready to do a release, turn off the heat. For a natural release, let the pot sit. For a quick release, you turn the pressure valve to let out the steam.

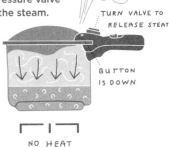

Using Your
Electric Pressure Cooker

If you have an electric pressure cooker, you follow a similar procedure, but the timing and heat regulation become automated. Add your ingredients to the pot; if sautéing any ingredients, use the sauté or brown function. To bring your food to pressure, turn on the pressure setting, set the timer, and lock on the lid. The cooker will beep when time is up, or it will switch to the "keep warm" setting. Turning off the "keep warm" function helps the pot cool more quickly. You can then do a quick release or natural release. The natural release on these cookers can take longer than with stovetop cookers, often 10 to 20 minutes or more.

Read the Instruction Manual

It's important to read the manual that comes with your cooker. The pressure cooker manufacturer will give you advice, guidelines, and warnings about using the cooker and show you the various parts of the cooker. But beware: I suspect that many pressure cooker manual writers have not actually used a pressure cooker as the directions can be less than accurate.

A Note on the Recipe Style

Most of the recipes in my previous books were written for the stovetop cooker, but now with electric cookers becoming so popular, I've written the recipes to apply to both. But for space and clarity considerations, I've condensed the directions for bringing pots to pressure so that they apply to both kinds of appliances. So keep in mind, when the instructions say to "Bring to high pressure; cook for 3 minutes. Release the pressure naturally," if you are cooking in a stovetop cooker, once you achieve pressure by using high heat, you'll need to reduce the heat to low or medium-low, then keep an eye on the pressure to make sure it is maintained, increasing or reducing the heat as necessary.

Electric Pressure Cooker

The electric pressure cooker lid has only a few visible parts that are important.

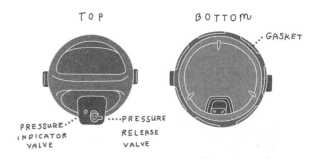

Most cooker manufacturers are following a practice that is referred to as CYB (cover your butt). They often tell you to take every precaution, but not in the interest of producing great-tasting food. I am all for safety but I cook because I want to eat well.

Here is my first bit of conflicting advice but please don't let it confuse you. Many manufacturers tell you to add a minimum amount of water to your cooker, which is often ½ to 1 cup, or more. Some of my quick cooking recipes use less liquid than that. It's important for you to pay attention to your particular pressure cooker and how it cooks, to see if you need to adjust the liquid in recipes so that your cooker works best. (See The Test Run, page 17, to learn how to establish your cooker's minimum liquid amount.) I have not heard from my students or readers about problems with using less liquid in my recipes but as a precautionary note, I want you to know that it can happen. You might end up with burnt material on the bottom of your cooker. See Don't Cry Over a Burnt Pot (page 25) for instructions on how to clean this up.

What a Pressure Cooker Can Do

Pressure cooking often involves more than just throwing all the ingredients into the cooker, although if that's your style, that's OK. Knowing the different ways you can use your cooker can help you achieve better tasting and more varied results. Here's what you can do in your pressure cooker:

Brown or sauté foods before adding other ingredients. Use the sauté or brown function on an electric cooker, or place a stovetop cooker over medium to medium-high heat. I often sauté aromatic and other vegetables and toast spices to increase the flavor components in a dish. I either sauté with oil or dry sauté (see page 20), which uses the hot pot without oil. This works well for anyone who follows an oil-free diet and/or is watching calorie intake. The caution with dry sautéing is to be sure that no food sticks to the bottom of the pot, checking and adding liquid (a tablespoon at a time) as necessary to prevent this.

Braise, which is cooking first in a little fat and then adding liquid and continuing to cook. This is one of my favorite ways to use the pressure cooker. The liquid can be water, stock, wine, juice, or anything else. And even if you start by dry sautéing without fat, you will still get wonderful results.

Poach, which is actually a braise without the initial sautéing. There are few vegetarian foods that respond well to this type of cooking, although seitan cooked in liquid is actually poaching.

Steam by using the rack that comes with your cooker or a collapsible steamer basket over water or other liquid. I do this only occasionally, mostly for whole beets, corn, sweet or regular potatoes, winter squash, and artichokes, as I find food cooked directly in the liquid in the cooker to have better flavor.

Boil, which is perfect for grains and beans. But I find that boiling dilutes flavor in most other foods, especially vegetables. Boiling in the pressure cooker does not mean covering the food with liquid since you are cooking with steam, not the liquid.

Stew, where everything is simply put into the pot and the lid is locked on. This usually involves less liquid than poaching.

Water bath or bain marie cooking, where you use the trivet that comes with your cooker and place another container on it, which contains the food to be cooked, and add liquid to the bottom of the pot. (See "Bowl in Pot" Pressure Cooking, below, for more information.) This is the method used for cooking cornbread, quiche, and some desserts.

Multi-step cooking, where you add foods that cook faster or slower at different times so that all ingredients are perfectly cooked. For instance, with Creamy Broccoli (or Any Vegetable) Soup (page 169), the potatoes need to be thoroughly cooked, which takes a total of 4 minutes. So you cook them at pressure for 3 minutes and quick release the pressure; then add the broccoli and cook for just 1 minute with a quick release so that both the potatoes and broccoli are cooked through but not overcooked.

There is one thing that you cannot do in a pressure cooker, and that is **fry:** You must always use liquid, even if it's just a small amount. Remember that you need steam to raise the pressure.

"Bowl in Pot" Pressure Cooking

One useful method to consider when cooking in the pressure cooker is the "Bowl in Pot" (or "Pan in Pot") method. You add food and liquid to a small 1- to 2-quart casserole dish, bowl, or other vessel, cover it, and place it inside the pressure cooker, elevated above water by a trivet or base. This method has traditionally been used by those following a macrobiotic diet to cook brown rice in an Ohsawa pot. It helps with cleanup when cooking foods such as oatmeal or polenta, although I generally find the flavor development of food cooked directly in the pot to be superior.

Here is the method: Add 1 cup water to the cooker. Put a trivet or standing basket in the cooker and place a casserole or bowl on the trivet or into the basket. Make sure there is at least 1 inch of space between your insert and the sides of the cooker. If required, cover the bowl with a lid or a make-shift foil lid. If your trivet or basket does not have a handle, you will also need to make a helper handle (see below) to pull out the hot food when it is done.

This method works well for any of the cakes (page 287) cooked in a 1- or 2-quart round Corning (or other heat-proof) dish that fits easily on a trivet. Indeed, these recipes would be impossible to make without using this cooking technique. Casserole type dishes can be made in the same way.

Stainless steel, glass, and ceramic bowls all make great inserts. Food cooked in metal containers cook more quickly than the same food cooked in glass, although you might not need to make any time adjustments.

While this technique isn't at the top of my pressure cook-ing favorite list, it is an option to consider for certain foods, especially if you dislike scrubbing your pressure cooker, or the food needs to be contained, like cakes and vegetable pies.

MAKING A "HELPER HANDLE"

I have not yet discovered the perfect material to use to make a handle that raises and lowers hot dishes into and out of the pressure cooker. The more that I think about this handle, the more ideas I have come up with for how to make it—but none is perfect.

The best method I have found so far is to use heavy-duty aluminum foil. Let me stress *heavy-duty,* because the cheapo foil does not work well at all. I tried and failed. You want to make a handle that is 16 to 24 inches long, so that it is easy to grip and pull the container out of the pressure cooker.

Here is how to make a helper handle to use in either a stovetop or electric cooker:

Fold a 2-foot-long piece of heavy-duty aluminum foil lengthwise into quarters to make a long, thick strip that is at least 2 to 4 inches wide. Twist the ends together tightly so it is a secure loop or put a staple through the ends to join them. Pour 1 cup water into the cooker. Fold the foil loop into a strip "handle," then bend into a U-shape. Place the bottom of the U on the trivet. Then place the not-yet-hot container directly on the foil. Be sure that you have a lid on the container, if called for, and then fold the handle ends over the top of the lid.

Cook as directed. When time is up and the pressure has released, remove the lid carefully. Holding the handle close to the container, one piece in each hand, carefully lift the container out. Use silicone oven mitts so that if you accidentally touch the sides of the pressure cooker, you will not get burned.

If you want to shore up your handle to make it feel heftier you can reinforce it by putting plastic wrap, waxed paper, or parchment paper inside the foil before folding. Or you can use twine and make a basket with it.

My most recent discovery is that using more than one han-dle makes lifting even easier and provides more of a feeling of security. Cross two handles perpendicular to each other and staple to hold them together. Place on the trivet, put your dish on top, and lower into the pressure cooker.

I suggest practicing with this before you actually have to use the handle to see what might work best for you.

The nice thing is that your helper handle is reusable. I let mine dry out and store it near my pressure cooker so that I have it when I need it.

Make Helper Handles

To make helper handles, start with 2 pieces of heavy-duty aluminum foil that is at least 24 inches long.

Fold the foil into thirds so that you have a long strip at least 2 to 4 inches wide. You can fold it in quarters if you find that easiest.

Crisscross the two handles so that they form an X shape. Staple in the middle so that they are joined.

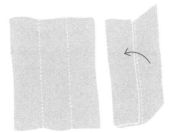

"Bowl in Pot" Pressure Cooking

Add at least 1 cup of water, or the amount according to the recipe directions, to the cooker, then the trivet, and then the helper handles so that the ends extend beyond the cooker.

Add your dish with the food inside. Add a cover if directed in the recipe. Fold the helper handles in on top of the cover or dish so that you can lock the lid on the cooker.

Once the pressure is released, use an oven mitt to carefully lift the dish out of the cooker, using the helper handles. Place on a heatproof surface. Save the handle to reuse in the future.

General Pressure Cooking Guidelines

While a pressure cooker is easy to use, it requires a new way of thinking about cooking, since your food is cooking in pressurized steam and liquid, which behaves differently than food cooked other ways, and you can't see or do anything to your food while it is at pressure. Until you get familiar with this cooking process, it is important to follow each recipe's specific instructions. So if a recipe states, "do not stir," there is a reason—usually it's to prevent food with a high sugar content from sticking to the bottom of the cooker at the high heat needed to achieve pressure and possibly burning.

The most important thing to do before using your cooker is to read the manual that comes with it. Then, give it a test run.

The Test Run

Once you've taken your pressure cooker out of the box and read the manual, you want to become familiar with how it works in action. The easiest way to do this is with the "water test": Add 2 cups water to your cooker, lock on the lid, and bring to high pressure, indicated by the pressure valve rising. If using a stovetop cooker, reduce the heat to maintain high pressure. Cook at high pressure for 5 minutes. Remove the pot from the heat if using a stovetop model, or turn the pot off if using an electric model. Quick release the pressure by turning the knob, first turning it to the low pressure setting (if you have one) to gradually release the pressure, then turning it all the way to the release setting, in order to get a feel for how the pressure comes out of your cooker. Note the direction in which the steam comes out. **Always be sure to keep away from the steam release valve as steam burns are quite painful.**

Measure the liquid left in the pot and note how much liquid was lost; you'll see that the pressure cooker does not lose liquid to evaporation in the same way as a pot on the stove. If you like, you can repeat this with 1 cup of liquid to determine liquid loss when using less liquid, but it's not necessary unless it will make you feel comfortable with your pot. It is unusual for a lot of liquid to be lost. If it is,

It's Fickle, Fresh, and Often Forgiving

If this sounds like your partner, child, or other family member, it's not. It's food. Foods that come directly from Mother Earth are far different than foods processed in a factory. They are not the same every time. In fact, the opposite is often true.

I once cut up 6 pounds of potatoes to make a batch of Garlic Parsley Mashed Potatoes (page 217) for a cooking demonstration and as I was cutting them, I noticed that I had to slide my knife through some of them with a bit more force than I typically do. They seemed tougher and older and likely needed a longer cooking time.

While doing the cooking demonstration, I prepped two apples to go into the food processor; one had a mushy texture, while the other was firm. I had bought them from the same farmer and they might have even come from the same tree. There is no accounting for the fickleness of fresh food, or even foods that used to be fresh, such as dried beans, which are sometimes more dehydrated than you'd like. The drier the grain or bean, the longer it will take to pressure cook. Unfortunately, you don't always know how long these dried foods have been sitting in a warehouse or on a store shelf.

Luckily, food, more than many people, is forgiving, if you know how to treat it. Cook your food with care, and taste it to be sure that it is cooked as you like it. Mother Nature has a plan and we must abide by it. Learn how to season food so that its fickleness becomes part of your plan, maybe even your dinner.

then there might be an issue with how the gasket is inserted or with the sealing of the pressure valve.

Next, you'll want to determine the minimum amount of liquid necessary for your cooker. Add a small amount of water (¼ to ½ cup) to your cooker. Put the stovetop cooker pot over high heat, or set an electric cooker to manual high pressure for 5 minutes; then lock on the lid and bring to pressure. Lower the heat to medium or low on the stovetop cooker (the electric cooker will do this automatically), and wait 5 minutes to see if the pot maintains pressure. If so, then you can likely use less liquid than the manufacturer states. Note the amount of liquid you need to use to get the pot to pressure and to maintain it for 5 minutes. This is your minimum liquid requirement.

Foaming Foods

Older pressure cooker books and manufacturer manuals report that you cannot safely cook pearl barley, applesauce, cranberries, split peas, oatmeal or other cereals, rhubarb, and pasta due to their foaming. If the foam reaches the top of the cooker it can clog the pressure valve. This is problematic with all cookers but was an extreme issue with the jiggle top cooker, which would then build up too much pressure and blow the lid. But I'm here to tell you that, with just a few adjustments, I have successfully cooked all of these ingredients.

If you cook foods that foam, and you are concerned, add a tablespoon of oil to reduce the foaming, or use a 6-quart or larger pressure cooker to reduce any potential problems. Never fill the cooker more than half full with these foods and always use a natural pressure release (unless otherwise instructed). Be sure to thoroughly clean your vent pipe and pressure valve after cooking these foods to avoid potential blockage issues the next time you cook.

Cooking Food in Your Pressure Cooker

Even more so than with other types of cooking, I suggest that you have all your ingredients prepped and ready to go at the start of the process, which is called *mise en place*. With traditional stovetop cooking you often have a few minutes to grab last-minute items, but pressure cooking happens quickly, so be prepared. Have any additional equipment such as helper handles, trivets, baskets, or steamers handy as well.

What Are You Cooking?

Certain foods cook better in the pressure cooker than others and how you prepare the food matters more in pressure cooking than with other cooking methods.

Fast-cooking foods such as summer squash, eggplant, okra, broccoli, and green beans require you to be vigilant with the timing. Pasta, especially gluten-free, sometimes doesn't cook as well as it would on the stove top.

As with any other type of cooking, cutting your ingredients into even pieces is important so that they cook through in the same amount of time.

You can use ingredients that are at room temperature, cold, or even frozen. In fact, one of the benefits of using a pressure cooker is that you can bypass defrosting and add frozen ingredients directly to the pot, as they will generally thaw with added liquid and the heat of the cooker.

If you will be doing multi-step cooking, be sure to know which foods go into the cooker when. Ingredients with the longest cooking time must get the full time to cook for best results.

Some fast-cooking vegetables such as English peas, green beans, and summer squash, when added to very hot dishes such as risotto, soup, and stew, do not even need any time under pressure. Sometimes just stirring them in or locking on the lid for a minute provides enough heat to cook them through.

Liquid Is Essential

Pressure cooking depends upon having liquid in the cooker to raise the pressure. When water boils, it creates steam, which pushes up the pressure valve to seal the pressure cooker and create pressure. Liquid is also important because it is the liquid that helps to infuse flavor into food. Whether the liquid comes from the food being cooked itself or from added liquid, you've got to have it in the proper ratio and quantity for your pressure cooker to function best.

HOW MUCH LIQUID? IT DEPENDS . . .

Manufacturers' instructions typically tell you the minimum amount of liquid that they think you need to make the pressure cooker work. In an effort to have the pressure cooker be "one size fits all" for the quantity of added liquid, the amount recommended might be more than you actually need.

I look at pressure cooking from a culinary, not technical, point of view (always keeping in mind that the cooker must perform correctly to make a dish turn out great). Many manufacturers state that you need a minimum of ½ to 1 cup water to get your cooker to pressure. I have cooked many dishes with less liquid than that.

SIZE MATTERS, AND SO DOES TIMING

The most important considerations when deciding how much liquid to add are the size, make, and model of the pressure cooker that you are using and what you are putting into it. A quick-cooking dish such as Asparagus, Shiitake Mushrooms, and Snow Peas (page 123), cooked for just a minute or two in a 3-quart pressure cooker, requires less liquid than the same dish cooked in a 6-quart or 8-quart cooker. This is based on how long it takes the water to boil, produce steam, and reach the pressure valve. A smaller cooker has a smaller space for the steam to rise.

The height, diameter, and size of the pot will also make a difference in how much liquid your pot requires. A short, wide pot will most likely come to pressure more quickly than the same size cooker that is taller and narrower, so you will need less liquid in the short, wide pot.

GET COMFORTABLE WITH SMALL AMOUNTS OF LIQUID

For some recipes, I use as little as ¼ cup of liquid. As long as the cooker creates enough steam to get to pressure, it will work. If you use a large cooker, such as an 8- or 10-quart, you will often need to use more water or wait longer for the cooker to get to pressure. You may need to do some experimentation with your cooker to determine how much liquid to use for various types of foods.

When you are cooking with watery vegetables you can actually use less than the minimum liquid requirement. Summer squash, cabbage, bok choy, and tomatoes are some of the vegetables that give off a lot of liquid. Mushrooms also do, but to a lesser degree. The released liquid can be figured into the total liquid needed.

My goal in pressure cooking is to end up with the perfect texture, which for me means that my food is not swimming in liquid unless you are intentionally making a soup or stew. By using the right amount of liquid, your pressure-cooked food will make its own flavorful sauce with just the right consistency. I use as little liquid as I can get away with, sometimes using less than the manufacturer's

Using Liquid to Increase Digestibility and Flavor

Flavorful liquid added to vegetable recipes actually gets absorbed and breaks down the fiber in the cell walls of the plant, making the vegetable tastier and more digestible. Any extra liquid after cooking contains nutrients that are better absorbed back into the food than poured down the drain. My goal is to have food cooked to perfection, which means that it will not be swimming in liquid. If you *do* end up with more leftover liquid than you need, save it and add to soups, stews, or your next batch of cooked vegetables.

directions. And remember that you do not need to cover your food with liquid, especially beans, as you do for stovetop cooking since you are pressure cooking, not boiling.

Using less liquid when cooking helps assure that the nutrients in the food remain within the finished dish and don't end up down the drain. You can, though, save any remaining cooking liquid and incorporate it into grain dishes, stews, or soup, if you like.

Sautéing and Dry Sautéing

Traditionally, sautéing involves heating oil in a medium-hot pan and then adding the food and cooking it in the hot oil, stirring frequently. Sautéing provides much more flavor than if you were to proceed directly to pressure cooking your ingredients in liquid.

However, after years of teaching low-fat cooking, I realized that omitting the oil and sautéing ingredients in a dry pot does not alter the flavor of most pressure-cooked dishes, as the high heat of the pressure cooker and its fast flavor infusion produces a tasty dish. And this way you easily cut 100 to 200 or so calories from your diet. Here I share my method for doing a dry sauté.

Many of my recipes will start with the dry sauté, but if you want to use oil, please do. In cases where sautéing in oil will more noticeably add flavor to the finished dish, I give both options in a recipe, and sometimes suggest using vegetable cooking spray. And there are a few recipes where I really think it is important to use some oil, and so give instructions for regular sautéing.

TO DRY SAUTÉ

Heat a stovetop pressure cooker over medium heat for a few minutes, or set an electric pressure cooker to the sauté or brown setting to get the insert heating up. Add whatever ingredients you will dry sauté to the hot pan (without any liquid or fat), in the order listed and for the recommended

cooking times. The key to preventing burning is to stir occasionally and look at the ingredients to be sure nothing is sticking or burning. If that starts happening, add liquid—water, stock, juice, or wine—a tablespoon at a time so you can easily scrape off the stuck-on food particles. Do not add so much liquid that the ingredients get soggy, or you will not be sautéing. You generally want to dry sauté onions or garlic until they start becoming translucent.

Before continuing with the recipe, make sure there is no stuck-on food at the bottom of the pot by adding a tablespoon or two of liquid that will release any browned bits. Remember that when you turn the heat to high to bring the cooker to pressure, any stuck-on food will burn.

Dry sautéing works well in the stovetop pressure cooker due to its thick triple-ply bottom. If your electric cooker has a thinner pot, it might be harder to achieve. You might also choose to skip this initial sauté step and move immediately to the recipe. The choice is yours.

Fast Flavor Infusion

One of the highlights of pressure cooking is the amazing flavor that happens quickly. Herb and spices penetrate food in a way that doesn't happen with most other quick-cooking methods, such as steaming.

And making a flavorful stock in the pressure cooker is easy (see Taking Stock of Stock, page 156). Then you can use that stock as cooking liquid (instead of water), elevating the depth of flavor in your dishes.

The pressure cooker is all about fresh food, heat, liquid, aromatics, seasonings, and food alchemy. Pressure-cooked food is vibrant despite what you've heard about the life being cooked out of vegetables. Vegetables and other vegan foods never made it to the table so quickly and deliciously.

Bringing to Pressure

A pressure cooker comes to pressure when you apply heat. With a stovetop cooker, you start out with the cooker over high heat to bring it to pressure, then lower the heat to maintain the pressure and keep the pressure valve up. With the electric cooker, this happens automatically. After you lock on the lid and turn on the cooker, it will come to pressure, and then automatically regulate heat and start the timer within a minute or two of the pressure valve rising and the pot sealing.

One of the biggest differences between stovetop and electric pressure cooking is how long it takes for the pressure to come up and down. You don't have to "babysit" your electric cooker, but it generally takes significantly more time for the pot to come to pressure and for the pressure to come down naturally. The stovetop cooker almost always gets to pressure and comes down more quickly than the electric cooker, so factor in that time when planning meals.

Timing Is Almost Everything

In order to pressure cook effectively, you need to have a timer. It can be the timer on your oven or microwave, a handheld digital kitchen timer, the timer on your smart phone, or simply the one that's built into your electric pressure cooker. Your timer needs to be accurate.

Cooking at high heat means that an extra minute or two can negatively affect the outcome of some dishes, especially vegetables. In fact, with tender and fast-cooking vegetables like broccoli, asparagus, snow or sugar snap peas, or zucchini, even 30 seconds can be the difference between a bright green, crisp stalk and a gray-green, limp one. This is one of the drawbacks of using an electric pressure cooker. But such precise timing is not needed for long-cooking foods like beans, grains, soups, and stews.

On the other hand, there is a lot of variability in the cooking times of vegetables, beans, and grains. Most of the time potatoes cooked for 3 minutes turn out perfectly. Yet, "new" potatoes, which are the freshly harvested, first-of-the-season potatoes, might need to cook for only 1½ minutes, and will turn into overcooked mashed potatoes at 3 minutes under pressure. Newly harvested heirloom beans might not need a full 7 minutes, while beans that have been on your grocer's shelf for a year or longer might need twice as long. The same holds true for grains and greens. The times that I list are what have worked for me generally, but you always want to pay attention to the food you have on hand, where it came from, and how fresh it is.

Undercooking is better than overcooking, as you can always bring the pot back to pressure and continue cooking—but overcooked food can't be cooked less. If you do overcook, there's no need to toss out your food: It's time to become creative, turning your soft food into soup, burgers, loaves, or dips, depending upon what you are working with. Even overcooked green vegetables can become part of a blended soup with fresh greens or Italian parsley added to brighten the flavor and color.

High-Altitude Cooking

Cooking at high altitudes is different. The temperature at which water boils is lower at higher altitudes; so water can boil at 200°F or even less (rather than 212°F), which means it will take longer to cook your food. Although the pressure cooker raises the temperature at which water boils, it is still less than pressure cooking at sea level. So the timings of my recipes are for sea level cooking, which is up to 2,000 feet. To cook at altitudes higher than 2,000 feet, increase the cooking time by 5 percent or more for every 1,000 feet. This is usually just another minute or two. If you've lived at higher altitudes for a while, you know that there are challenges with any type of cooking. But pressure cooking at high altitudes should help open up more cooking possibilities, making it possible to thoroughly cook beans and whole grains without much time or effort.

Tools You'll Want to Have When Pressure Cooking

Here are some wonderful items to have when you are cooking with your pressure cooker. A few are necessary for preparing some of the recipes in the book. Others are nice to have but not essential.

* A **steamer basket** is important if you plan to steam in the cooker, so invest in one if your cooker didn't come with one. It can be as simple as a collapsible stainless steel or silicone basket with a post and ring in the middle for easy lifting out of the cooker. Some people like to use a deeper pasta insert, to which they add vegetables, but finding one that fits your pot can be a challenge.

* Similarly, if your cooker did not come with a **trivet** (for the steamer basket to stand on), you can make one out of heavy-duty foil by folding into a thick ring. Or use a clean small can, like a cat food or tuna can, with both ends cut off so that it is just a ring to balance the steamer basket or casserole dish on.

* **Glass or ceramic casserole dish(es)**—if you can find them with lids that fit on the dish but not tightly, that's great. Make sure that the dish fits into the cooker with at least 1 inch of space all around. If the dish doesn't have handles, make a helper handle (page 15) to raise and lower the dish.

* **Metal bowls**—choose the sizes that fit into the cooker. Never overfill them or your contents will end up in the water in the cooker.

* An **immersion blender** makes blending hot soup directly in the pressure cooker easy, but it is not essential. You can also transfer the soup to a blender (see below) to blend until smooth. (Do not use an immersion blender in a pressure cooker that has a nonstick interior as you can easily damage the nonstick finish and then it's finished.)

* **Blender**—a high-speed blender is a luxury item; if you can afford one, you will have the smoothest possible soups and sauces, but it's not necessary except to make super smooth cheezecake. A good blender will do as well.

* **Mini-loaf metal pan or other glass containers**—small square or rectangular pans for turning burger mixtures into loaves. Best with their own glass lids.

* **Spice grinder**—this is important for grinding spices and seeds, such as chia or flax, and nuts. These can be ground in a blender but for small amounts, a grinder is most efficient.

* **Microplane zester**—use for grating citrus zest, chocolate, ginger, and garlic.

* **Citrus squeezer**—a ceramic coated or metal squeezer is a great tool for lemon, lime, or other citrus juice.

* **Food mill for applesauce**—buy the best stainless steel one that you can. Mine comes with 3 interchangeable disks so that they mill in different sizes from fine to coarse.

* **Ohsawa pot**—people who follow a macrobiotic diet love these pots for cooking rice in the pressure cooker. They have a lid and a rope handle so that they are easy to get in and out of the cooker. They still need to be elevated off the bottom of the cooker with a trivet to be used well and they are pricey.

Releasing Pressure

Once you've cooked your food at pressure for the recommended cooking time, now it's time to learn how to release the pressure so that you can open it up, take out your food, and then serve. Due to major improvements in safety with the newer cookers, you cannot open the cooker until the pressure is down and has released. There are three methods for releasing pressure in your cooker.

Quick Release

One of the best features of the modern cooker, stovetop or electric, is the quick pressure release. There is a mechanism on your cooker that will allow you to flip a switch, turn a dial, or push on something to quickly release the pressure from the cooker. This stops the cooking right

away and is the method I use for quick-cooking vegetables. Be sure that you know the direction that your steam will be releasing so that you can avoid spraying steam on yourself or your cabinets. Some cookers vent upward and some vent outward. Depending upon the size and fullness of your cooker, this type of pressure release will take a few seconds to a minute or more.

If you use an older style, jiggle-top cooker, the quick-release method will not apply. You will have to use the running water method (see page 24) to release pressure.

QUICK RELEASE WITH A FULL POT

If you have pot full of food such as risotto or a soup with tender vegetables added at the end, you might need to quick release the pressure to stop the cooking. However, quick-releasing pressure in a full pot can cause liquid to spew out of the pressure valve.

If your pressure cooker has multiple pressure settings, not just high and low, you can quickly release a full pot by very slowly turning the dial from high to low to release pressure, reducing the chance of spewing liquid.

If you only have high and low, you can release the pressure in bursts: Turn the knob to low pressure or to pressure release in short bursts until the pressure is released. If at any point liquid starts to exude from your pressure valve, turn the switch back to high pressure. Continue like this until the pressure is released.

If the pot is more than half full with liquid or you want to release without the potential of spewing, you can also use the running water release (see page 24), but heaving a hot, heavy pot to the sink is not my idea of fun, either. If you do take your pot to the sink, take care to run water only over the edges of the top and sides of the cooker and not on the pressure release valve, ever.

A Note on Stovetop Burners

If you are using a stovetop pressure cooker on an electric stove, in order to help regulate and maintain consistent pressure, sometimes it is necessary to have two burners going, one on high and another on low. This allows you to quickly move the pressure cooker from high to low heat once pressure is achieved. If you have a gas stove, or an electric stove that goes from high to low quickly and easily, you won't need to use multiple burners. You will have to determine what works best with your stove.

But if you have an electric stove and have two burners going at once, be sure that you do not accidentally put the pressure lid down on a hot burner. You risk having your lid or handle—or even worse, pressure valve—melt.

In addition, if you have a gas stove with high BTU burners, you might need a flame tamer so that your low setting will be low enough for your cooker. Never let the flames go up the sides of the cooker as you risk burning or melting the handles.

RUNNING WATER RELEASE

Sometimes you might want or need to do a running water release. This is the only quick-release method available for older model jiggle-top pressure cookers. And it's handy if you are using a smaller stovetop cooker and making risotto or another liquid-filled food that might spurt out the release valve when you go to release pressure.

To do this, transfer the stovetop cooker to the sink and run the water over the sides of the pot until the pressure releases, avoiding the pressure vent since this can cause the pot to get damaged. This will take a minute or more, depending upon the size of the cooker and what it contains.

You may also need to use a running water release if pressure remains in your pot after a quick release, even when it looks like the release valve is all the way down. You will know that this is the case if you can't open the cooker. If this happens, try a running water release and then open the pot. If you still can't open the pot, bring back to pressure and then try the running water release again. In almost 20 years of pressure cooking, I have only encountered this a couple of times, for unknown reasons. But I have always been able to open my pot this way.

Important note: The running water release works only for a stovetop cooker: **Do not ever run water on the top of an electric cooker.** (If you have an electric pressure cooker, you certainly will not be doing anything with your pot and the sink.) But you can approximate cool running water by draping a damp kitchen towel over the top of the pot for a few minutes to cool down the pot. Be careful touching the towel as it can be quite hot. You can also let the pressure out in short bursts, as described above.

Natural Pressure Release

The natural release method requires you to move your pressure cooker off the heat and wait for the pressure valve to drop. This will take anywhere from 30 seconds to 10 minutes or more, depending upon the size of the cooker and what is in it. If you have an electric pressure cooker, the natural release will often take twice as long as with a stovetop cooker. Often you can wait a certain period of time, say 15 to 20 minutes, for the pressure to come down and then quick release the remaining pressure, without having any detrimental effects on the food. If the pot is very full with soup or oatmeal, then it's best to simply wait for the pressure to come down so that you don't have spewing liquid.

Often with grains you might need to allow some additional sitting time with the lid on after the pressure releases, to let the grains continue to steam and become fully tender. This is clearly stated in the recipes. Remember that during the natural release method, the food is still cooking in the pot. With grains, beans, and other legumes, you *need* this additional time to continue cooking. Using a quick release method with a pot of beans might cause the beans to split apart. This is also the time that soups and stews develop flavor so always follow recipe instructions for natural release, if that's what's called for.

Recipe Adjustments for Electric Cookers

All of the recipes in this book have been tested in both electric and stovetop cookers. However, there are a few things to keep in mind when cooking from my recipes.

For Electric Cookers

Some electric cooker models (which work better for some foods such as beans and grains) don't reach the pressure levels that stovetop cookers do. When testing the recipes for this book using an electric cooker at 11 psi (vs 15 on a stovetop cooker), I found that the lower pressure was offset by the longer time needed to reach and come down from pressure. As a result, recipes ended up cooking in the same amount of time at pressure in both electric and stovetop models. If you find you need to cook foods longer in your electric cooker, it may be because of the lower level of pressure.

Many of my recipes involve multi-stage cooking at pressure, where some ingredients are added, the pot comes to pressure, the pressure is released, more ingredients are added and the pot comes to pressure again. Because the electric cooker takes longer to come to pressure and longer to come down, these recipes might take longer than they would with a stovetop cooker, although the actual "at pressure" time needn't change.

But, because the food is cooking when the pressure is building and releasing, it's possible that food may overcook. There are a couple of ways to fix this. First, when bringing the pot back to pressure for the second time, cook in an electric cooker for a minute shorter than the specified time. Second, if the cooking time is only a minute or two, don't even bother bringing the pot back to pressure. Stir in the ingredients, lock the lid on, and let sit for 3 to 5 minutes. Generally the residual heat will cook the most recently added ingredients.

Another potential issue with the electric cooker is simmering or reducing liquid in the dish after the food has been cooked. The general way to do that with the electric cooker

is with the brown or sauté function. But the heat with this function can be higher than what you would use on the stove, which can cause the ingredients to scorch or burn. Some models have a "low" sauté, which is the best choice for doing this. If you don't have low sauté, use sauté but be sure to cook quickly and stir frequently.

Don't Cry Over a Burnt Pot

If you accidentally burnt your pot you might think that your pressure cooker is unusable. This is not true. I know from experience that unless you've burnt the outer part of the pot, causing the triple-ply bottom to melt off, the inner part can be salvaged despite how it looks.

The first thing to do is to figure out what you'll be eating for dinner. Then, remove as much of the food in the cooker as possible, and put it in the compost pile, the garbage, or your garbage disposal.

Second, add at least 2 cups water to the cooker, lock on the lid, and bring to high pressure over high heat and cook for a few minutes. Remove from the heat, let the pot sit until the pressure comes down, then let the pot sit another 10 minutes or more. Carefully open the pot. Dump out the hot water. Get your muscles ready for some good pot scrubbing with an abrasive sponge, not steel wool or metal pad. If you cannot see the bottom of the pot, add a few tablespoons of baking soda and another few cups of water, put the lid back on the pot, and bring to high pressure for a few minutes. Repeat as above until your pot is back to normal.

White vinegar is also good for removing stains in the pot, but don't add it when adding baking soda. You'll have to do that separately.

Caring for Your Cooker

The pressure cooker does not have an abundance of parts, which makes it easy to take care of. It does require more care than your average skillet or saucepan, but it requires less know-how than using your food processor.

The Lid

The lid has most of the moving parts of the cooker. Like the other parts, it requires care after each use.

I always wash and dry my lid by hand, never in the dishwasher, to make sure it does not get damaged. Store the lid upside down in the pot, with the pressure valve in place (assuring that you don't lose the valve), and the gasket ajar or inside it. If you lock the lid on the pot, the smells that are in the gasket get trapped in the pot.

If the pot seems difficult to open or close, drip a bit of cooking oil under the lid, rub it around the edges, and then replace the gasket. This often makes it easy to open and close.

THE GASKET

The gasket, made of silicone or sometimes rubber, along with the pressure valve, is what helps seal the pot so that it can get to pressure. The gasket sits inside the lid of the cooker, making a seal between the lid and the cooker base. It is recommended that it be removed and washed and dried each time you use the cooker. Put it back on the cooker once you have cleaned and dried the lid. If your gasket gets smelly, soak it in baking soda or white vinegar. When your gasket is no longer pliable, has any cracks, or doesn't seal your cooker, it's time to get a new one. Some manufacturers recommend replacing the gasket once a year. Mine usually

Oh, No, I Have a Pressure Problem

There are only a few problems you might encounter when cooking in your pressure cooker.

The pot is making a lot of noise and a lot of steam is releasing: You might have the heat too high. Remember to adjust the heat to medium or low on a stovetop cooker after it has reached pressure.

The safety valve is releasing pressure: An overfilled cooker (more than half full for beans or grains, or two-thirds full for other foods that don't expand) can cause particles of food to get trapped in the pressure valve, which can result in built-up pressure, causing pressure to be released out of one of the safety valves or the pressure not releasing properly or completely. If this happens, remove the valve and rinse thoroughly to remove any debris.

The pot does not seem to come to pressure as it has before: Check your pressure regulator valve; it can become blocked with food particles or not be functioning correctly. If you are able to remove the valve, take it off, clean it, and run water through it, then try again. If that doesn't help, replace it to see if that resolves the issue.

Trouble getting the lid on or having to force it: Inspect your gasket and make sure that it is still flexible and fits into the lid of your cooker. Place a few drops of oil under the cooker rim and spread with your finger and then replace the gasket. This will often remedy the problem.

Not able to bring the pot to pressure: Be sure that you are using enough liquid to build up pressure. Larger cookers often require more liquid than smaller ones.

Not able to bring the pot to pressure but have done so previously: Check the gasket for nicks, cracks, and splits. A gasket will generally last a year or more. (Although I had one that lasted almost 5 years with almost daily use before I had to replace it.)

last much longer. Remember, if your gasket fails, you will not be able to use your cooker until you replace it. Most manufacturers sell extra gaskets, which you can buy online or in cookware stores.

THE PRESSURE VALVE

One of the most important parts of the lid assembly is the pressure release valve, a dial that is necessary for bringing the cooker to pressure. The valve can be removed on many cookers; if yours can be removed do so after each use and rinse and dry it, along with the pressure vent, which is found on the underside of the lid. It is a stationery piece, and food particles can get in it. Run water through it after each use. Always be sure that the valve turns easily and the pressure indicator button (which cannot be removed) moves the way that it should (most often that means up and down).

If somehow your pressure valve gets lost, some manufacturers will sell a replacement valve, but your cooker will be unusable as a pressure pot until it arrives.

The Pot

Wash the base (the pot) of your stovetop cooker after each use. Do not use abrasive materials. There are a few products that can help you keep your cooker shiny and looking new: Bar Keepers Friend, a professional cleaning polish meant for metals, and the sponge-type product called Magic Eraser. A mixture of white vinegar and water also works well for cleaning your cooker. If the manufacturer says that you can put your base in the dishwasher, it's OK to do so. Otherwise, hand wash and dry the base.

For the electric cooker, the pot is the insert, which can be stainless steel, ceramic, or have a nonstick coating. You want to be sure to wash it well each time that you use it. Depending upon what it's made of you can put it in the dishwasher. If it has a nonstick coating, do not use metal in it or any abrasive cleaners on it. Clean the inner pot as you would the stovetop cooker.

The Handles

Depending upon the make and model of your cooker, you might need to take care of the handles that hold the pressure lid or on the base of the pot. Some handles attach with screws, either visible from the outside, or hidden under the handle. Look at your cooker to determine if your screws are adjustable. It often takes quite some time before you'll notice that the handle or handles become wobbly. If that happens, look for the screws and tighten them. Some cookers have integrated handles that do not require much care, while some other models have a removable handle that requires that you reattach it properly should you decide to take it off to put the lid in the dishwasher.

Adapting Traditional Recipes for the Pressure Cooker

Most anything that requires cooking in even a little bit of liquid can be adapted for the pressure cooker, although it is best suited for longer-cooking foods such as beans, grains, soups, and stews, and for making incredibly fresh crisp-cooked vegetables in just a minute or two.

Experience and experimentation are the best teachers when it comes to adapting recipes, but you can use similar recipes and their cooking times to create other recipes. Take notes as you cook to refer to when making a particular type of recipe again. You'll need to determine if the quick or natural release method is best for your recipe, based upon ingredients used, keeping in mind that the natural release happens more quickly with the stovetop cooker than the electric.

Here are three quick rules of thumb for adapting conventional recipes for the pressure cooker:

1. Reduce the liquid used by at least 25 percent but often up to 50 percent, depending upon the food you are cooking.

2. Increase the seasoning by as much as twice the amount (start with at least fifty percent more during cooking, then taste and add more if needed after cooking), except for hot chiles, as their heat is intensified by the pressure cooker. As always, it's best to add salt at the end of cooking.

3. Decrease the cooking time at pressure by 75 percent for vegetables, beans, and mixed dishes and by 50 percent for grain dishes.

Remember that foods that contain liquid, such as watery vegetables, will release their liquid into the recipe. Once you try a recipe, you'll need to determine if there's too much or too little liquid and then adjust it the next time you make it, keeping in mind the liquid minimum for your cooker.

I generally start by cutting the cooking time in half when adapting traditional recipes. You can also refer to the At-a-Glance cooking charts (see pages 51, 53, 95, and 119) for general guidelines for cooking times. But when experimenting with the cooking times, err on the side of less time. If the food is not cooked completely, it is easy to get the pot back up to high pressure and continue cooking, but once you have overcooked certain foods they are not especially appealing (this can challenge your creativity, which might be fun, or not).

Some more additional tips for adapting recipes for your pressure cooker:

* If you end up with an overcooked dish or vegetable, you can always turn it into a puree to use later in soups, make into a sauce, or see if the dish is suitable for burgers or patties (see page 232).

Adapting Slow Cooker Recipes to the Pressure Cooker

Slow cooker recipes can easily be adapted for the pressure cooker. The advantage to using a pressure cooker is obviously time, but also that the pressure cooker lets you layer flavors and add ingredients at different stages so that you don't end up with a homogenous batch of mush.

To figure out total cooking time, use guidelines from a similar pressure cooker recipe, or use the At-a-Glance cooking charts (see pages 51, 53, 95, and 119) to determine the time necessary for the longest-cooking ingredient. You will definitely need to use less liquid in the pressure cooker as there is very little liquid loss during cooking. Decrease the liquid by 25 to 50 percent, depending upon the dish. Grains work best with 25 percent less liquid while most bean dishes will need 50 percent less liquid.

You don't need as much advance planning but a well-stocked pantry is an asset. You can also add frozen ingredients to the cooker and they will defrost during their time in the cooker.

Pressure Cooking Tips

- Never fry in your pressure cooker under pressure.

- Follow the manufacturer's directions regarding the minimum amount of liquid to add to your cooker, unless you discover otherwise (see The Test Run, page 17).

- Never fill your cooker more than one-half to two-thirds full, depending upon what you are cooking. With beans and grains filling halfway is the limit; most everything else can go up to two-thirds.

- When adapting traditional recipes to the pressure cooker, you will usually need to add more herbs and spices and less liquid (see page 28).

- Cut all of the same ingredient into similar sizes and shapes, ensuring more even cooking. Cut longer-cooking foods into smaller pieces or add to the cooker first.

- The more food that's in the cooker, the longer it will take for the cooker to reach full pressure and the longer it will take for the pressure to come down when using a natural pressure release.

- Adding boiling or near-boiling water or stock to your pressure cooker will help your pot quickly reach high pressure. This may not be generally energy efficient, but might save time overall. You can bring the water or stock to a boil in a separate pot on the stove or an electric kettle while you are prepping the ingredients and sautéing in the cooker pot. (If you have an electric cooker that heats with the lid off, you can do this step while prepping.)

- When you double or triple a recipe, you do *not* need to lengthen the cooking time at pressure; however, it will take longer to get to pressure.

- Be careful when sautéing ingredients containing natural sugars—onions, leeks, carrots, and tomatoes. Anything that sticks to the bottom of the cooker will burn when the heat is turned up to high. To prevent this problem, add some water or other liquid and give a good stir on the bottom of the pot to loosen any stuck-on bits of food.

- Do not stir any soup that contains lentils, split peas, or grains and then return it to the heat, since those ingredients will often sink to the bottom and burn the food and the pressure cooker.

- For stovetop cookers: Be sure to set your timer when the cooker reaches the specified pressure and turn the heat down to maintain that pressure setting. Always set a timer and don't walk away, take a long shower, or leave the house as cooking times for these dishes are generally less than 30 minutes. It's wise to glance at the cooker every now and then as your food cooks to be sure that the pressure valve is still raised, indicating that your cooker is at pressure. If it is not, raise the heat to bring it to pressure again and then lower the heat to maintain high pressure.

- When opening the cooker, be sure to tilt the lid away from you so that the extremely hot steam does not burn you.

- Remember that food coming out of the cooker will be hotter than food cooked by other methods, so warn people accordingly or let the food cool a bit. This is especially true for soups.

* If you are using mixed foods that cook at different times, cut the longer-cooking vegetables into smaller pieces. For instance, if you are cooking potatoes and carrots together, cut the potatoes smaller than the carrots so that they both cook in about 2 minutes, without overcooking.

* If you didn't add enough liquid to the recipe, the first sign might be the smell of burnt food. If this happens, immediately remove the stovetop cooker from the heat and run the pot under cool water or do a quick release. If using an electric cooker, immediately quick release the pressure (see page 23). Then carefully remove the lid and taste the dish. If the scorched part has not affected the rest of the food, carefully spoon the unscorched food out and serve. Then see Don't Cry Over a Burnt Pot (page 25) for instructions for cleaning a burnt cooker.

* Be sure to keep foods high in natural sugar, such as tomatoes in any form, off the bottom of the cooker. Always layer them on top and do NOT stir until after cooking is complete.

* To prevent sticking and burning after sautéing, add the liquid and scrape the bottom of the cooker to free any browned bits before bringing to pressure. Naturally high sugar foods such as onions, leeks, and garlic, and some spices, tend to stick.

Ready, Set, Go

Are you ready to take the first step in pressure cooking? If you haven't already determined how much liquid your cooker needs, now is the time; see page 17.

If you don't yet feel confident enough to cook something that could burn, try making stock (page 156). You'll be happy that you learned how to do this. By making your own stock, instead of buying it, you can save enough to make your pressure cooker pay off quickly and deliciously. It's time to thumb through the recipes and choose the ones that appeal to you. Then put your pressure cooker to work.

Glossary of Ingredients

Learn about the ingredients used in the recipes with which you might be unfamiliar.

Agave nectar: The liquid sweetener that comes from the agave cactus. It is also called agave syrup. I always choose organic agave. Use sparingly. Feel free to choose any other liquid sweetener that you prefer for the recipes.

Arrowroot powder: From the arrowroot plant, this starch is often used as a thickener instead of the more highly processed cornstarch. To use, mix arrowroot powder with a small amount of cool liquid, stirring well to remove lumps. While it can be added directly to the ingredients in hot pots or pans, to avoid clumping, first remove the pan from direct heat. You can substitute cornstarch mixed with water for arrowroot but cornstarch thickens only at the time of cooking and it loses its thickening power during reheating. As arrowroot is less refined than cornstarch it is my thickener of choice for cooked foods. Purchase in bulk for the best price.

Berbere: Also known as *berber,* this spice blend is used in Middle Eastern and Moroccan cuisines. It is usually hot and spicy but you can make it to suit your taste. See recipe on page 36.

Bragg liquid aminos: Use this salty fermented condiment in the same way as tamari or soy sauce. Derived from soybeans, it contains amino acids and is gluten-free.

Cashew meal or flour: Cashews can be purchased finely ground as meal or flour. If you cannot find either, you can grind your own cashews in a spice grinder or blender until powdered.

Chia seeds: High in omega-3 fatty acids, ground chia seeds make a wonderful binder for veggie burgers and in cakes. Ground chia can also take the place of eggs when mixed with liquid, and is often used in place of ground flax.

Chili paste with garlic (sometimes called chili garlic sauce): This is a fermented chili sauce that is somewhat salty and definitely garlicky. I buy it in my local supermarket, but you might have to get it in an Asian grocery or online. My favorite brand is Lee Kum Kee's Panda Brand because it doesn't have any preservatives or unfamiliar ingredients.

Chipotle chile: This is a dried smoked pepper, most often a jalapeño, that is available dried whole, dried ground, and canned in adobo sauce. If you cannot find chipotle powder, you can buy the dried peppers whole and process them in a spice grinder. If you can't get either of these, you can always substitute canned chipotle in adobo, although they often contain vinegar or other seasonings. Simply drain them of the sauce and mince.

Coconut palm sugar: My sugar of choice comes from the coconut tree and is not heavily processed. You can often find it in dark and blonde versions. If you cannot find it, substitute Sucanat, organic cane sugar, or your favorite sugar.

Flax seeds: A good source of omega-3 fatty acids. Ground flax seeds mixed with liquid make an egg substitute, plus they can also be sprinkled on hot cereal or other foods, but note that they tend to get gelatinous. They are best purchased ground, and stored in the freezer to keep them fresh; or as whole seeds stored in the refrigerator or freezer. Grind flax seeds in a blender or spice grinder—a food processor will not work.

Gluten-free flour: My recipes that call for flour will always include a gluten-free option. There are a number of gluten-free blends on the market. Read the labels to see that they are just flours or starches without any added baking powder or soda since the recipes are written for the flour only. Also read the label as some flour blends have added dairy. If you choose not to use gluten-free flour, you can substitute spelt or whole-wheat pastry flour. Combine carefully, without too much stirring, as gluten-containing flour can get tough if overmixed.

Lemongrass: The stalk of a lemongrass plant. You can grow it outdoors in the ground or in a pot, or find it in Asian groceries, natural food stores, and some supermarkets. When using it, remove some of the outer stalk. Then bruise the stalk by carefully hitting it with the blunt part of your knife. Cut into 1-inch or larger pieces. Be sure to fish these out after cooking, as they are woody and tough. You can use a bit of grated lemon zest or dried lemongrass to replicate the flavor if you cannot find fresh lemongrass.

Miso: A fermented soybean paste that is very salty and provides umami flavor. There are many types and brands of miso, and the flavor of each differs. In my refrigerator you'll find mellow white miso, which is mild; brown rice miso, which is also relatively mild; and barley miso, which is aged longer and has a stronger flavor. You might need to try a few to find what you like. Miso lasts for a year or more in the refrigerator. Westbrae and Eden brands are commonly available, although South River miso is extremely delicious and more delicate. Add miso only at the end of cooking soup or stews as it has probiotic activity (beneficial bacteria) that is inactivated when cooked. Use it sparingly or it can overpower your food.

Nondairy milk: Choose any nondairy milk that you like. I use a number of them, such as rice, hemp, almond, multigrain, and soy. They are generally interchangeable in cooking. If the recipe calls for unsweetened, it is usually because the recipe is savory. Read the labels to choose what works for you. The recipes in this book only use nondairy milk.

Nutritional yeast: A yellow powder or flakes used as a dietary supplement and seasoning. It has a nutty, cheesy taste and is easily added to soups, stews, gravies, salad dressings, and sauces. Yeast powder is best used when you want to maintain a smooth consistency, as in a sauce; yeast flakes are better for seasoning. It is not the same as brewer's or baking yeast, and the three cannot be used interchangeably. Purchase it in bulk, or in containers, at natural food stores. Store in the refrigerator for up to a few months, although I can't imagine it spoiling.

Oil: I often call for canola or another neutral-tasting oil such as grapeseed, sunflower, untoasted sesame, avocado, or rice bran in the recipes; feel free to use your favorite daily neutral-tasting oil. Since neutral oil has little to no flavor, a full-flavored olive oil or toasted sesame oil is not generally a good substitute. If a recipe calls for olive oil at the start of the recipe, extra virgin is not needed; if olive oil is added after, use extra virgin. Most of my recipes are easy to adapt and make without any oil. If you choose to omit oil, that's fine (see Sautéing and Dry Sautéing, page 20).

Paprika, Spanish smoked (aka pimentón): Often available in gourmet stores, smoked Spanish paprika adds a smoky flavor to foods. It comes in mild and hot. I use mild in all my recipes but if you like spicier food, choose the one that works best for you. It is also available from WholeSpice.com and MountainRoseHerbs.com.

Porcini powder: Porcini mushrooms add a lot of umami flavor to dishes. To make porcini powder you need dried porcini mushrooms. Grind them in a spice grinder or blender and store in a cool, dark place for 3 to 6 months. You can also purchase porcini powder from WineForest.com or other online sources (see Resources, page 304).

Seitan: This is gluten, the protein part of wheat. If you eat gluten-free, you will definitely want to avoid seitan. If you don't eat gluten-free, seitan is often a good substitute for tofu or tempeh as a protein source in recipes. It is ready-to-eat when you purchase it so feel free to substitute. I share my technique for making it on page 212. Make your own and you will save money and be able to flavor your seitan any way that you like. One batch makes about 24 ounces, or the equivalent of 3 boxes of store-bought seitan.

Soy sauce: Traditionally made soy sauce is often called shoyu. It is generally not gluten-free. Read the labels on soy sauce to see what they contain and choose the ones without salt and caramel coloring. Soy sauce can be used interchangeably with tamari and Bragg liquid aminos.

Sucanat: Natural sugar cane juice. It is unrefined and substitutes one to one for sugar, although the color is darker. I like to use it because it contains slightly more minerals than white sugar. But it is still quite sweet, so use sparingly, as you would brown or white sugar.

Tahini: Raw or roasted sesame seed paste. I prefer raw but buy what you can find in jars or cans at the natural food store, supermarket, or Middle Eastern grocery. Store in the refrigerator to keep fresh.

Tamari: A dark, wheat-free sauce made from fermented soybeans. The flavor is much better than standard soy sauce, which is mostly salt, water, and coloring. Japanese shoyu is a good substitute, although it contains wheat. I often use San-J Reduced Sodium Tamari since it is widely available at most natural food stores and some supermarkets.

Tamarind paste: From a fruit with a sour taste, tamarind paste is available in jars, which I find at the Asian grocery. A little bit goes a long way. I only use it in one recipe here, Spicy White and Sweet Potatoes on page 142, but feel free to get creative with it. I love it paired with the sweetness of corn. It lasts a long time in the refrigerator.

Tempeh: A fermented soybean cake with origins in Indonesia, where it has been enjoyed for several hundred years. It has more fiber and is less processed than tofu, with a nutty taste and firm texture. You can buy it in natural food stores and some supermarkets. You will often find it in the freezer case or the refrigerated section of the store. Once opened it must be refrigerated, but can be refrozen to use later. If your tempeh turns colors or has an off-smell, toss it. Tempeh can be substituted in many recipes that call for firm tofu.

Thai curry paste: This paste comes in three colors: red, yellow, and green. I prefer red but you might like a different kind. Read the labels as many brands contain fish sauce. My go-to curry paste is from Thai Kitchen.

Tofu: A wonderful source of soy protein. For most cooking, and especially pressure cooking, I prefer to use a firm or extra firm tofu from a vacuum-packed refrigerated container (rather than those found in water). You might need to drain or squeeze some water out of the tofu, depending upon its consistency. If the tofu is somewhat firm, you can do this by actually squeezing the tofu gently between your hands. Alternatively, you can lay the tofu on a cutting board set on an angle next to the sink and put another board on top to create pressure and let the liquid drain out for at least 15 minutes. I prefer very firm tofu that does not need this treatment, but sometimes all I can get is a less firm tofu. In that case, remove as much liquid as possible. If you can find "sprouted" tofu, you will find that it is generally very firm. Buy organic, non-GMO tofu, if available. In the pressure cooker, tofu gets firmer as it cooks.

Tofu, silken: Made by Mori-Nu, silken tofu currently comes in a 12.3-ounce aseptic box that is shelf-stable and good for up to a year from the date it's made. Once opened, the tofu must be refrigerated. To keep it fresh in the refrigerator for up to a week, change the water the tofu is kept in daily. I use silken tofu only for blending in soups, sauces, or dressings to add creaminess, and not for braises, stir-fries, or for baking, as it tends to crumble when used for those purposes. You can also buy water-packed, refrigerated silken tofu if that's all that you can find.

Vegetable cooking spray: Using spray oil helps you cut down on the amount of fat in cooking. Vegetable cooking spray generally refers to a commercial spray oil product, which usually contains lecithin and burns at a lower temperature than oil, making your cookware permanently sticky. So I prefer putting the oil of my choice, usually canola, olive, or a combination of the two, in a spray bottle, such as a Misto sprayer.

Zest: The outer, colored part of the peel on citrus fruit. Use any citrus except grapefruit since it is too bitter. Citrus zest has anti-cancer properties and adds incredible flavor with no fat. Avoid the white pith under the peel, as it is bitter. Use only organic fruit when zesting. The best way to do this is with a tool called a zester or a Microplane fine grater.

THREE

Spice Blends
and Other
Seasonings

I can't imagine how vegan food would taste without using herbs and spices to dress up the simple ingredients. When pressure cooking, it's even more important to spice up your dishes since the flavors can get muted. I often use twice the quantity of herbs and spices when pressure cooking as I do in regular cooking. The spices don't need to be hot but they are flavorful. Dried herbs add grassy and woody notes, and spice and herb blends often have a synergistic combination of flavors, rounding out a dish easily.

You don't have to make your own blends, but there are benefits to doing so. You'll usually save money and have fresher, more flavorful blends. You can also customize the blends to suit your tastes, as you'll see in the recipes. Buy your herbs and spices in bulk if you can, as you often pay a premium for those small jars. Whole spices such as cumin or mustard seeds can last for years and most powdered spices and dried herbs will retain their freshness if used within 6 months. Storing them in a cool, dark spot is optimal.

One of the best pieces of equipment to grind toasted spices is a spice, or coffee, grinder (see page 22). You might need to grind some blends in batches as the grinder only holds a few tablespoons. A regular blender, but not a food processor, will also accomplish the important task of grinding spices.

I've provided a range of blends, and they all appear in the recipes in this book. But I encourage you to find new uses for them, or try an herb or spice which is new to you. Broadening your herb and spice palette will enliven the foods that hit your palate.

Berbere Spice Blend

¼ cup ground cayenne

3 tablespoons paprika

¾ teaspoon ground ginger

½ teaspoon garlic powder

½ teaspoon ground fenugreek

½ teaspoon ground cinnamon

½ teaspoon ground turmeric

½ teaspoon ground coriander

½ teaspoon ground black pepper (omit if you prefer less heat)

¼ teaspoon ground cardamom

⅛ teaspoon freshly ground nutmeg

⅛ teaspoon freshly ground allspice

Pinch of ground cloves

½ teaspoon salt, optional

This is the traditional spice mixture used in Ethiopian and Eritrean cooking that adds not only heat but the aromas and flavors of warm spices, including cinnamon, coriander, and cardamom. Just like curry, there are probably as many variations of berbere as there are people who make it.

Traditionally berbere is added to cooked red lentils, but it also works as a seasoning for mixed vegetable dishes and whole grains. If you want this to be flavorful but not hot, replace some or most of the cayenne with a mild chili powder. If you cannot find ground fenugreek or good-quality ground coriander, buy the whole seeds and grind them in a spice grinder.

MAKES ABOUT ½ CUP (MAKE HALF IF YOU WON'T BE USING THIS OFTEN)

1. Toast all the ingredients in a large, dry pan over medium heat until the mixture smells toasted, about 5 minutes. Alternately, you can put the ingredients on a rimmed baking sheet and bake in a 300°F oven for 5 to 10 minutes.

2. Let cool and put into a jar. Store in a cool, dark place for up to 6 months.

Cajun Seasoning

When you want to add a little heat, spice, and flavor to a dish, this blend will do the trick. If you like milder blends, reduce the cayenne to ½ to 1 teaspoon. Always use the freshest dried spices that you can, especially when it comes to paprika. The flavor difference is substantial. Since this blend is salt-free, make sure to taste your dish for salt before serving.

MAKES ABOUT ⅓ CUP

Combine all ingredients in a small bowl and stir to blend. Store in an airtight container for up to 6 months.

2 tablespoons sweet paprika

1 tablespoon onion powder, or 2 teaspoons minced dried onion

1 tablespoon garlic powder, or 2 teaspoons minced dried garlic

1 tablespoon ground cayenne

2 teaspoons dried thyme

2 teaspoons dried oregano

1 teaspoon freshly ground black pepper

½ teaspoon freshly ground nutmeg

Curry Powder

1 tablespoon cumin seeds

1 teaspoon coriander seeds

1 teaspoon fenugreek seeds

½ teaspoon mustard seeds, yellow or black

½ teaspoon whole black peppercorns

¼ teaspoon fennel seeds

2 cloves

Seeds from 2 green cardamom pods

1 tablespoon ground turmeric

1 teaspoon ground cinnamon

1 teaspoon ground ginger

Curry powder can be made to your liking. Mine contains plenty of the spices that I like and less of the spices that I don't care for, such as fennel and cloves. The mixture is flexible, so if there's a spice that you don't like or don't have, leave it out. If you like your curry powder spicy, add a pinch or more of cayenne or another hot pepper powder. Toasting the seeds adds a rich flavor that I like, but you can skip this step.

If you fall in love with this blend, I suggest doubling or tripling it, but don't make more than what you can use within a couple months as it will lose its fresh taste.

MAKES ABOUT ¼ CUP

1. Combine the cumin, coriander, fenugreek, mustard, peppercorns, fennel, cloves, and cardamom seeds in a large skillet. Toast the spices over medium heat until the mustard seeds begin to pop, 15 seconds to 1 minute. Transfer the toasted seeds to a small bowl and cool.

2. When cool, grind the mixture in a spice grinder until powdered. Return the mixture to the bowl and stir in the turmeric, cinnamon, and ginger. Transfer to a jar or container and store in a cool, dark place for up to 2 months.

Garam Masala

Garam masala, like curry powder, is a versatile blend that can be made to your taste preference. I tend to leave out the cloves entirely, but since they are so typical in the traditional spice blend, I've included some in this recipe. Like other spice blends, it is best to store in an airtight container, in the dark, away from heat, and use within 2 to 6 months—which ought to be easy if you use seasonings as much as I do.

MAKES ABOUT ⅓ CUP

1. Toast the coriander, cumin, and peppercorns in a dry skillet over medium heat until the cumin smells toasty and turns slightly brown, about 3 to 5 minutes. Once cool, grind in a spice grinder with the cloves until everything is powdered. Transfer to a small bowl.

2. Add the remaining spices and stir to combine. Transfer to an airtight container and store in a cool, dark place for up to 6 months.

2½ teaspoons coriander seeds

1½ teaspoons cumin seeds

¾ teaspoon black peppercorns, or less if you prefer less heat

8 to 10 cloves

1 tablespoon ground cinnamon

1½ teaspoons ground allspice

1½ teaspoons ground cardamom

1½ teaspoons mild chili powder

1 teaspoon ground ginger

¾ teaspoon freshly ground nutmeg

Harissa Spice Blend

1 tablespoon cumin seeds

1½ teaspoons coriander seeds

1 tablespoon paprika

1 tablespoon chile powder

1 teaspoon ground cayenne

¼ teaspoon caraway seeds

½ teaspoon salt, optional

This hot spice blend with toasty undertones is used in Moroccan cooking. Sometimes it contains dried garlic, too. Since it's so easy to use fresh garlic in your cooking, I think that it's redundant in a spice blend, so I have left it out.

If you prefer your food less fiery, use more paprika and less cayenne. Also, be aware that the heat level of cayenne powder can vary, so feel free to adjust the amounts in this blend.

MAKES ABOUT ¼ CUP

1. Toast the cumin and coriander seeds in a dry skillet over medium heat until the cumin smells fragrant, about 2 minutes. Let cool.

2. Combine the toasted spices with the remaining ingredients in a spice grinder, and grind until it is powdered. Store in an airtight container in the dark for up to 6 months.

Italian Seasoning

Just a sprinkling of this blend transforms a pot of beans into something special. It is a bit different from a number of other Italian blends you might find, as I like to use dried minced garlic and onion, rather than powdered, which provides better flavor and texture. I also include summer savory because it goes so well with beans. If you love lemon, don't bypass the dried lemon peel or lemon verbena.

MAKES JUST MORE THAN ½ CUP

Mix all the ingredients together. If you prefer a finer mixture, you can give this a few pulses in a blender or spice grinder, in batches. Transfer the mix to a jar and store in a cool, dark place. This will maintain its potency for 3 to 6 months, so use it often.

3 tablespoons dried basil

2 tablespoons dried oregano

1 tablespoon dried marjoram

1 tablespoon dried parsley

2 teaspoons dried thyme

1 teaspoon dried summer savory

1 teaspoon dried rosemary, chopped fine or crushed

1 tablespoon dried minced garlic

2 teaspoons dried minced onion

¼ to ½ teaspoon crushed red pepper flakes

2 teaspoons minced dried lemon peel or lemon verbena, optional

1 tablespoon ground allspice

1 tablespoon dried thyme

1½ teaspoons ground cayenne
or your favorite chile powder

1½ teaspoons freshly ground
black pepper

¾ teaspoon freshly ground
nutmeg

¾ teaspoon ground cinnamon

Jerk Seasoning

This spicy, dry blend is often mixed with wet seasonings (including minced garlic, citrus juice, and onion or scallions), and used to marinate foods destined for the grill (see Jerk Marinade, below). You could also add fresh minced chile pepper to the jerk paste, but remember that pressure cooking intensifies the heat of chiles.

This is a spicy blend, and because sweet often balances out hot spices, sugar is often added. But it can make the blend cake up, so wait and add the sugar when you are cooking, up to ½ teaspoon (or to taste) for each tablespoon of blend.

MAKES ABOUT ¼ CUP

Combine all the ingredients in a small bowl. Transfer to a jar or other container. Store in a cool, dark place for up to 3 months.

Jerk Marinade: To marinate tofu, tempeh, or seitan, mix 1 tablespoon (or more to taste) of the Jerk Seasoning with ¼ cup orange, lemon, or lime juice (or a combination), 2 tablespoons minced onion, and 2 minced cloves garlic. Rub onto your food and let it marinate for at least 1 hour or up to 4 hours in the refrigerator. Grill your food, or cook in your pressure cooker with vegetables and liquid to make a complete dish.

Mexican Spice Blend

I suspect that in Mexico they might call this a *gringa* seasoning because it includes garlic and orange peel, but I love them in my Mexican blend. Like other cultures, in Mexico seasonings vary according to region and it's likely that most people cook by adding a little of this or that rather than following a strict recipe. Here you can put it all together and use it often when you want to add Mexican flavorings.

MAKES ABOUT ¼ CUP

Combine the ingredients in a small bowl. Transfer to a jar or container. Store in a cool, dark place for up to 3 months.

Smoky Mexican Spice Blend: If you like a smoky flavor, use 1⅔ tablespoons chili powder and 1 teaspoon chipotle chili powder instead of the ground ancho.

2 tablespoons ground ancho or other chile, or ground cayenne

2 teaspoons dried oregano

2 teaspoons garlic powder

2 teaspoons cumin seeds, toasted and ground

2 teaspoons dried cilantro

½ teaspoon dried orange peel, ground, optional

⅛ teaspoon ground black pepper

Pumpkin Pie Spice

2 tablespoons ground cinnamon

1 tablespoon ground ginger

1 teaspoon allspice

1 teaspoon freshly grated nutmeg

½ teaspoon ground cloves

Why buy it when you can make your own? I am a huge cinnamon fan but not as much a clove lover, so clove is minimized here. Feel free to adjust the quantities to your liking. That's the joy of making your own blends! I prefer to grate my nutmeg with a fine grater and to grind my own cloves in a spice grinder.

MAKES ALMOST ¼ CUP

Combine all the spices and transfer to a bottle or other container. Store in a cool, dark place for 1 to 2 months.

Salt-Free Spicy Mix

This mix works well when you are cutting down on salt because it adds a lot of flavor. If you make it and decide you like it, make a quadruple batch so it will last you at least 1 month.

MAKES ABOUT ¼ CUP

Combine all ingredients in a blender and process until powdered to combine flavors. Transfer to a nice bottle or tin. Store in a cool, dark place for up to 2 months.

1½ teaspoons dried parsley

1½ teaspoons dried sage

1½ teaspoons dried thyme

1 teaspoon dried rosemary

1 teaspoon paprika

1 teaspoon dried oregano

1 teaspoon dried celery seed

1 teaspoon garlic powder

1 teaspoon onion powder

1 teaspoon freshly ground black pepper

3 tablespoons nutritional yeast flakes

Using Your Spice (Sometimes Called Coffee) Grinder

A spice grinder is a wonderful kitchen tool that makes grinding hard seeds (spices) easier. I like to toast many of my spices before grinding to boost the flavor way beyond what you get with store-bought ground spices. One spice that I am always grinding is cumin because I like it—a lot.

Sometimes, though, you grind something like cumin but then don't want everything else you put in your spice grinder, such as other nuts or seeds, to taste like cumin.

To clean the grinder to get rid of residual spices, grind some dry white rice or a piece of white bread. Either will help pull out the volatile oils from the inside of the grinder between uses. Most grinders should not be submerged in water so after you grind and discard the white bread or rice, use a slightly damp paper towel to wipe out the area near the blades and then rinse the top well and dry.

Although spice grinders are fairly inexpensive to purchase, if you don't have one and want to grind spices, use your blender for grinding. The food processor will not work. Trust me, I have tried: The seeds just spin around the bowl.

Make friends with your grinder and spices. They will change how you cook and how your food tastes.

FOUR

Grains

One of the best uses for the pressure cooker is for cooking whole grains. You can expect grains to cook in about 50 percent less time than with traditional stovetop cooking, and they turn out great, as long as you follow the recommended cooking times and liquid ratios. You will find many types of grains—ancient, traditional, and gluten-free—in this chapter. No longer will you say that cooking whole grains takes too long.

I like to cook a pot of grain at least once a week to combine with cooked beans and vegetables or to serve as a base for chili or stew. Whole grains fill you up with "good for you" fiber and are a perfect complement to other vegan food.

Keeping cooked whole grains in your refrigerator or freezer allows you to easily put together cold or hot grain salads, side dishes, and even desserts. Leftover grains get used to make veggie burgers or can be added to soup. You'll learn about soaking grains for faster cooking and how to cook "perfect" grains. You'll find a wide variety of recipes to satisfy your whole grain desires, including one for cornbread "baked" in the pressure cooker.

Ancient Grains

Often also called heirloom grains, ancient grains were eaten by our ancestors. There is a movement to reintroduce these grains instead of relying so heavily on hybridized modern wheat. Many of these ancient grains are gluten-free, as they tend to be the seed heads of grasses rather than cultivated grains. But there is also a growing array of gluten-containing grains available in specialty and natural-food stores, as well as online.

Gluten-Free Ancient Grains

The most popular gluten-free grains are amaranth, buckwheat, millet, quinoa, sorghum, and teff. (Kaniwa, fonio, and Job's tears are gaining notice, but are much more difficult to find and quite pricey so I'll only mention them here.) Wild rice is also gluten-free and although it's a grass (which might not be considered an ancient grain), I include it in this chapter as it's cooked like many grains.

Amaranth, possibly 8,000 years old, was grown in Central and South America. It is a tiny grain which tastes toasty and grassy. It becomes gelatinous when cooked, like hot cereal but unlike quinoa (which has individual grains). I like adding it to recipes where it's not the star but plays a good supporting role, in both savory and sweet grain dishes or in soup or stew.

Buckwheat, sometimes referred to as beech wheat, is not a true grain, and not related to wheat, but part of the rhubarb family. It has been cultivated since 6,000 B.C. Buckwheat has a distinct texture and flavor, which some people grow to love. It comes in two forms: raw, and toasted—in which case it's called kasha or buckwheat groats. Raw buckwheat often has a greenish hue while toasted buckwheat is reddish brown. This is a fast-cooking grain so pay attention when using it.

Millet is not commonly eaten in the United States but is popular in many parts of the world, including India, China, Russia, South America, and Africa. It is very easy to digest and goes well with many dishes and herbs and spices. In America, we know it best as bird seed. Lucky birds.

Quinoa has become so popular in the United States that its cost has almost quadrupled in the last few years. It is called the mother grain because it was one of the foods that sustained people in the Andes Mountains in Peru, Bolivia, and Ecuador for hundreds of years. Hopefully the indigenous farmers can increase sustainable production, make a living, and ship more quinoa to the United States. Or perhaps more American farmers can start growing quinoa. It grows best at high altitudes but I recently met a California farmer who successfully grew quinoa near sea level.

Sorghum is an ancient grain that originated in Africa and is used there and in India. It grows well in the Southern United States but it is another grain most often used for bird food in this country. It makes an amazing gluten-free, whole grain stand-in for Israeli couscous. You will most often find it whole but it also comes pearled. It is a longer-cooking grain, so using the pressure cooker is almost essential.

Teff is a teeny tiny grain that I find to be similar in texture to amaranth when cooked. I often use them interchangeably in recipes and rarely on their own as the texture and flavor are too distinctive for my taste. It is the staple grain in Ethiopia, where it sustains up to two-thirds of the population, often by being ground into flour to make the fermented flatbread, injera.

Wild rice is a grass that is not related to traditional Asian rice. It is grown in areas with shallow water and streams. It tends to be expensive so it is often eaten for special occasions and holidays, but it's tasty all year long. It has a dark, chewy outer covering and a tender, grassy, almost vegetal tasting inside. When fully cooked the grains pop open.

Gluten-Containing Ancient Grains

Most of the gluten-containing ancient grains are related to wheat, except for barley. They include triticale, spelt, farro, Kamut, einkorn, and emmer. There are also "heirloom" varieties of wheat, such as Sonoran, which have not been hybridized to have high gluten content, which makes them

Grain Cooking Basics

more digestible for many people. These tough hulled whole grains benefit from soaking overnight, or longer. They will then cook more quickly and potentially be easier to digest.

Barley was supposedly included in Esau's porridge mentioned in the Bible. It is available in a few versions: *whole,* which is also called hulled; *hull-less,* which is almost whole, but has a thin hull which falls off during processing; and *pearl,* which is not a whole grain because the husk has been removed. The whole and hull-less versions are nutritionally superior. There is purple hull-less barley (sometimes called black barley), which is quite pretty, looking similar to black rice.

The pressure cooker works well with these and all whole grains.

People often avoid cooking whole grains because they take about twice as long to cook as polished or white grains. The pressure cooker generally cuts cooking time by 50 percent. On the stovetop, brown rice cooks in 45 minutes, but takes only 22 minutes in the pressure cooker. Cooking time reductions are similar for white rice.

The chart on page 51 gives an approximate time for each grain. A rule of thumb is to read the package instructions for stovetop cooking and cut that time in half—that's how long to cook it at pressure.

But grains, like other whole foods, can vary from batch to batch, and the cooking time can vary accordingly. Grains (like beans) lose moisture and dry out as they age. Older grains therefore take longer to cook than fresher grains, which is rarely something that we, as consumers, can determine.

If you cook a grain according to the directions and discover it is not thoroughly cooked, or if there is liquid remaining,

Soaking Grains

Maria Speck, who has written books on whole grains, recommends soaking all "chewy" whole grains for better digestibility. I agree, and soak a number of grains: whole barley, hull-less barley, farro, Kamut, whole oat groats, wheat and rye berries (and any wheat relatives, like emmer), spelt, and triticale. You can cook any whole grain without soaking if you don't have time. Just be sure to add at least 10 minutes to the time listed in Grain Cooking At-a-Glance (page 51).

Overnight Soak: A long, slow soak in cool water is best for activating the nutrients within the grain. This is similar to how you'd soak beans. In a bowl or jar, cover the grains by more than double their volume of water and let sit on the countertop to soak for 4 hours, unless the temperature of your kitchen is above 80 degrees, which will speed up the soaking process. Grains won't soak as well in the refrigerator, but if that is your only choice, increase the soak time to 12 hours. Drain the soaking water (try watering your plants with it), and cook according to directions.

Quick Soak: This technique is also often used with beans. Put the grains in a pot and add water to cover the grains by 3 inches. Bring to a boil and boil for 1 minute. Turn off the heat, cover, and let sit for 1 hour. Drain and continue cooking.

In macrobiotic cooking, they also suggest that you soak your brown rice for at least 8 hours or overnight in the amount of cooking water that you would use. Then cook according to standard cooking directions, using the soaked rice and the water it was soaked in.

usually locking the lid back on and waiting for a few minutes will remedy this issue. This allows the grain to keep cooking in the residual heat and absorbing liquid. If that doesn't work you can bring the pot back to high pressure for a minute or two and then let the pressure come down again naturally.

Over time, you may come up with your own method for cooking grains in the pressure cooker. There are many ways to achieve good results; whatever method gets the grains cooked how you like them is the one that you want to use. There is no absolute perfection in cooking grains, but the times that I have provided work for me almost always.

Grain Cooking Timetable

The chart that follows highlights the amount of liquid needed, timing, and amount of cooked grain produced for pressure cooking a wide variety of whole grains. Use it as a quick reference for simple cooking of your grains, to adapt one of my recipes to cook a different type of grain, or to adapt conventional grain recipes.

Cook all grains at high pressure and use a natural release. The amounts given are for cooking 1 cup of dry grains. To double or triple the amounts, see Cooking Multiple Cups of Grain, page 52. The first time you cook a grain, cook it at pressure for the lowest time given in the range. If the grain is not yet done to your preference, bring it back to pressure for a bit longer. Over time you'll learn how you like to cook each grain.

I recommend soaking some grains before cooking, as indicated in the chart. If you don't have time to soak, skip the soaking and add 10 minutes to the cooking time.

You can toast grains if you like before cooking, but I find toasting for 2 to 3 minutes over medium heat only really improves the flavor of millet and quinoa, or when making a grain pilaf.

Adding salt to whole grains before cooking can make them tough, so I suggest salting after cooking. This also lets you decrease the amount of salt you use, since its taste is more apparent when sprinkled on the grain rather than cooked into it.

Grain Cooking At-a-Glance

Grain, dry (1 cup)	Liquid	Time (at high pressure with natural release)	Yield
Amaranth	2 cups	3 minutes	2½ cups
Barley, pearl	2½ cups	19–22 minutes	3–3¼ cups
*Barley, hulled or hull-less, soaked**	3 cups	25–35 minutes	3½–4 cups
Barley, black or purple, hull-less	3 cups	25 minutes	3½–4 cups
Buckwheat, raw or toasted (kasha)	1¾ cups	3	2–2½ cups
Cornmeal, coarse (polenta or grits)	4 cups	5 minutes	4–4½ cups
Farro, semiperlato	2–2½ cups	6–7 minutes	2–2½ cups
*Farro, whole, soaked**	1½–2 cups	15–20 minutes	3 cups
Freekeh, cracked	1½–1¾ cups	7–8 minutes	3 cups
*Kamut, soaked**	2 cups	10–15 minutes	2½ cups
Millet	1¾ cups	10 minutes	3–3½ cups
Oats, rolled ("Bowl in Pot" method, see page 14)	2½ cups	2–4 minutes	3–3½ cups
Oats, steel-cut	3 cups	3–5 minutes	3 cups
*Oats, whole groats, soaked**	2 cups	20–22 minutes	2–2½ cups
Quinoa	1¼ cups	5 minutes	3–3½ cups
*Rye, whole, berries, soaked**	1½–2 cups	25 minutes	2–2½ cups
*Spelt, soaked**	1½ cups	22 minutes	3 cups
Sorghum	2½ cups	30–35 minutes	3½ cups
Teff	2½ cups	3 minutes	3 cups
*Triticale, soaked**	2 cups	20 minutes	2–2½ cups
*Wheat berries, soaked**	2 cups	10–15 minutes	2–2½ cups
Wild rice	2½ cups	25 minutes	3–4 cups

*Cooks best when soaked or quick soaked. See Soaking Grains, page 49.

Cooking Multiple Cups of Grain

Cooking time under pressure does not change when cooking larger quantities of grains. However, the pressure cooker will take longer to get to pressure and longer to come down.

I am not sure of the exact science, but to avoid soggy grains when you double a grain quantity, it is important to use less than double the amount of water. (I use a similar formula when adding salt to recipes so that they don't end up too salty.) I subtract ¼ cup of liquid for each additional cup of grain used. So to cook 1 cup of brown rice, I use 1½ cups water. To cook 2 cups of brown rice, I use 1½ cups plus 1¼ cups, or 2¾ cup water. And so on, as the chart below shows. Please adjust for grains that start with a different ratio of grain to water—still subtracting ¼ cup liquid for each additional cup of grain. (If the math has you stymied, you can always just double the water and have your slotted spoon handy to remove any excess liquid.)

Quinoa	Liquid
1 cup	1¼ cups
2 cups	2¼ cups (1¼ cups + 1 cup)
3 cups	3 cups (2¼ cups + ¾ cup)
4 cups	3½ cups (3 cups + ½ cup)

Brown Rice	Liquid
1 cup	1½ cups
2 cups	2¾ cups (1½ cups + 1¼ cups)
3 cups	3¾ cups (2¾ cups + 1 cup)
4 cups	4½ cups (3¾ cups + ¾ cup)

Rice

Often when we think of rice, we think mostly about white or brown. But there is truly a world of rice varieties available, as rice is eaten in many parts of the world. If you are seeking a way to broaden your vegan options, especially for whole grains, then it's time to explore some new-to-you varieties of rice. You might be amazed at the array of colors and resulting textures and flavors. All rice is definitely not the same.

When I want to wow people I like to make black or red rice. For everyday eating, I like Indonesian Volcano or Mekong Flower rice because they are still brown but cook more quickly and are more exotic and flavorful than standard brown rice. Sometimes I mix black rice in with my brown rice and cook that for the full 22 minutes at pressure with good results.

Rice Cooking Timetable

The chart that follows highlights the amount of liquid needed, timing, and amount of cooked rice yielded for pressure cooking a wide variety of rices. Use it as a quick reference for simple cooking of your rice, to adapt one of my recipes to cook a different type of rice, or to adapt conventional rice recipes.

Rice Cooking At-a-Glance

Rice, dry (1 cup)	Liquid	Time	Yield
WHITE RICE			
Arborio, carnaroli	3–3½ cups	5–7 minutes	4 cups
Kalijira, white	1 cup	5 minutes	3 cups
Most all other white rice, including basmati, jasmine, sushi	1–1¼ cups	3 minutes	3 cups
WHOLE GRAIN RICE			
Black (Forbidden)	1½ cups	15 minutes	3 cups
Brown, most, including basmati, jasmine, sushi	1½ cups	22 minutes	2½–3 cups
Brown, basmati, (aged)	1¼–1½ cups	12–15 minutes	3 cups
Indonesian Volcano	1½ cups	15 minutes	3 cups
Jade Pearl (bamboo)*	1½ cups	10 minutes	3 cups
Jasmine, black	1¼ cups	8 minutes	3 cups
Jasmine, coral	1¼ cups	7–8 minutes	3 cups
Jasmine, purple	1½ cups	3 minutes	3 cups
Jasmine, ruby red	1½ cups	9 minutes	3 cups
Mekong Flower	1¼ cups	15 minutes	3 cups
Pink, Madagascar	1¼ cups	10 minutes	3 cups
Red, long-grain*	1½–1¾ cups	9 minutes	3 cups
Red, short-grain*	1¼ cups	10 minutes	3 cups
Red, Bhutanese*	1¼ cups	10 minutes	3 cups
Red, Colusari	1½ cups	15 minutes	3 cups
Red, Wehani	1½ cups	20–22 minutes	3 cups
Purple	1¼–1½ cups	3–5 minutes	3 cups

* Let the pot sit for at least 10 minutes after the pressure comes down before removing the lid.

13 minutes high pressure,
natural release

⅓ cup millet

¼ cup red or pink rice

¼ cup Mekong Flower or brown
Volcano rice

2 tablespoons amaranth or teff

1¾ cups water or vegetable
stock

Mixed-Grain Blend
for Any Time of Day

Do you ever have small amounts of several different dried grains hanging
around the pantry and wonder what to do with them all? Well, I did one
morning and thought, Why not combine them together? This is the result:
It's quite tasty, has good texture, is very digestible, and gluten-free. See the
variations for other mixtures that work if you don't have this group of more
unusual grains.

The recipe is unseasoned so that you can make it your own, going either
sweet or savory, or leave it just as it is. I bet that it would make wonderful
veggie burgers but I haven't yet tried that. If you want to make this a one-pot
meal, add ½ cup dried lentils along with the grains and increase the water by
1 cup. The types of rice used here do matter because they have similar cooking
times.

You can mix any blend of grains that share the same cooking time,
although you will have to do some math to get the liquid quantity correct. See
the charts for cooking grain and rice on pages 51 and 53.

If you want to use standard brown rice instead of more exotic rice, soak it
overnight and drain before using. It will cook in the 13-minute time frame.

MAKES AT LEAST 3 CUPS

1. Combine all the grains and add to the cooker. Stir in the water
   or stock. Lock on the lid and bring to high pressure; cook for 13
   minutes. Let the pressure release naturally. Carefully remove the lid,
   tilting it away from you.

2. Stir the mixture to fluff up the grains and season as you like (see
   Seasoning Ideas, right).

   Brown and Black Rice with Barley: Use ½ cup brown rice, ¼ cup
   black rice, and ¼ cup pearl barley with 1¾ cups water or stock.
   Cook for 22 minutes.

   Kamut (or Rye or Wheat Berries), Wild Rice, and Red Rice: Use
   ½ cup Kamut, ⅓ cup wild rice, and 3 tablespoons red rice with
   2 cups water or stock. Cook for 25 minutes.

Seasoning Ideas for Plain Grains, Beans, or Any Food

The herb and spice blends found in Chapter 3 offer ways to vary the flavor of a pot of beans, grains, or even vegetables every time you make them. How much seasoning to add? It depends upon whether you are adding them before cooking or after cooking, and how spiced you like your food. Some people like to add the spices when cooking and also after the food is cooked to punch up the flavor. Generally, 1 tablespoon of spice blend is enough to flavor 1 cup of dry beans or grains.

Here are some additional ideas for cooking mild grains, such as millet, rice, buckwheat, and quinoa: Combine (to taste) ground cinnamon, nutmeg, cardamom, and star anise together and use as is, or add dried fruit or sweetener to make it sweet, or add 1 to 2 teaspoons ground cumin to keep it savory. Or head to the Mediterranean, with a twist, by adding 1 tablespoon Italian Seasoning (page 41) when cooking, and 1 more teaspoon after cooking, along with 1 to 2 tablespoons nutritional yeast, 2 to 3 tablespoons finely chopped walnuts or pine nuts, and 1 to 2 tablespoons chopped fresh flat-leaf parsley and/or basil, if in season.

For beans, I tend to use more assertive flavoring, although these combinations would work well with hearty grains such as whole oat groats, wheat or rye berries, or barley: Before cooking, add 1 tablespoon Curry Powder (page 38), 1 teaspoon ground ginger, and 2 minced cloves garlic. After cooking, top with 2 tablespoons chopped cilantro. For a more Southern feel, sauté 1 cup chopped red bell pepper and 1 cup diced onion, then add 1 tablespoon Cajun Seasoning (page 37) before cooking the beans or grains. After cooking, top with chopped flat-leaf parsley.

Don't be afraid to experiment with the seasoning blends in this book and other blends available in stores and online. Seasoning your food turns it from blah to brilliant with very little effort. Remember though, that just like dressing up your wardrobe with accessories, sometimes a little can go a long way and too much is too much.

1 cup chopped red or yellow
onion

1½ cups chopped red cabbage
plus 1½ cups thinly sliced red
cabbage

1 cup rye berries, soaked
overnight and drained

1 teaspoon caraway seeds

2 bay leaves

¾ cup vegetable stock or water

2 tablespoons whole-grain
mustard

1 tablespoon date or maple
syrup

1 to 2 tablespoons fresh lemon
juice

1 medium carrot, grated
(½ to 1 cup)

¼ cup chopped fresh chives

Salt, optional

Lots of freshly ground black
pepper

4 C's Warm Rye Berry Salad

Photo, page I-2

This hearty salad tastes great but has very simple ingredients, including cabbage, caraway, carrots, and chives. If you've never cooked rye berries before, you might be surprised by their firm texture and amazing flavor. You can also make a salad with other whole grains such as farro, Kamut, spelt, wheat berries, or—if you want it to be gluten-free—whole oat groats (refer to Grain Cooking At-a-Glance, page 51, for the right times and liquid ratios).

SERVES 4 TO 6

1. Heat a stovetop cooker over medium heat, or set an electric cooker to sauté. Add the onion and the 1½ cups chopped cabbage and dry sauté until the onion starts to look translucent. Add water by the tablespoon as needed to prevent any sticking.

2. Add the rye berries, caraway seeds, bay leaves, and stock. Lock the lid on the cooker. Bring to high pressure; cook for 25 minutes. Let the pressure come down naturally. Remove the lid, tilting it away from you.

3. Carefully remove and discard the bay leaves. Transfer the grain mixture to a large bowl and let cool until almost room temperature. Once cool, drain and discard any remaining cooking liquid.

4. Combine the mustard, date or maple syrup, and lemon juice in a small bowl. Add the dressing to the cooled rye.

5. Stir in the sliced cabbage, carrot, and chives. Add salt (if you like) and pepper to taste. Serve immediately or store in the refrigerator for up to 5 days. Taste and adjust seasonings before serving.

Kamut Salad
with a Kick

If you like spice, as I do, then this salad will make you smile and perhaps bring a few small tears to your eyes. The heat of the chiles is tempered by the mint and lemon juice. If you prefer less heat, seed the chilies before adding to the dressing. The salad also works well with any whole grain such as barley, whole oats, wheat berries, spelt, or sorghum. See Grain Cooking At-a-Glance, page 51, for cooking times and liquid ratios. If fresh corn is in season, add 1 cup to the Kamut when it comes out of the pressure cooker. It will cook in the residual heat.

SERVES 4 TO 6

1. Heat a stovetop pressure cooker over medium heat, or set an electric cooker to sauté. Add 2 teaspoons of the garlic and dry sauté for 30 seconds, until softened but not browned. Add the Kamut, stock, and bay leaf.

2. Lock on the lid. Bring to high pressure; cook for 15 minutes. Let the pressure come down naturally. Remove the lid carefully, tilting it away from you.

3. Transfer the cooked grains to a large bowl and let cool to room temperature.

4. To make the dressing, place the remaining 1 teaspoon garlic, the dates and their soaking water, mint, cilantro, chiles, scallions, lemon zest and juice, and salt in a blender. Blend until smooth, scraping down the sides as needed.

5. Remove the bay leaf from the Kamut and discard. Add the summer squash and tomatoes. Add the dressing and mix gently so that you don't smash the tomatoes.

6. Refrigerate until serving. Taste and adjust seasonings.

1 tablespoon chopped garlic

1½ cups Kamut, soaked overnight and drained

2¾ cups vegetable stock

1 bay leaf

2 pitted dates, soaked in 3 tablespoons hot water

½ cup chopped fresh mint (from 1 large bunch)

½ cup chopped cilantro

1 or 2 jalapeño chiles, stems cut off

1 serrano or other hot fresh chile, stem cut off

3 scallions, chopped, both white and green parts

2 teaspoons grated lemon zest

¼ cup fresh lemon juice

½ teaspoon salt

1 to 2 medium summer squash, cut into ¼-inch pieces to equal 2 cups

1 pint cherry tomatoes, halved

GRAINS

1 cup diced onion

5 cloves garlic, minced

2 tablespoons finely chopped
sun-dried tomato

1 tablespoon Italian Seasoning
(page 41), or your favorite
store-bought Italian
seasoning

1 cup whole farro (not pearled
or semiperlato), soaked
overnight and drained

1½ cups vegetable stock

2 tablespoons balsamic vinegar

2 tablespoons finely chopped
fresh flat-leaf parsley

1½ cups chopped ripe tomatoes,
ideally a mix of colors

1½ cups packed arugula,
chopped; plus additional
whole small leaves for
serving

Salt and freshly ground black
pepper

Farro Salad with Tomatoes and Arugula

Photo, page I-2

Any other hearty grain, such as spelt, rye, wheat berries, hull-less barley, and whole oat groats, can stand in for the farro in this salad (see Grain Cooking At-a-Glance, page 51, for times and ratios). Farro, however, is grown in the region where the salad originated: Italy. If you love fresh basil, feel free to add some to the cooked farro before putting it atop the arugula. The flavor of the salad depends upon having good ripe tomatoes, so choose them wisely. I love heirloom tomatoes, so I make this dish during summer's height of tomato season.

SERVES 4 TO 6

1. Heat a stovetop pressure cooker over medium heat, or set an electric cooker to sauté. Add the onion and about two-thirds of the garlic and dry sauté for 2 to 3 minutes, until the onion starts turning translucent.

2. Turn off the sauté function if using an electric cooker or turn up the heat on the stovetop cooker. Add the sun-dried tomatoes, seasoning, farro, and stock.

3. Lock on the lid. Bring to high pressure; cook for 15 minutes. Let the pressure come down naturally. Carefully remove the lid, tilting it away from you.

4. Transfer the grain mixture to a large glass dish or bowl and let cool for a few minutes. Add the remaining garlic and the balsamic vinegar and stir. Let cool to room temperature.

5. When cool, add the parsley, tomatoes, chopped arugula, and salt and pepper to taste, mixing gently. Serve the salad on top of a bed of arugula.

Barley, Wheat Berry, and Hazelnut Salad

Serve this simple, hearty winter salad on a bed of fresh greens (use whatever looks best in the supermarket or at the farmers' market). Any leftovers can go into pita bread halves or wraps. It is adapted from a recipe in Ginny Callan's *Horn of the Moon Cookbook*.

SERVES 4

1. Combine the barley, wheat berries, and water in a pressure cooker. Lock on the lid and bring to high pressure; cook for 25 minutes. Let the pressure come down naturally. Carefully remove the lid, tilting it away from you.

2. Transfer the grains to a large bowl. Let cool for at least 15 minutes.

3. While the grains are cooking, combine the lemon juice, olive oil, and salt and pepper to taste in a medium bowl. Set the dressing aside.

4. When the grains are cool, add the dressing, celery, carrot, parsley, hazelnuts, and garlic. Taste and adjust the seasonings.

5. Refrigerate for an hour or two before serving, or serve immediately at room temperature.

25 minutes high pressure, natural release

1 cup pearl barley (not quick-cooking)

⅓ cup wheat berries

2⅔ cups water

¼ cup lemon juice

3 tablespoons olive oil; or 2 tablespoons olive oil plus 1 tablespoon hazelnut oil

½ teaspoon salt

Freshly ground black pepper

2 stalks celery, finely chopped

1 carrot, finely chopped

½ cup finely chopped fresh parsley of any kind

¼ cup halved or chopped toasted hazelnuts or toasted almonds

4 large cloves garlic, minced

GRAINS

2 cups assorted green and yellow beans, cut into 1-inch pieces

½ to 1 cup broccoli florets

3⅓ cups vegetable stock or water

1¼ cups whole (or hulled) barley, soaked overnight and drained

2 tablespoons tamari or soy sauce

1 tablespoon rice vinegar or balsamic vinegar

1 teaspoon toasted sesame oil

½ to 1 tablespoon grated fresh ginger

2 to 3 cloves garlic, minced

½ cup diced carrot (1 medium)

½ cup diced unpeeled Japanese, Middle Eastern, or English cucumber

½ cup sliced scallions

2 tablespoons toasted sesame seeds

Gingery Barley Salad

This substantial dish is easy to put together. Some of the vegetables are lightly cooked and others are raw, providing contrast. If you didn't remember to soak the barley, cook it for 30 minutes. If you only eat gluten-free grains, you can make this with whole oat groats and adjust the cooking time to 20 to 22 minutes at pressure.

SERVES 4 TO 6 (PLUS LEFTOVER COOKED BARLEY*)

1. Combine the green beans and broccoli in a pressure cooker with ⅓ cup of the stock. Bring to high pressure; cook for 1 minute. Quick release the pressure. Carefully remove the lid, tilting it away from you. Transfer the cooked vegetables to a medium bowl and set aside.

2. Drain the liquid from the pressure cooker. Add the barley and remaining 3 cups stock. Lock on the lid. Bring to high pressure; cook for 15 minutes. Let the pressure come down naturally. Carefully open the cooker, tilting the lid away from you.

3. While the barley is cooking, combine the tamari, vinegar, sesame oil, and ginger and garlic (to taste) in a small bowl. Set the dressing aside.

4. Transfer half the barley to the bowl with the cooked beans and broccoli (reserve the other half for another use*). Add the carrot, cucumber, scallions, and dressing and stir well to combine.

5. Let sit for at least 15 minutes before serving. Serve immediately or store in the refrigerator for up to 5 days. Garnish with the toasted sesame seeds just before serving.

*One great way to use the remaining barley mixture is with the Barley, Shiitake, and Walnut Burgers, page 236.

Late Summer or Early Fall Vegetable Quinoa Salad

Tomatillos are an underutilized vegetable with a tart flavor and crunchy texture. Here they are paired with other veggies to make a tasty quinoa salad. Tomatillos are used often in Mexican cooking and work best with those types of seasonings. If you like your food spicy, add part of a hot chile when blending the tomatillos.

My favorite grain for this dish is quinoa but other cooked grains will also work. Follow cooking directions and liquid ratios at Grain Cooking At-a-Glance, page 51.

SERVES 4 TO 6

¾ pound tomatillos, husks removed, rinsed

1 clove garlic, minced or crushed

2 tablespoons lime juice or mild vinegar

1 cup quinoa, rinsed and drained

1 red bell pepper, cored, seeded, and diced

1¼ cups vegetable stock or water

2 scallions, chopped

3 tablespoons chopped cilantro

1 cup diced fresh tomato

Salt and freshly ground black pepper

1. Chop half of the tomatillos into bite-sized pieces and set aside. Place the remaining tomatillos in a blender along with the garlic and lime juice. Blend until smooth. Set aside.

2. Heat a stovetop pressure cooker over medium heat or set an electric cooker to sauté. Add the quinoa and toast for 1 to 2 minutes. Add the bell pepper and dry sauté 1 minute. Add the stock.

3. Lock the lid on the pressure cooker. Bring to high pressure; cook for 5 minutes. Let the pressure come down naturally. Remove the lid, carefully tilting it away from you.

4. Check to be sure that the quinoa is fully cooked: It should have little white rings and be translucent and puffed up. If not cooked through, lock on the lid and let sit for 2 to 3 minutes longer.

5. Transfer the quinoa to a large bowl or platter. Add the reserved tomatillos, the scallions, cilantro, and tomato. Add the pureed tomatillo mixture and toss to combine.

6. Taste and add salt and pepper. Serve warm or at room temperature.

1 cup quinoa, rinsed and drained

¼ cup raw sunflower seeds

½ teaspoon ground cinnamon

Pinch each ground cardamom and ground coriander, optional

¼ teaspoon freshly ground black pepper

½ cup diced onion or shallots

¼ cup dried cranberries

1¼ cups vegetable stock

Salt

2 to 3 tablespoons chopped fresh flat-leaf parsley or cilantro

Quinoa Stuffing for Squash or Anything Else

One morning I had a brilliant idea: Cut a squash in half, fill it with uncooked quinoa as a stuffing, and it would come out as squash stuffed with cooked quinoa. But that's not quite what happened. I ended up with cooked squash halves, which I enjoyed eating, but the quinoa stuffing was not cooked. I had to cook it separately and that's what this is. It's delicious stuffed into already cooked squash halves, but also worth making on its own to serve with greens.

SERVES 4, OR ENOUGH TO FILL 4 TO 6 SMALL SQUASH HALVES

1. Heat a stovetop pressure cooker over medium heat or set an electric cooker to sauté. Add the quinoa and toast for a minute, until it smells toasty. Add the sunflower seeds, spices, and onion and dry sauté for 2 minutes. Add the cranberries and stock.

2. Lock the lid on the cooker and bring to high pressure. Cook for 5 minutes. Let the pressure come down naturally. Remove the lid, carefully tilting it away from you.

3. Transfer the contents to a medium serving bowl and add salt to taste. Stir in the parsley and serve.

To use as stuffing for cooked winter squash halves: Cook 4 to 6 small squash halves, such as acorn or delicata, according to the chart on page 120. Spoon stuffing into the centers and place on a baking sheet. Broil for 3 to 5 minutes, until the filling is slightly crispy; or bake at 350°F for 10 to 20 minutes, until the squash and filling are both warm.

Quinoa with Pistachios and Currants

Quinoa takes on flavors so well. Here it becomes exotic with a hint of the Middle East from cardamom and pistachios. If you want to serve this as a main-dish salad, chill it and add 1 cup cooked chickpeas and ¼ cup diced red onion. Add more lemon juice and zest too, if you like.

SERVES 4

1. Heat a stovetop pressure cooker over medium heat, or set an electric cooker to sauté. Add the oil, or spray the bottom with cooking spray, or omit the oil if you prefer to dry sauté. Add the shallots and garlic and sauté or dry sauté for 2 minutes, or until the shallots just start to soften. Add the quinoa and cardamom and stir for 2 minutes to toast lightly. Add the carrot, stock, cinnamon stick, and currants. Stir once.

2. Lock on the lid. Bring to high pressure; cook for 5 minutes. Let the pressure come down naturally. Remove the lid, carefully tilting it away from you.

3. Remove and discard the cinnamon stick. Add salt and pepper to taste. Stir to fluff. Stir in the cilantro, pistachios, and lemon zest and juice.

4. Transfer to a bowl or platter. Garnish with scallion, if desired, and serve.

1 to 2 teaspoons vegetable oil; or vegetable cooking spray, optional

2 shallots, minced, or ¼ cup minced onion

1 clove garlic, minced

1 cup quinoa, rinsed and drained

1 teaspoon ground cardamom

½ cup thinly sliced carrot

1¼ cups vegetable stock or water

1 (1-inch) cinnamon stick

3 tablespoons dried currants

¼ teaspoon salt

Freshly ground black pepper

¼ cup chopped cilantro

3 tablespoons toasted pistachios, chopped

½ teaspoon grated lemon zest

1 to 2 tablespoons fresh lemon juice

1 scallion, chopped, for garnish, optional

GRAINS

1 cup quinoa, rinsed and
drained

2 cups nondairy milk, such as
vanilla almond, hemp, soy, or
coconut

1½ cups mixed berries

1 to 2 tablespoons agave or
other sweetener

3 tablespoons toasted sliced or
slivered almonds

1 to 2 tablespoons
unsweetened shredded or
flaked coconut, optional

Red, White, and Blue Quinoa

In the summer, I prepare quinoa a lot, as it's filling but also light, especially when mixed with berries or other summer fruit. I developed this recipe for a cooking demonstration at a farmers' market on July Fourth. I wanted to use market-fresh ingredients, so I chose blueberries, blackberries, and strawberries. The result was a tasty, lightly sweet surprise that you can enjoy for breakfast or dessert.

———————

SERVES 4

1. Heat a stovetop cooker over medium heat or set an electric cooker to sauté. Add the quinoa and toast for 1 minute. Add the milk and stir.

2. Lock the lid on the cooker. Bring to high pressure; cook for 5 minutes. Let the pressure come down naturally. Remove the lid, carefully tilting it away from you.

3. Stir in the berries and sweetener to taste. Spoon into bowls and top with the almonds and coconut, if using.

Freekeh with Eggplant and Tomato

Don't know what freekeh is? It's OK. I didn't know either until a short time ago. It's cracked roasted green wheat. I would say that it's similar to bulgur, which it resembles, but that just wouldn't be true. It has an exotic smoky aroma that I truly enjoy. I like this recipe so much that I once added it to a burger mixture—which you can do, too—instead of another cooked grain.

Cooking freekeh in the pressure cooker is so easy. It can be paired with almost any vegetable at all. This summery eggplant and tomato version can be enjoyed hot, warm, or cold.

SERVES 4 TO 6

1. Heat a stovetop pressure cooker over medium heat or set an electric cooker to sauté. Add the onion and dry sauté for 2 minutes. Add the garlic and bell pepper and cook 1 minute longer. Add the freekeh, eggplant, and stock.

2. Lock the lid on the pressure cooker. Bring to high pressure; cook for 7 minutes. Let the pressure come down naturally. Remove the lid, carefully tilting it away from you.

3. Stir the tomatoes into the freekeh. Lock the lid on and let sit for 2 minutes.

4. Remove the lid, add salt and pepper to taste, and stir in the parsley. Transfer to a platter and serve.

1 cup diced red onion

3 cloves garlic, minced

1 cup chopped red, yellow, or orange bell pepper

1 cup cracked freekeh

½ cup diced eggplant

1¾ cups vegetable stock

½ cup diced fresh or canned tomatoes

Salt and freshly ground black pepper

¼ cup finely chopped fresh flat-leaf parsley

1½ cups millet

2½ cups water

Salt

Basic Mmmm...Millet

Here is plain, pressure-cooked millet that you can season any way you like, sweet or savory (see Seasoning Ideas, page 55). Millet looks nice, with its sunny yellow color, and it's easy to digest. Think about having it for breakfast when oats aren't on the menu.

SERVES 4 TO 6

1. Heat a stovetop pressure cooker over medium heat or set an electric cooker to sauté. Add the millet and toast, stirring often, until it begins to pop and smell toasty.

2. Add the water and lock on the lid. Bring to high pressure; cook for 10 minutes. Let the pot rest for a full 10 minutes. If the pressure has not released at 10 minutes, quick release any remaining pressure. Remove the lid, carefully tilting it away from you.

3. Check to see if the millet is cooked. The grains will be all yellow without white areas. If not fully cooked, lock on the lid for another 5 minutes and let sit undisturbed. Fluff the millet, adding salt to taste.

Lemon-Scented Millet with Greens

This is an adaptation of a recipe by my pressure cooking mentor, Lorna Sass. The millet is well-cooked, with a moist consistency, which makes it wonderful for eating and also for making into burgers. Use this cooked mixture instead of plain cooked millet in any burger recipe (see pages 242 and 243).

SERVES 4

1. Heat a stovetop pressure cooker over medium heat or set an electric cooker to sauté. Add the millet and dry sauté until it smells toasty. Add the leek and garlic and cook for 1 minute. Add the stock.

2. Lock the lid and bring the mixture to high pressure; cook for 10 minutes. Let the pressure come down naturally. Remove the lid, carefully tilting it away from you.

3. Add the greens to the pot. Replace the cover and let sit for 3 minutes while the greens steam.

4. Carefully remove the lid again and stir in the lemon zest and juice. Add salt to taste.

10 minutes high pressure, natural release for 10 minutes

1 cup millet, rinsed

1 cup sliced leek or onion

2 cloves garlic, minced

3 cups vegetable stock or water

2 cups chopped greens (such as tatsoi, bok choy, kale, or collards)

1 tablespoon grated lemon or lemon zest

1 to 3 tablespoons lemon juice

Salt

Vegetable cooking spray

½ cup coarse polenta

1 cup cornmeal (finer grind
than polenta)

½ cup gluten-free flour mix
or all-purpose flour

¼ cup millet

1 tablespoon arrowroot
powder

1 teaspoon baking powder

1 teaspoon baking soda

½ teaspoon salt, optional

3 tablespoons golden or other
flax seeds, finely ground in a
blender or spice grinder

¼ cup water

1 cup nondairy milk of your
choice

1 tablespoon white or cider
vinegar

3 tablespoons maple syrup

2 tablespoons raw tahini

½ cup fresh or frozen (not
thawed) corn kernels

Creamy Cornbread
with Millet Photo, page I-15

This oil-free cornbread has more moisture than most, as it's not baked but cooked in the pressure cooker, which helps keep your kitchen cool in summer. You will need a 1½-quart casserole or glass dish with a lid that fits inside your cooker. Use foil if you don't have a lid.

If you want to crisp up the finished cornbread, place it in a hot, dry skillet for a few minutes on each side. It's quite moist, so it will only last a couple of days without refrigeration.

SERVES AT LEAST 8

1. Add 1 cup water to a pressure cooker. Add a trivet or rack to elevate the dish above the water (see page 14). Create a set of helper handles (see page 15) and set them on the trivet.

2. Spray the inside of a 1½- to 2-quart casserole dish that fits inside your pressure cooker with cooking spray.

3. In a large bowl, combine the polenta, cornmeal, flour blend, millet, arrowroot, baking powder, baking soda, and salt, if using, and stir well to blend.

4. In a medium bowl, combine the ground flax seeds and ¼ cup water. Stir. Add the milk and vinegar and let sit for a few minutes until the flax starts thickening.

5. Add the maple syrup, tahini, and corn kernels to the flax mixture and stir well so that the mixture is liquid and well combined.

6. Add the liquid mixture to the dry mixture, combining quickly and thoroughly. Do not overmix

7. Pour the batter into the prepared dish. Cover the dish and put in the pressure cooker. Lock on the lid. Bring to high pressure; cook for 25 minutes. Let the pressure come down naturally. Carefully remove the lid, tilting it away from you.

8. Using the helper handles, carefully lift the dish out of the pressure cooker. Carefully remove the cover to the dish, making sure not to get any liquid on the cornbread. Let cool on a rack, then cut into slices.

Brown Rice Biryani

I like to make my own biryani so that I can control what goes in it and decrease the fat. This two-step recipe requires you to prep and partially cook the vegetables in a marinade, and then cook the rice. The cooked vegetables are then added to the rice and left to steam in the heat of the pot.

Pragati Sawhney Coder of the Rugrat Chow blog gave me some tips on the spices that she likes to use in her biryani. "I use the usual whole spices (cumin, black peppercorns, cinnamon stick, cloves, cardamom, bay leaves) and just before I place the lid on (after tossing everything), I'll sprinkle some garam masala on top. I tend not to use mushrooms because they become mushy."

The resulting dish is well spiced but not hot, and the vegetables elevate its status from just "another rice side dish."

SERVES 4 TO 6

1. Combine the carrot, green beans, sweet potato, and cauliflower in a medium bowl. Combine the lime juice, garlic, chile, and ginger in a small bowl. Pour over the vegetables, toss, and let marinate for at least 10 minutes.

2. Add the vegetables and their marinade, along with ⅓ cup of the vegetable stock, to the pressure cooker. Lock the lid. Bring to high pressure; cook for 2 minutes. Quick release the pressure. Carefully remove the lid, tilting it away from you.

3. Transfer everything to a medium bowl. Cover and set aside.

4. Heat a stovetop pressure cooker over medium heat or set an electric cooker to sauté; add the oil, if using. Add the onion and sauté or dry sauté for 2 to 3 minutes, until the onion starts turning translucent. Stir in the spices and herbs. Add the tomatoes, rice, and remaining 1½ cups stock.

5. Lock the lid. Bring to high pressure; cook for 15 minutes. Let the pressure come down naturally. Remove the lid, carefully tilting it away from you. Add the reserved vegetables and any marinade. Lock the lid and let sit for 3 minutes.

6. Remove the lid and stir, adding salt to taste and more cilantro, if desired. Remove the bay leaf before serving.

1 cup diced carrot

1 cup green beans, cut into ½-inch pieces

1 cup diced sweet potato (peeled if desired)

1 cup cauliflower florets

2 tablespoons lime or lemon juice

3 cloves garlic, minced

½ small minced hot chile, such as serrano or jalapeño, or to taste

1 teaspoon grated or minced fresh ginger

1½ cups plus ⅓ cup vegetable stock

1 tablespoon oil, optional

1½ cups thinly sliced onion

½ cup chopped fresh or canned tomatoes

1 teaspoon cumin seeds

1½ teaspoons garam masala, store-bought or homemade (page 39)

½ teaspoon ground turmeric

1 bay leaf

2 tablespoons chopped cilantro, plus more for garnish

1 cup brown basmati rice, rinsed and soaked for 20 minutes to 1 hour, then drained

Salt

GRAINS

69

1 to 2 tablespoons olive oil, optional

½ cup finely chopped onion

2 or more teaspoons minced garlic

4 cups vegetable stock or water

1 teaspoon salt

1 bay leaf

2 teaspoons chopped fresh oregano, or ½ teaspoon dried

1 teaspoon chopped fresh rosemary, or ¼ teaspoon dried

3 tablespoons chopped fresh basil

2 tablespoons chopped fresh flat-leaf parsley

1 cup coarse polenta

Herbed Polenta

Polenta has gone upscale, but it's easy to make at home for pennies. Another bonus: Pressure-cooked polenta doesn't need stirring. You might end up with a lump or two (see Note), but cooking this way saves a lot of time. Adding dried mushrooms or sun-dried tomatoes (see variations on page 71) when cooking polenta adds big flavor.

Be sure to use coarse polenta (sometimes called coarse corn grits), rather than cornmeal or corn flour, which are much finer and will turn your pressure cooker into a fine mess.

SERVES 4 TO 6

1. Heat a stovetop pressure cooker over medium heat or set an electric cooker to sauté; add the oil, if using. Add the onion and sauté or dry sauté for 1 minute. Add the garlic and cook for another minute.

2. Add the water, salt, bay leaf, oregano, and rosemary, along with half of both the basil and parsley; stir. Sprinkle the polenta over the water; do not stir.

3. Lock the lid in place. Bring to high pressure; cook for 5 minutes. Let the pressure come down naturally for 10 minutes, then release any remaining pressure. If the pressure releases before 10 minutes is up, let the polenta sit in the pot for the full 10 minutes. Remove the lid, carefully tilting it away from you.

4. Remove and discard the bay leaf. Whisk the polenta to smooth out any lumps. If the polenta seems too thin, stir and simmer over medium heat for a few minutes, or lock the lid back on the cooker and let sit for 5 minutes.

5. Serve as is, or pour into glass pans to cool to at least room temperature. Once cool, bake, grill, or panfry.

✱ **Note:** If you can't stand lumps, you can cook polenta in a dish instead of cooking directly in the pot. (See "Bowl in Pot" method on page 14.) Add the ingredients to a bowl that fits inside the cooker. Put 1 cup water into the cooker, along with a rack and set the bowl on top, using helper handles (see page 15) if necessary. Lock on the lid and cook at high pressure for 5 minutes with natural release.

Sun-Dried Tomato and Olive Polenta: Add ⅓ cup finely diced sun-dried tomatoes before cooking the polenta. After the polenta is finished cooking, stir in ¼ cup chopped olives of your choice.

Mushroom Polenta: Add ½ cup chopped dried mushroom pieces and 1 cup chopped mushrooms before cooking the polenta. After the polenta is finished cooking, sprinkle with fresh herbs.

POLENTA CROUTONS

Use to top soups, stews, and salads or eat as a snack. They are versatile and tasty.

1. Pour 1 cup of the cooked polenta mixture into an 8 x 8-inch or larger glass pan, spreading it very thin, about ¼ inch thick.

2. Let cool at room temperature or in the refrigerator for a few hours.

3. When the mixture has completely set, which will take at least 30 minutes, cut the polenta into squares or rectangles the size of croutons.

4. Dry sauté the pieces, working in batches, in a nonstick skillet over medium to high heat until crispy. Or place them on a parchment-lined baking sheet sprayed with cooking spray or oil and bake at 400°F until crispy on one side, about 5 minutes. Flip over and bake the other side for 5 minutes. These will stay fresh in a container in the refrigerator for up to 5 days.

1 cup diced onion

1 cup sorghum

¾ cup diced dried apricots

2½ cups water or mild vegetable
broth

½ teaspoon salt, optional

½ cup sliced or slivered
almonds, toasted

¼ cup lemon or orange juice

2 tablespoons chopped fresh
mint, for garnish

Sorghum with Apricots, Almonds, and Mint

I had not cooked sorghum before developing this recipe. I have now discovered that when I want a gluten-free change of pace with a bit more texture, sorghum, an ancient grain, is the one to reach for. It is like Israeli couscous in size and texture, with a mild taste. I love this combo of sorghum, apricots, mint, and lemon as a side dish or salad. It also makes a pleasant base for serving cauliflower or other curry.

SERVES 4 TO 6

1. Heat a stovetop pressure cooker over medium heat, or set an electric cooker to sauté. Add the onion and dry sauté for a minute or two, until the onion starts getting translucent. Add the sorghum and toast for 10 seconds. Add ½ cup of the apricots, the water, and salt, if using.

2. Lock on the lid. Bring to high pressure; cook for 35 minutes. Let the pressure come down naturally. Carefully remove the lid, tilting it away from you.

3. Transfer the sorghum to a large bowl. Add the remaining ¼ cup apricots and the almonds, then stir in the juice. Let cool a little and garnish with the mint. Serve hot or at room temperature. This will keep in the refrigerator for up to 4 days.

Mushroom and Buckwheat "Risotto"

This is a nutritional improvement over the white rice used in traditional risotto. If you love buckwheat, you'll like the simplicity of this nutty and earthy dish. If you can't find ground mushroom powder, simply put dried mushrooms into your spice grinder or blender and process until powdered.

SERVES 4 TO 6

1. Heat a stovetop pressure cooker over medium heat or set an electric cooker to sauté; add the oil. Add the onion and sauté for about 5 minutes, stirring often. Add the garlic and buckwheat. Stir to coat the buckwheat with oil. Add the bay leaf and fresh and ground mushrooms and cook for 2 to 3 minutes. Add the stock.

2. Lock the lid. Bring to high pressure; cook for 3 minutes. Let the pressure come down naturally. Remove the lid, carefully tilting it away from you.

3. If using heartier greens, add them now, along with balsamic vinegar to taste; stir to combine. Add more liquid if necessary, or cook over medium heat or on the sauté function for a couple of minutes to thicken the risotto further, until it's the consistency that you like.

4. Remove and discard the bay leaf. Add the parsley, if using, and salt to taste.

3 minutes high pressure, natural release

1 tablespoon olive oil

2 cups finely chopped onion

2 cloves garlic, minced

1½ cups buckwheat groats (kasha)

1 bay leaf

2 cups chopped crimini or other mushrooms

1 to 2 tablespoons ground dried shiitake or porcini mushrooms

4 cups mushroom or vegetable stock (to make your own, see page 156)

3 tablespoons chopped fresh parsley or finely sliced greens such as Swiss chard or kale

1 to 2 teaspoons balsamic vinegar

Salt

2 cups water

1 cup nondairy milk, water, or apple or other fruit juice

Pinch of salt

1 cup steel-cut oats

Steel-Cut Oats in Just a Few Minutes

This is the basic recipe for steel-cut oats. Many people avoid preparing them because they take so long to cook on the stovetop. But they're ready in only a few minutes at pressure.

When I make a batch for myself, it lasts 4 to 5 days. You could even double the recipe and freeze some, to defrost and reheat later.

SERVES 4

1. Add the water and milk to the pressure cooker. Stir in the salt. Add the oats but do not stir.

2. Lock the lid on the cooker. Bring to high pressure; cook for 3 minutes. Let the pressure come down naturally. Carefully remove the lid, tilting it away from you.

3. Stir the mixture. If it seems watery or too loose, lock the lid back on and let sit for 5 minutes. Open carefully.

4. Transfer the oats to a bowl and serve. Store any uneaten oats in a container in the refrigerator for up to 5 days or freeze for up to 1 month.

   To flavor steel-cut oats: Add cinnamon sticks, grated nutmeg, cardamom, star anise, or your favorite spices, either before or after cooking the oats. Add a chopped apple or pear and up to ½ cup of your favorite chopped dried fruit before cooking if you like it soft, or after for more texture. Top with sunflower, pumpkin, or hemp seeds. Add sweetener and more cinnamon, or other spices.

Pumpkin-Spice Steel-Cut Oats

Photo, page I-15

The pumpkin bug hits each fall; I think that part of the appeal is the warming spices that usually accompany it. I like this pumpkin oatmeal with dried cranberries instead of raisins, which I use in more traditional oats. If you like nuts such as walnuts or pecans, as I do, be sure to add those, too, after cooking. If you prefer not to use maple syrup, you can sweeten with chopped dates; add to the cooker before cooking the oats.

SERVES 4

1. Combine the water and milk in a pressure cooker. Stir in the salt, spices, and cranberries. Add the oats and pumpkin, but do not stir.

2. Lock the lid on the cooker. Bring to high pressure; cook for 3 minutes. Let the pressure come down naturally. Carefully remove the lid, tilting it away from you.

3. Stir the mixture. If it seems watery, lock the lid back on and let sit for 5 minutes. Open carefully.

4. Use long tongs to remove and discard the cinnamon sticks. Add the pumpkin pie spice and maple syrup to taste. Top each bowl with toasted nuts.

   Pumpkin-Spice Buckwheat: Make this dish with buckwheat groats (kasha) instead of steel-cut oats. Follow the same directions.

3 minutes high pressure, natural release

2¼ cups water

1 cup vanilla nondairy milk

Pinch of salt

½ teaspoon grated nutmeg

¼ teaspoon ground cardamom

1 to 2 cinnamon sticks

¼ cup dried cranberries

1 cup steel-cut oats

½ cup diced pumpkin or other squash; or ½ cup pumpkin puree

1 to 2 teaspoons pumpkin pie spice

Maple syrup

¼ cup chopped toasted pecans or walnuts

3 minutes high pressure, natural release

½ cup diced onion or leek

½ cup diced carrot

½ cup diced celery

1 teaspoon minced garlic

⅛ teaspoon freshly ground black pepper

½ teaspoon smoked paprika or chipotle chile powder

1 cup ½-inch diced sweet potato

3½ cups vegetable stock; or 2½ cups vegetable stock plus 1 cup unsweetened nondairy milk

1 tablespoon tamari

1 cup steel-cut oats

2 cups chopped greens of your choice, such as kale, chard, or collards

2 tablespoons nutritional yeast, optional

1 to 2 tablespoons mellow white or other miso

2 to 3 teaspoons fresh lemon juice

¼ cup sliced scallions

2 tablespoons chopped fresh herbs such as flat-leaf parsley or cilantro

Smoky, Cheesy Steel-Cut Oats
WITH SWEET POTATO AND GREENS

If you like to start your day in a savory way, like I generally do, then you'll like this version of steel-cut oats for breakfast. If not, enjoy it for lunch or dinner.

You can add any leftover cooked vegetables that you have, along with the sliced scallions and herbs, in addition to my recommendations. Since I try to eat probiotic foods daily, I stir in a tablespoon or two of miso along with the final seasonings.

SERVES 4

1. Heat a stovetop pressure cooker over medium heat, or set an electric cooker to sauté. Add the onion, carrot, and celery and dry sauté for 3 minutes. Add the garlic, pepper, and smoked paprika and cook another minute.

2. Add the sweet potato, stock or stock and milk, and tamari. Stir. Add the oats and stir once.

3. Lock the lid. Bring to high pressure; cook for 3 minutes. Let the pressure come down naturally. Quick release any remaining pressure after 20 minutes. Remove the lid, carefully tilting it away from you.

4. Add the greens and nutritional yeast, if using. Stir once. Lock the lid back on the cooker. Let sit for 3 minutes.

5. Open the cooker carefully. Add miso, lemon juice, scallions, and herbs to each serving.

✱ Note: The miso should be added just before serving, as its probiotic qualities can cause the oats to break down if it sits, and reheating will diminish or destroy its beneficial properties. If you won't be serving this all at once, add the miso, a teaspoon or two at a time, into each serving.

Smoky, Cheesy Grits with Sweet Potato and Greens: Instead of steel-cut oats, you can make this with grits ("coarse polenta," for those not living in the South). Use 1 cup grits (or polenta) and 4 cups stock. Add the grits when the oats would be added but do not stir. Lock on the lid and continue with the recipe but cook for 5 minutes at pressure.

Brown Rice of Almost Any Kind

This is a standard brown rice recipe for the pressure cooker for all the standard rice that I buy in bulk, including short-, medium-, and long-grain rice and blends. Pressure cooking rice takes half the time as cooking on the stovetop. Be forewarned, though, that not all rice is the same. Some brands have shorter cooking times. If you have a package with a label, read it, and cut the cooking time in half. It works almost every time. If you want to double this recipe, see Cooking Multiple Cups of Grain, page 52.

SERVES 4 TO 6

1. Combine the rice and water in the pressure cooker.

2. Lock the lid. Bring to high pressure; cook for 22 minutes. Let the pressure come down naturally. Remove the lid, carefully tilting it away from you.

3. Transfer the rice to a bowl. Stir to fluff, adding salt, if desired.

22 minutes high pressure, natural release

1 cup brown rice

1½ cups water

¼ to ½ teaspoon salt

2 teaspoons olive or other oil

½ cup diced onion or leek

2 cloves garlic, minced

1½ cups arborio or carnaroli rice

3½ to 4 cups vegetable stock

Salt and freshly ground black pepper

Squeeze of lemon juice or vinegar, or sprinkle of grated soy cheese, optional

Basic Risotto

This is a recipe where you can really see the pressure cooker work its magic. Risotto can be fairly plain or enhanced with all manner of ingredients, from wild mushrooms to winter squash. When you add those ingredients depends upon how long they take to cook, so see the variations.

I became a risotto expert when my son was 5 years old. His friend Jordan would come over weekly and always asked if I had any risotto. I made it each and every time. He liked it simple: onions, leeks, stock. That's it. It's a wonderful comfort dish with which to experiment.

SERVES 4

1. Heat a stovetop pressure cooker over medium heat, or set an electric cooker to sauté; add the oil. Add the onion and sauté for 1 minute. Add the garlic and sauté another 2 minutes. Stir in the rice to coat with the oil.

2. Add 3½ cups stock to the cooker. Lock on the lid. Bring to high pressure; cook for 5 minutes. Quick release the pressure by turning the pressure valve in short bursts so that the liquid doesn't come spewing out. Carefully remove the lid, tilting it away from you.

3. Stir in more stock if needed to get the consistency as creamy as you want it. Season with salt and pepper, and add lemon juice, vinegar, and/or soy cheese, if you like.

Winter Squash and Kale Risotto: Add 1 cup diced peeled winter squash after adding the rice. Add 2 to 3 cups thinly sliced kale after opening the lid. Stir and lock the lid back on and let sit for 3 minutes. When you open the cooker, add 1 teaspoon grated lemon zest.

Spinach Risotto: After removing the lid, stir in 3 cups spinach or 1 (10-ounce) package drained thawed frozen spinach, 2 tablespoons chopped parsley, a grating of fresh nutmeg, and a squeeze of lemon juice. Lock the lid back on and let sit for 3 minutes to let the spinach wilt or warm up.

Mushroom Risotto: Use 1 cup leeks instead of the onions. After adding the rice, add 1 to 2 cups sliced mushrooms, ½ ounce soaked dried porcini mushrooms (include the soaking water as part of the liquid), 3 to 4 chopped rehydrated sun-dried tomatoes, and 1 tablespoon porcini mushroom powder. Stir 3 tablespoons chopped fresh flat-leaf parsley into the finished risotto.

Spring Saffron Risotto with Peas and Asparagus: Use 1 tablespoon olive oil, 1 chopped leek instead of the onion, and 3 to 4 minced stalks green garlic or 3 to 4 minced cloves regular garlic. Add 2 teaspoons grated lemon zest and ½ teaspoon saffron soaked in 2 tablespoons hot water after adding the rice. After removing the lid, stir in 1 cup thawed frozen peas or 1 cup halved sugar snap or snow peas, and 1 cup asparagus spears cut into 1-inch pieces. Stir until the peas and asparagus are cooked through or lock on the lid and let the pot sit for 3 minutes. Garnish with chopped chives (and their flowers, if available) or parsley.

Risotto with Green Beans and Tomato: Add ¼ to ½ teaspoon saffron, soaked in 2 tablespoons hot water, if desired before cooking. After removing the lid, add 1 cup diced seeded tomatoes and 1 cup green beans cut into 1-inch pieces; cook for a minute or two until they are cooked through or lock on the lid and let sit for 2 to 3 minutes. Add 2 teaspoons golden or white balsamic vinegar or lemon juice and 2 tablespoons minced fresh basil just before serving.

- ⅔ cup dried borlotti beans, soaked and drained

- 4 cups vegetable stock, plus more if needed

- 1 tablespoon olive oil

- ½ cup finely chopped onion

- 1½ cups arborio or carnaroli rice

- 2 to 3 tablespoons nutritional yeast, optional

- ½ cup finely chopped Beef-Style Seitan (page 213) or Bean Sausages (page 98)

- Salt and freshly ground black pepper

- 2 to 3 tablespoons chopped fresh flat-leaf parsley, for garnish

Risotto con Fagioli Borlotti

Marcella Hazan, the late *gran dama* of Italian cooking, made a risotto with *borlotti* (cranberry) beans and sausage. (Beans in risotto? Only in Italy.) I adapted the recipe from *Marcella Cucina*. This vegan version uses beefy seitan or bean sausage. We'll precook the beans as Marcella did, although I suspect that there is a way to cook the rice and beans together. For now, we'll follow Marcella's tradition, minus the meat of course.

SERVES 4 TO 6

1. Combine the beans and ½ cup of the stock in a pressure cooker. Lock on the lid. Bring to high pressure; cook for 6 to 8 minutes. Let the pressure come down naturally. Remove the lid carefully, tilting it away from you.

2. Transfer the beans to a bowl and let them sit in their cooking liquid. Wash and dry the pressure cooker.

3. Heat the stovetop pressure cooker over medium heat or set the electric cooker to sauté; add the oil. Add the onion and sauté for 3 to 5 minutes, stirring frequently, until it starts turning translucent.

4. Remove the beans from their cooking liquid and add to the pressure cooker. Add 3 tablespoons bean water to the cooker and mash up about half the beans with a potato masher or a fork. Cook for a minute, stirring well. Add the rice and stir. Add the remaining 3½ cups stock and stir well, making sure that nothing is stuck to the bottom of the cooker.

5. Lock on the lid and bring to high pressure; cook for 5 minutes. Quick release the pressure in short bursts so that you do not end up with "rice juice" coming out of the cooker. Remove the lid, carefully tilting it away from you.

6. Stir the risotto. Add more stock, if needed, so that it's soupy, as it firms up as it cools. Add the nutritional yeast, if using, and seitan or bean sausage. Season with salt and pepper to taste.

7. Transfer to a warm platter. Garnish with parsley and serve immediately.

Three-Minute Spiced White Basmati Rice

White rice is not a staple in my house, but my son really liked it so I became good at cooking it. This one is seasoned with aromatic whole spices and pepper.

Let the cooker sit for the full 7 minutes even if the release valve drops before then. If you find the rice is too sticky or wet for your liking, you can reduce the liquid to 1 cup per 1 cup of rice, although there is more of a chance that the rice will stick to the bottom of the cooker.

MAKES 3 CUPS OR 4 SERVINGS

1. Heat a stovetop pressure cooker over medium heat or set an electric cooker to sauté; add the oil. Add the cumin, mustard seeds, and red pepper and sauté for 1 minute. Add the rice and stir to coat with oil.

2. Add the water and salt. Stir. Lock on the lid. Bring to high pressure; cook for 3 minutes. Remove from heat and let sit for at least 7 minutes for the pressure to come down naturally. Remove the lid, tilting it away from you.

3. Transfer to a bowl. Fluff and serve hot.

3 minutes high pressure, natural release

1 teaspoon canola oil

½ teaspoon cumin seeds

½ teaspoon mustard seeds

Pinch of crushed red pepper

1 cup white basmati rice

1¼ cups water or vegetable stock

½ teaspoon salt

1 cup coconut milk, light or
regular

¾ cup water

1 cup diced fresh or canned
pineapple with ¼ cup juice
(add water if needed to make
¼ cup)

1 cup brown rice, long-,
medium-, or short-grain

¼ cup unsweetened shredded
coconut

1 cinnamon stick

Pinch of sea salt, optional

Chopped scallions and
cilantro, for garnish

Coconut Pineapple Rice

Photo, page I-11

This dish pairs well with many main courses, especially Indian spiced curry dishes. It is rich, fruity, and sweet with savory notes from the fresh herbs. You can also add more sweetener and serve it for dessert. This will cook more quickly if you use Volcano or Mekong Flower rice. You can also use the technique with quinoa or millet. (See the cooking charts for grain and rice, pages 51 and 53, for information.) Feel free to take the idea and run with it.

SERVES 4

1. Combine the coconut milk, water, pineapple and juice, rice, coconut, and cinnamon stick in the pressure cooker. Stir.

2. Lock on the lid. Bring to high pressure; cook for 20 minutes. Let the pressure come down naturally. Remove the lid, carefully tilting it away from you.

3. Remove and discard the cinnamon stick with a pair of tongs. Add salt, if using. Transfer to a large dish.

4. Garnish with scallions and cilantro. Or serve as dessert with ground cinnamon, more coconut, and your favorite sweetener. Serve hot, warm, or chilled.

Wild Rice and Winter Fruit Salad

Cooking wild rice in the pressure cooker is a snap since it takes less than 30 minutes at pressure and turns out "just right" with the grains popped open but not mushy. Combine the cooked rice with raw winter fruit for an easy lunch or dinner accompaniment. If you like dried cranberries, this would be a wonderful dish to add them to, after the rice is cooked.

SERVES 4

1. Combine the spices in a small bowl.

2. Heat a stovetop pressure cooker over medium heat or set an electric cooker to sauté. Spray the pressure cooker with vegetable cooking spray or add the oil, if using. Add the shallots and half of the spice mixture and cook for 3 minutes.

3. Add the rice, water, and juice. Stir well. Lock on the lid and bring to high pressure; cook for 25 minutes. Let the pressure come down naturally. Quick release any remaining pressure after 10 minutes. Carefully remove the lid, tilting it away from you.

4. Check to be sure that the grains are thoroughly cooked: They should be slightly split. If you don't see this, bring the cooker back to high pressure and cook for another 2 to 3 minutes and then quick release. Remove the lid carefully. Transfer the rice to a bowl and let cool for 10 minutes.

5. Once the rice has cooled, drain the cubed apples and pears and add to the rice, along with the orange sections.

6. In a small bowl, combine the grated orange zest and juice, the remaining spices, and the oil, if using. Whisk to combine. Pour over the wild rice mixture. Taste and season with salt and pepper. Top with toasted almonds or seeds. Serve at room temperature or chilled.

½ teaspoon ground coriander

½ teaspoon ground cardamom

1 teaspoon ground cinnamon

⅛ teaspoon freshly grated nutmeg

Vegetable cooking spray or 2 teaspoons oil, optional

½ cup minced shallots or onions

1 cup wild rice

2 cups water

1 cup apple juice

1 medium apple, peeled, cored, and cubed, then soaked in a bowl of lemon juice and water

1 medium pear, cored, cubed, and soaked in the same lemon water

1 navel orange, zested, peeled, and sectioned

½ cup fresh squeezed orange juice

1 tablespoon flax oil, extra virgin olive, or other oil, optional

Salt and freshly ground black pepper

¼ cup slivered almonds or pumpkin seeds, toasted

GRAINS

1 teaspoon olive oil, optional

1 cup diced onion

3 cloves garlic, minced

1 tablespoon diced poblano or jalapeño chile

1 cup brown basmati or other long-grain rice

1 (8-ounce) can or box tomato sauce

1 cup water or vegetable stock

½ teaspoon salt and freshly ground pepper

"Spanish" Brown Rice

I am not sure whether this ought to be called Spanish or Mexican, but in any case it is rice seasoned with onion, garlic, peppers, and a tomato-y coating. You must add more liquid than usual to get the rice to cook thoroughly. *Muy bueno.*

If you want to add a more Mexican flair, add 2 teaspoons ground cumin along with the garlic and chile.

SERVES 4 TO 6

1. Heat a stovetop pressure cooker over medium heat or set an electric cooker to sauté; add the oil if using. Add the onion and sauté or dry sauté for a couple of minutes. Add the garlic and chile pepper and cook for 1 minute longer. Add the rice and stir. Add the tomato sauce and stock and give everything a good stir.

2. Lock the lid. Bring to high pressure; cook for 25 minutes. Let the pressure come down naturally. Remove the lid, carefully tilting it away from you.

3. Taste the rice and if you find that it's too chewy, put the lid back on and let sit for 10 to 20 minutes. Add the salt, season to taste with pepper, and serve.

Black Rice and French Green Lentils

This rice-lentil combination has a firm texture with two complementary flavors. The black rice is high in antioxidants and cooks more quickly than brown rice. You can use regular green or brown lentils, but do not substitute red lentils as they will fall apart and get mushy.

If you find that there is a little liquid in the bottom of your cooker after cooking, lock the lid and let the rice stand for 5 to 10 minutes and it should be absorbed. If not, use a slotted spoon to transfer the contents to another dish. This looks better garnished with something green, such as parsley, cilantro, or even finely chopped kale or chard.

SERVES 4

1. Combine the rice, lentils, and stock in the pressure cooker.

2. Lock the lid. Bring to high pressure; cook for 15 minutes. Let the pressure come down naturally, which will take 10 to 15 minutes. Carefully remove the lid, tilting it away from you. Season to taste with salt and pepper and stir.

1 cup black Forbidden rice, rinsed

½ cup French green (de puy) or black beluga lentils

2½ cups vegetable stock

Salt and freshly ground black pepper

GRAINS

2 minutes high pressure,
quick release; 15
minutes high pressure,
natural release

½ cup diced peeled sweet
   potato

½ cup diced peeled parsnip

¼ cup diced carrot

½ cup diced peeled beets

2 cups black Forbidden rice
   or Thai long-grain black rice
   (see Note), rinsed

2¾ cups water

¼ cup diced watermelon radish
   or daikon radish (for both
   color and flavor)

2 to 3 tablespoons minced
   shallot

¼ cup chopped fresh flat-leaf
   parsley or cilantro

1 to 2 teaspoons grated lime
   zest

2 tablespoons or more lime
   juice

1 tablespoon ume vinegar

1 to 2 teaspoons low-sodium
   tamari, or to taste

1 to 2 teaspoons toasted
   sesame oil, optional

1 to 2 tablespoons brown or
   black sesame seeds, for
   garnish

Bejeweled Black Rice Salad

This is a colorful dish with many tasty vegetable nuggets, but does take more time than most weeknight cooking allows. I first made it for a large gathering, and it stood out among many more ordinary dishes. Any vegetables will do, but I chose sweeter ones for contrast with the earthiness of the rice. Ume vinegar is not a true vinegar but the leftover juice from fermented Japanese plums. It is salty, not tangy. It's one of my secret weapons in cooking. I often drizzle it on salad, but I must warn you that it can be addictive, so be careful. If you don't have any on hand, you can substitute tamari or soy sauce.

SERVES 6 TO 8

1. Add 1 cup water to the pressure cooker and place a steamer basket inside. Add the sweet potato, parsnip, and carrot to the basket.

2. Lock the lid on the cooker and bring to high pressure. Cook for 2 minutes. Quick release the pressure. Remove the lid, carefully tilting it away from you.

3. Transfer the cooked vegetables to a small bowl. Set aside.

4. Add the beets to the basket in the pressure cooker. Lock on the lid. Bring to high pressure; cook for 2 minutes. Quick release the pressure. Remove the lid, carefully tilting it away from you.

5. Make sure that the beets are cooked through. If not, lock on the lid and bring to pressure for 1 more minute and quick release. Remove the lid carefully. Transfer the beets to another small bowl and set aside.

6. Remove the steaming basket, discard the steaming water, and dry the cooker.

7. Add the black rice and 2¾ cups water to the pressure cooker. Lock on the lid. Bring to high pressure; cook for 15 minutes. Let the pressure come down naturally; wait at least 10 minutes before opening the cooker, even if the pressure drops. Carefully remove the lid, tilting it away from you.

8. If there is still liquid left, cover and let the rice sit for 5 more minutes, or until all the liquid is absorbed. Transfer the rice to a large bowl.

9. Add the beets and other cooked vegetables to the rice. Then add the raw radish, shallot, parsley, and lime zest and juice. Stir. Sprinkle with the ume vinegar, tamari, and sesame oil, if using. Stir the rice gently. Taste and adjust seasonings. Sprinkle on the sesame seeds and serve.

✱ **Note:** Thai long-grain black rice cooks in only 10 minutes at pressure and uses 2 cups water for the 2 cups of rice.

1 tablespoon olive oil, optional

2 cups finely chopped onion

3 cloves garlic, minced

1 cup sliced red, yellow, and/or orange bell pepper

2 to 3 teaspoons paprika

2 bay leaves

¼ teaspoon saffron threads, soaked in ¼ cup hot water or stock

1½ cups short- or medium-grain brown rice, soaked overnight and drained

½ cup dried chickpeas, soaked overnight and drained (soak in the same bowl as the rice)

1 (15-ounce) can artichoke hearts in water or 1½ cups frozen artichoke hearts, chopped

2¾ cups vegetable stock

1½ cups green or romano beans cut into 1½-inch lengths

1 cup frozen or fresh peas

2 to 3 tablespoons fresh lemon juice

½ cup sliced roasted red pepper

Salt and freshly ground black pepper

Chopped fresh flat-leaf parsley, for garnish

Veggie Paella

This is non-traditional paella, but it includes what I consider the cornerstone of the real thing: saffron threads. You might be tempted to omit the saffron because you've heard that it's very expensive. While saffron is pricey, it lasts a very long time and you don't need to use a lot. And the aroma of food cooked with saffron is quite intoxicating.

I use brown rice, which would not happen in Spain—it's white, medium-grain, starchy rice most of the time. I cook chickpeas and some of the vegetables with the rice, and add the remaining vegetables to cook for just a few minutes at the end. Use any fresh, seasonal vegetables that you have on hand. Paella usually has a lot of oil, but I don't like to bog it down too much. If you like, drizzle some olive oil over the dish at the end and stir it in.

SERVES 6 TO 8

1. Heat a stovetop pressure cooker over medium heat or set an electric cooker to sauté; add the olive oil, if using. Add the onion and sauté or dry sauté for a minute or two. Add the garlic, bell pepper, and paprika and cook another minute or two. Add the bay leaves, saffron and its soaking liquid, and the rice and chickpeas. Stir, making sure that nothing is stuck to the bottom of the cooker. (If using an electric cooker, turn off sauté function now.)

2. Add half the artichoke hearts and all of the stock. Lock on the lid. Bring to high pressure; cook for 15 minutes. Let the pressure come down naturally. If the pressure has not released by 20 minutes, quick release any remaining pressure. Carefully remove the lid, tilting it away from you.

3. Add the green beans on top, along with the peas. Do not stir. Lock on the lid. Let sit for 5 minutes with the lid on but without any heat. If pressure builds, quick release it. Add the remaining artichoke hearts, the lemon juice, and roasted red pepper and stir everything up. Season to taste with salt and pepper. Garnish with parsley and serve.

Any Grain and Vegetable Salad

This recipe is highly adaptable to whatever in-season vegetables you have on hand. Combine them with any pressure-cooked grain made using the charts on pages 51 and 53 (one of my favorites for this salad is a premade brown and black rice blend), and stir in nuts or seeds, dried fruit (or not), and a simple vinaigrette made with chopped herbs.

SERVES 6

1. Combine the bell pepper, tomato, scallions, dried fruit, and nuts in a large bowl. Mix lightly with fork. Season to taste with salt and pepper.

2. Fluff the cooled grains with a fork and season to taste with salt and pepper. Transfer to the bowl with the salad ingredients, mixing it in lightly with a fork.

3. Pour the lime juice, oil, and herbs into a small container with a tight-fitting lid. Cover and shake well until combined. Drizzle over the salad and mix lightly with a fork.

4. Serve or refrigerate, covered, for up to 2 days.

1 cup chopped red bell pepper (1 small)

½ tomato, seeded and cut into bite-size pieces; or ½ cup cherry tomatoes, cut in half

¼ cup chopped scallions or red onion

¼ cup finely chopped dried fruit (apricots, raisins, dates, or cherries)

2 tablespoons toasted pine nuts, sunflower seeds, chopped almonds, or chopped walnuts

Salt and freshly ground black pepper

3 cups cooked brown and black rice blend, or your favorite cooked whole grain (see Grain Cooking At-a-Glance, page 51), cooled

Juice of 1 lime (2 to 3 tablespoons)

2 tablespoons extra virgin olive oil

2 tablespoons finely chopped fresh chives or flat-leaf parsley; or 2 teaspoons dried

2 tablespoons finely chopped fresh mint or cilantro; or 2 teaspoons dried

FIVE

Beans

One of the best reasons to use your pressure cooker is for legumes: beans, peas, and lentils. They cook in a fraction of the time of stovetop cooking, and when you add seasonings the beans are infused with flavor at the same time.

Legumes, which have sustained people for thousands of years, are the pillars of a vegan diet and a great source of generally inexpensive fiber-filled low-fat protein (except for the soybean, which is the highest-fat bean). Many people eat canned beans, and stick to the big four types: black, pinto, kidney, and chickpeas. There is, however, a world of beans beyond these, and incorporating them into my diet has changed my life for the better. It will likely do the same for you.

Legumes have made the leap from peasant-style, home-cooked fare to upscale dishes available at tony restaurants. They now grace the shelves of specialty and natural food stores. Beans that have been cultivated for a long time are called heirloom beans. While grown from "old stock," they are usually more recently harvested than the bags of more ordinary beans sitting on your grocery shelf. Truly old beans might be tough and may not become completely tender during cooking. Beans from a natural food store rather than a bag from the supermarket are usually from a more recent crop, although you never know. (See Resources, page 304, for two good suppliers, Rancho Gordo and Purcell Mountain Farms.)

I praise beans for their versatility and variety, but their taste holds the allure. The flavors vary greatly. Lentils, which don't need soaking, go beyond the familiar brown, coming in black, red, and deep green varieties from various parts of the world, and cook in about 6 minutes at pressure.

Making at least one pot of beans a week will lead to a happier and healthier, and certainly easier, life. Say goodbye to cans and hello to a more delicious and natural way of eating. You've likely heard that little ditty, "Beans, beans, good for your heart . . ." They're good for your soul, too.

Bean Cooking Basics

I like to think of a pot of beans like the gold at the end of the rainbow. I really like rainbows. I like beans even more because they are far less elusive. I can cook them when I feel like it, which is often. Cooking a pot of beans means sustenance to me. Here are some important first steps in cooking your beans.

✳ Decide the quantity of beans that you want to cook. One cup of most dry beans will yield 2 to 3 cups of cooked beans, depending upon their size and shape.

✳ Measure your beans with a dry measuring cup, not the glass kind with a handle, to get the most accurate measure. Sort through the beans to pick out any rocks or twigs since beans grow on bushes and sometimes debris clings to the beans.

✳ After sorting through the beans, rinse them.

✳ Now it's decision time: To soak or not to soak?

To Soak or Not to Soak?

I almost always soak my beans. I have heard varying opinions about cooking beans.

Saving energy is one of the reasons that I soak my beans. Another is that beans cook more uniformly when they have been soaked.

But the main reason most people even think about soaking beans is because of the gas they produce in your intestines. Gas is the result of fermentation in your gut, which is produced for a variety of reasons. One reason is that beans contain a lot of fiber, some of which is indigestible, and some people with more sensitive digestive systems notice that eating a lot of beans causes bloating and gas. You have likely heard of probiotics, which can help with digestion. Well, beans are prebiotics, which are important because their fiber helps promote probiotic activity in your intestines. (Some people who have problems digesting beans actually have other gut issues, which should be addressed. If you are one of them, speak to your doctor, a competent Registered Dietitian, or a nutritionist about this.) Soaking beans before cooking them often results in more thoroughly cooked beans, which might be easier to digest. It's also a good idea to introduce beans into your diet slowly by adding just a few tablespoons a day, working up to a full cup as your body adjusts to the fiber. The good news is that for many people, the more beans you eat, the less gas you produce.

Overnight Soak: For energy purposes and to most thoroughly and evenly rehydrate beans, soak overnight: Fill a bowl, jar, or pot with beans and then cover them sufficiently, usually with at least double the volume of water. Remember, they are going to at least double in size, so be sure to use a vessel that is large enough to allow room for expansion. The beans need to soak for at least 8 hours, which means you can set them out in the morning for the evening, or soak them at night for the next day's meal. When you are ready to cook the beans, drain and cook according to directions (use the soaking water to feed your plants, indoor or out).

Quick Soak: Since I rarely plan too far in advance, I most often do what's called the quick soak. To do this, add beans to a pot and add water to cover the beans by 3 inches. Bring to a boil and boil for 1 minute. Turn off the heat, cover the pot, and let it sit for 1 hour. Drain the beans and cook as directed.

Soaked beans can be frozen and cooked later. This way, you will always have soaked beans at the ready.

Some people find that sprouting beans helps with their digestion. It is easy to do and it also reduces the cooking time, which you might find doubly helpful. See How to Sprout Beans, page 93.

Your Basic Pot of Beans

Now that you have rinsed, and maybe soaked or sprouted your beans, use the At-a-Glance chart that follows to cook them.

The rule of thumb for cooking beans in the pressure cooker: For each cup of dry beans that you have soaked, which equals 2 to 3 cups of soaked beans, use ½ to ¾ cup liquid to cook. One of the biggest differences with pressure cooking versus stovetop cooking is that you do not have to cover soaked beans with liquid. If you do, it takes much longer to bring the beans to pressure—and much longer for the pressure to come down—neither of which will save you much time or energy. Dry beans need at least 2 cups of liquid for each cup of beans.

Keep in mind that each batch of beans is different, as some might be older and more dehydrated. That's why I usually give a range of times for each type of bean. Cook them for the minimum time indicated, then test the beans, by tasting them and squishing one between your fingers. If they aren't tender, lock the lid, bring back to pressure, and cook for 1 or 2 more minutes. And note that sometimes older beans will never become thoroughly tender, even if they are cooked for a very long time.

How to Sprout Beans

Sprouting beans changes them from a dry, hard food to a fresh, living, and growing food. Each bean has the potential to become an entire bean plant, so each has to provide a lot of nutrition for the plant it will eventually grow into. It's a simple process that involves only beans, water, and time.

Note: Kidney, cannellini, and flageolet beans contain a toxin that might cause food poisoning, so do not sprout them unless you intend to cook them thoroughly (pressure cooking for at least 5 minutes, as recommended in Bean Cooking At-a-Glance, page 95).

The easiest method for soaking beans is the jar method. Put 1 to 2 cups beans in a large jar with room for them to expand two to three times their size. (So 2 cups of dry beans requires a jar larger than 1 quart.)

Cover the beans with at least double the volume of fresh, clean (not chlorinated) water. Cover the jar with a sprout lid or cheesecloth or a thick paper towel, and secure with a rubber band. Soak overnight on the countertop. The ideal temperature is 70°F. If it is too warm, your beans might get moldy before they sprout. (If your kitchen is above 80°F, soak in the refrigerator for a longer period of time.)

After soaking overnight, dump out the water. Rinse the beans by adding fresh water and dumping it out. Invert the jar, covered with cheesecloth, a paper towel, or a sprouting lid, into a bowl so that any water can

drain and place the whole thing in a dark cabinet or cupboard. (You can also sprout in a colander set in a bowl, if that is easier.) Keep the beans covered with a paper towel or cheesecloth. Repeat the rinsing process twice each day, dumping out any water that accumulates in the bowl.

By day 2 after the initial soak, you will see little tails on your beans, which means it's time to cook. (You can also eat the beans raw at this point, if you like, except for kidney, cannellini, or flageolet beans.) You can sprout up to 3 days if you prefer a longer tail and an even fresher taste, rinsing twice each day so that your beans do not spoil or sour. Since the beans have been so well hydrated, use less water to cook them, or use the same amount as for soaked beans. They will, however, likely take less time to cook.

You will have to experiment with your sprouted beans to discover the most appropriate cooking times. I would start by shaving off 25 percent of the time I give in the At-a-Glance. So for 8-minute beans, cook sprouted beans for 6 minutes. Remember that you can always bring them back to pressure, but overcooked beans will have to become dip, soup, or burgers or loaves.

If you don't cook all your sprouted beans at once, store them in the refrigerator for up to 3 days. I do not freeze sprouted beans since I can eat them as fresh beans.

If you like your beans to have some "pot liquor," the leftover liquid from cooking beans, you can certainly add more liquid than the minimum amount. Many people from the South like to dip their cornbread or bread into the broth. You can use the pot liquor to cook rice or vegetables, add it to soup, or use it in any recipe with added liquid, such as Rajma Curry Burgers (page 246). The choice is yours.

Do not add salt or acidic foods, such as tomatoes or molasses, to beans before or during cooking or else your beans might become tough. You can add them at the end of cooking, when the beans are already tender.

To season the beans during cooking, you might add a 3-inch strip of kombu seaweed, which contributes minerals and potentially increases digestibility. Boost flavor by adding aromatic vegetables, such as onions and garlic, and fresh herbs, such as bay leaf, thyme, oregano, or a small amount of rosemary at the beginning of cooking, as well as adding any spices. A teaspoon or two of dried herbs per cup of dried beans works as well. Often, I cook my "pot of beans" simply so that I can season them for different uses. If you want to salt your beans, do it after they are cooked.

I almost always use natural release when cooking beans. When the pressure-cooking time is up, let your pot rest and wait for the pressure to come down. This could take up to 20 minutes (especially with an electric pressure cooker, since the pot is so well insulated). Carefully release any remaining pressure after 20 minutes. Open the pot, tilting the lid away from you, and remove your beans with a long slotted or regular spoon. Reserve any leftover liquid, if you will be using it, or discard it along with any herb stems or large bay leaves. If you included kombu, don't throw it away. I consider it the prize in the pot and often eat it or cut it up and add it to my beans. You are now ready to use or freeze your cooked beans.

Cooked beans will last in the refrigerator for 3 to 5 days, and in the freezer for a few months. When beans go bad they stink. This prevents you from eating spoiled beans—you'll know when they are no longer fresh.

Freezing Beans

Often, you might simply want to cook a plain pot of beans to use just as you would a store-bought can of beans. Keep them handy by storing them in the freezer in 1½-cup amounts, which is equivalent to a 15- or 16-ounce can. If you freeze them on waxed or parchment paper–lined baking sheets, and transfer to freezer containers, the beans remain separated. Then use as many beans as you need to top a salad or add to a grain dish.

Be sure to label and date the freezer container. My running joke is that grabbing frozen black beans instead of the blueberries makes for a very interesting smoothie.

You can also soak the beans before freezing them, which lets you cook beans without having to think about soaking. You've done the work in advance.

Bean Cooking Timetable

The chart on page 95 highlights the timing for pressure cooking beans. The preferred method to cook beans thoroughly is to use a natural release, as the beans stay intact this way. However, some people choose to use a quick release (though I don't recommend it). Therefore, the chart gives times for cooking both soaked and unsoaked beans with a natural release, as well as times for cooking soaked beans with a quick release. Use it as a quick reference for cooking beans, or to adapt one of my recipes to cook a different type of bean, or to adapt conventional bean recipes.

Lentils (which do not need soaking) can cook with as little as 1½ cups liquid per cup.

Remember that when it comes to beans and lentils, only fill your cooker halfway so that there is room for the legumes to expand and have space to achieve pressure. You can cook up to 1½ pounds (or 3 cups dry beans) that have been soaked in a 6-quart cooker, and obviously more in a larger cooker.

Bean Cooking Times At-a-Glance

Bean (1 cup dry, soaked if desired)	Soaked beans (at high pressure with natural release*)	Unsoaked beans (at high pressure with natural release*)	Soaked beans (at high pressure with quick release*) Not recommended	Yield
Adzuki (azuki)	5–9 minutes	10 minutes, plus 10 minutes sitting	NA	2 cups
Black	4–6 minutes	24–28 minutes	18–25 minutes	2–2½ cups
Black-eyed peas	3 minutes	6–7 minutes	10–11 minutes	2½ cups
Borlotti (cranberry)	7–10 minutes	25–35 minutes	20–25 minutes	2½ cups
Cannellini	5–8 minutes	20–30 minutes	22–25 minutes	2½ cups
Chickpeas	12–14 minutes	30–40 minutes	22–25 minutes	2½ cups
Fava (add oil as bean skins come off)	8–10 minutes (at low pressure)	NA	NA	2½–3 cups
Flageolet	6–10 minutes	25–30 minutes	17–22 minutes	2½ cups
Great Northern	5–8 minutes	25–30 minutes	25–30 minutes	2½ cups
Kidney, red	5–8 minutes	12–15 minutes	20–25 minutes	2 cups
Lentils, black beluga or French green	NA	4–6 minutes	10–12 minutes	2–2½ cups
Lentils, green/brown	NA	6 minutes	8–10 minutes	2–2½ cups
Lentils, red	NA	6 minutes	4–6 minutes	2½ cups
Lima, baby	6–8 minutes	20–25 minutes	20–25 minutes	3 cups
Lima, large	6–8 minutes	20–25 minutes	20–25 minutes	3 cups
Mung	NA	6–8 minutes, plus 10 minutes sitting	NA	2½ cups
Navy or white	4–7 minutes	20–25 minutes	15–17 minutes	2½ cups
Peas, split, yellow or green	NA	6–10 minutes	NA	2½ cups
Peas, whole	6–8 minutes	12–15 minutes	16–18 minutes	2½–3 cups
Peruano (aka mayacoba)	7–9 minutes	25–30 minutes	20–25 minutes	2½–3 cups
Pinto	4–6 minutes	20–25 minutes	20–25 minutes	2½ cups
Scarlett runner	5–8 minutes	22–28 minutes	20–25 minutes	2½–3 cups
Soy, yellow	17–20 minutes	35–45 minutes	NA	2–2½ cups
Soy, black (add oil as bean skins come off)	17–20 minutes	35–45 minutes	NA	2–2½ cups
White, giant	8–10 minutes	25–30 minutes	25–30 minutes	2½–3 cups

*It is best to use natural pressure release with beans so that they don't split apart when you release pressure. If you are using the beans for creamy soups or dips, it really doesn't matter.

BEANS

2 teaspoons vegetable oil, optional

2 cups very finely chopped onion

2 cups dry navy or other white beans, soaked and drained

2 tablespoons dry mustard

2 teaspoons smoked paprika

1 bay leaf

2 cups vegetable stock

¼ cup chopped dates

¼ cup tomato paste

3 tablespoons blackstrap molasses

2 tablespoons Dijon or other prepared mustard

1 tablespoon apple cider vinegar

Salt

"Baked" Beans

There's nothing like shaving hours off a traditional recipe. These beans might not be quite as creamy as the long-baked type, but if you aren't tasting them side by side, I find beans "baked" in the pressure cooker to be mighty good. The key is to get the beans well-cooked before adding the other ingredients, which tend to toughen them up. When it's hot out and you don't want your oven on but want baked beans, here you go.

SERVES 6 TO 8

1. Heat a stovetop pressure cooker over medium heat or set an electric cooker to sauté; add the oil if using. Add the onion and sauté or dry sauté for 3 minutes, until the onion starts to look translucent. Add water by the tablespoon if needed to prevent sticking. Add the beans, dry mustard, paprika, and bay leaf. Stir.

2. Add the stock. Lock on the lid. Bring to high pressure; cook for 15 minutes. Let the pressure come down naturally. Let the beans sit for 10 minutes after the pressure has come down, and then carefully open the pot, tilting the lid away from you.

3. Taste a few beans to make sure they are cooked through and soft enough to squish between your fingers. If not, lock the lid, return the cooker to high pressure, and cook for a few minutes longer. Let the pressure come down naturally. Remove the lid, carefully turning it away from you.

4. Remove and discard the bay leaf. Add the dates, tomato paste, molasses, Dijon mustard, and vinegar, then stir well.

5. Bring the mixture to a simmer and let it bubble gently for about 5 minutes so the flavors can blend, or lock on the lid and let it sit for 10 minutes. Adjust seasoning with salt and serve.

"Refried" Black (or Your Favorite) Beans

I usually soak my beans but these seem to turn out just fine without soaking; they just take a whole lot longer to cook. I think, though, that they absorb a lot of flavor during cooking, which is a good thing. This recipe was inspired by a post on my Facebook page by Michelle King Cohen. You can use your favorite standard bean, such as pinto or kidney, or any other unsoaked bean that usually cooks within the 30-minute time frame. Please note that to get beans soft enough to mash, you'll need to cook them at least 5 minutes longer than the time stated on the At-a-Glance Cooking Chart on page 95.

SERVES 4 TO 6

1. To make the salsa: Combine the tomatoes, onion, garlic, and chile in a small bowl to make a salsa and set aside. (Or you can use 1½ cups commercial salsa instead.)

2. To make the beans: Heat a stovetop pressure cooker over medium heat or set an electric cooker to sauté. Add the diced onion and dry sauté for 1 minute. Add the garlic, chile, cumin, chili powder, and oregano and cook another minute.

3. Add the beans, water, kombu, and epazote to the cooker. Lock the lid. Bring to high pressure; cook for 30 minutes. Let the pressure come down naturally. Carefully remove the lid, tilting it away from you.

4. Taste to be sure that the beans are cooked through. If not, bring the cooker back to pressure and cook for 5 minutes longer. Let the pressure come down naturally. Carefully remove the lid and use tongs to remove the kombu and sprigs of epazote.

5. Add the salsa. Do not stir. Lock the lid. Bring to high pressure; cook for 3 minutes. Let the pressure come down naturally. Carefully remove the lid.

6. Using a potato masher or immersion blender, mash or blend the beans to the consistency you like, adding salt if desired. Top with chopped cilantro and serve.

30 minutes high pressure, natural release; 3 minutes high pressure, natural release

Salsa

1½ cups finely chopped fresh or canned tomatoes

¼ cup minced onion

5 cloves garlic, minced

1 teaspoon (or more) minced hot chile, such as jalapeño or serrano

Beans

1 cup diced onion

4 cloves garlic, minced

1 teaspoon minced hot chile, such as jalapeño or serrano

1 tablespoon cumin powder, or 2 teaspoons cumin seeds

1 tablespoon mild chili powder

1 teaspoon dried oregano

1½ cups black or other beans

2½ cups water

1 (3-inch) piece kombu

1 to 2 sprigs fresh epazote, if available, or ½ teaspoon dried

½ to 1 teaspoon salt, optional

Chopped cilantro, for garnish

Spice Mixture

2 teaspoons Italian seasoning,
store-bought or homemade
(page 41)

½ to 1 teaspoon smoked paprika

¼ to ½ teaspoon ground fennel

Sausage Mixture

1 cup crimini mushrooms, diced

½ cup finely diced red onion

2 cloves garlic, minced

¾ cup black-eyed peas, or
white, black, or pinto beans,
soaked and drained

½ cup water or vegetable stock

⅓ cup gluten-containing flour
(such as all-purpose) plus
2 tablespoons pure wheat
gluten (see page 213); or
use ½ cup gluten-free flour,
such as brown rice, teff, or
buckwheat flour, plus
2 tablespoons ground chia or
flax seeds

2 tablespoons nutritional yeast

1 tablespoon tomato paste

2 tablespoons balsamic vinegar
or tamari

1 tablespoon vegan
Worcestershire sauce

2 teaspoons oil for sautéing,
optional

Bean Sausages

They may not have the firmness of true sausages unless you go with the glutinous flour, but either way they certainly look like sausages and make a good stand-in on a bun or with "Baked" Beans (page 96) on the side. They are also a wonderful addition to Multi-Bean Soup with Bean Sausages (page 184). I think that once you make them, you'll find many ways to eat them.

I like making my own sausages because I can use my favorite beans and season them my way. I sometimes add a touch of cayenne or chipotle pepper. My husband, not typically a mushroom fan, didn't even notice that his sausage contained mushrooms. I was thrilled, since mushrooms are nutritional powerhouses.

_____

MAKES 6 SAUSAGES

1. Prepare the spice mixture by mixing the spices in a small bowl; set aside.

2. To make the sausage mixture: Heat a stovetop pressure cooker over medium heat or set an electric cooker to sauté. Add the mushrooms and onion and dry sauté for 2 minutes. Add the garlic and cook 1 minute longer. Add the drained beans and water.

3. Lock on the lid. Bring to high pressure; cook for 6 minutes. Let the pressure come down naturally. Carefully remove the lid, tilting it away from you.

4. Taste a few beans to make sure they are cooked through and soft enough to squish between your fingers. If not, lock the lid, return the cooker to high pressure, and cook for 2 to 3 minutes longer. Let the pressure come down naturally. Remove the lid, carefully turning it away from you. Transfer the beans to a medium bowl to cool.

5. Mash the beans with a fork, potato masher, or your hands. Add the spice mixture, the gluten flour and gluten (or gluten-free flour and seeds), nutritional yeast, tomato paste, vinegar, and Worcestershire sauce. Mix until well blended. Let sit for at least 5 minutes for the beans to absorb any liquid and firm up.

6. Divide the mixture into 6 pieces and roll each into a sausage link shape. Wrap with foil. (If you don't want your food to touch foil, use plastic wrap or parchment paper to wrap each sausage, then wrap in foil.)

7. Rinse the pot and add 1 cup water. Place a rack and steamer basket inside. Place the sausages in the basket. Lock the lid on the cooker and bring to high pressure. Cook for 10 minutes. Let the pressure come down naturally. Remove the lid, carefully tilting it away from you.

8. Carefully remove the sausages and unwrap. Refrigerate at least 3 hours or overnight to get the firmest sausage.

9. To heat and crisp the sausages a bit, add them to a nonstick pan, with 2 teaspoons of oil, if desired, and cook for at least 10 minutes, turning to crisp each side, or put under the broiler until crispy for 3 to 4 minutes on each side.

13 minutes high pressure, natural release; 1 minute low pressure, quick release

Salad

¾ cup chickpeas, soaked and drained

3 cloves garlic, minced

1 (3-inch) piece of kombu

½ cup vegetable stock

½ pound broccoli florets or broccolini

½ cup sliced red onion

¼ cup chopped fresh flat-leaf parsley

3 tablespoons chopped Kalamata olives, optional

¼ to ½ teaspoon crushed red pepper flakes, to taste

Dressing

1 tablespoon fresh lemon juice

1 tablespoon red wine vinegar

2 teaspoons Dijon mustard

1 teaspoon minced fresh garlic

1 tablespoon extra-virgin olive oil

1 teaspoon white miso

Chickpea Broccoli Salad

Photo, page I-12

This simple, versatile salad can be served warm or chilled. It's a bright addition to any table but especially in winter when broccoli is in season. If you can find broccolini, or "baby broccoli," use it whole.

If your broccoli is young and tender, it won't require any pressure, just a few minutes sitting in the covered cooker. Otherwise, use larger broccoli florets and cook briefly at low pressure.

SERVES 4

1. Put the chickpeas, garlic, kombu, and stock in a pressure cooker and lock on the lid. Bring to high pressure; cook for 13 minutes. Let the pressure come down naturally.

2. While the chickpeas cook, in a small bowl whisk together the dressing ingredients. Set aside.

3. Open the lid of the cooker, carefully tilting it away from you. Add the broccoli and lock on the lid. Bring to low pressure, cook for 1 minute, then quick release. (In an electric cooker, set to 0, bring to pressure, then immediately quick release.) Alternatively, you can stir in the broccoli, lock on the lid, and let sit until the broccoli becomes tender, 3 minutes for broccolini or up to 5 minutes for larger florets.

4. Open the cooker carefully. Remove and discard the kombu or save it for another use. Using a slotted spoon, transfer the contents to a serving bowl.

5. Combine the dressing with the beans and broccoli. Add the onion, parsley, olives if using, and red pepper flakes and toss. Taste and adjust the seasonings. Serve warm or chilled (if serving chilled, taste it when cold to see if you need to adjust the seasonings again).

Cannellini Beans with Gremolata

I'm not sure if it's the elongated shape of the cannellini bean or the creaminess that wows me, but it is one bean that I am happy to eat in a variety of ways. Here they are simply cooked, then seasoned with gremolata, a nutty, tangy, and lemony herb topping that can also be used in other recipes, such as Artichokes in Minutes (page 122), Mixed-Grain Blend for Any Time of Day (page 54), or Greek Stewed Lima Beans with Fennel and Artichokes (page 109). I especially have a fondness for lemon zest, which tastes great and may have anti-cancer properties. (How can you not like an ingredient that contributes such pizzazz and adds virtually nothing in the way of salt, sugar, oil, and calories?) If you like your food with more spice, add a pinch of crushed red pepper to the gremolata.

———

SERVES 4

1. Combine the beans, garlic, bay leaves, and stock in a pressure cooker. Lock on the lid. Bring to high pressure; cook for 8 minutes. Let the pressure come down naturally.

2. While the beans are cooking, make the gremolata: Combine the gremolata ingredients, except for half the lemon zest, in a mini food processor and process briefly, until the mixture is coarsely chopped (or finely chop with a knife). Stir in the remaining lemon zest.

3. When the pressure has come down, carefully remove the pressure cooker lid, tilting it away from you.

4. Taste a few beans to make sure they are cooked through. If not, lock the lid and return to high pressure; cook for a few minutes longer and release naturally, then carefully remove the lid.

5. Using a pair of tongs, remove and discard the bay leaves. Transfer the beans to a large bowl or platter. Serve the beans sprinkled with gremolata or pass it alongside.

8 minutes high pressure, natural release

1½ cups cannellini beans, soaked and drained

4 cloves garlic, minced

2 bay leaves

1 cup vegetable stock

Gremolata

¼ cup slivered almonds

2 garlic cloves, peeled

¼ cup chopped fresh flat-leaf parsley or baby kale leaves

Grated zest of 2 lemons

Crushed red pepper flakes, optional

5 minutes high pressure,
quick release; 8 minutes
high pressure,
natural release

1¼ cups water or vegetable
stock

1 cup dried chickpeas, soaked
and drained

½ cup diced onion

2 bay leaves

1 (3-inch) piece kombu

1 teaspoon dried summer or
winter savory

1 cup kidney beans, soaked
and drained

1 cup pinto, pink, or white
beans, soaked and drained

¾ pound green, yellow, or
romano beans (a mix if
possible), cut or snapped into
2-inch pieces (at least
3 cups)

2 tablespoons Dijon mustard

2 tablespoons agave nectar or
other sweetener

3 tablespoons apple cider
vinegar

1 to 2 teaspoons Bragg liquid
aminos

½ cup finely diced scallions
(whites and tops), or red
onion

¼ cup finely chopped celery

½ teaspoon freshly ground
black pepper

Easy (En)Lightened Four-Bean Salad

Four-bean salads are a staple of summer potlucks. This version differs from most by starting from dried beans cooked quickly in your pressure cooker (even cooking the green beans at the same time), resulting in a salad with better texture and flavor than one made from canned beans.

If you're not going to a potluck, you may want to cut the recipe in half. Or make it all and enjoy the leftovers.

———————
SERVES 8

1. Combine the water, chickpeas, onion, bay leaves, kombu, and savory in a pressure cooker. Lock on the lid. Bring to high pressure; cook for 5 minutes. Quick release the pressure. Carefully remove the lid, tilting it away from you.

2. Add the kidney and pinto beans to the chickpeas. No need to stir. Place a steamer basket on top of the beans. Wrap the cut green beans in a square of parchment paper, securing with a rubber band if necessary. (I wrap this with a fold on the top and usually put the rubber band across the wide part of the package.) Put the packet on top of the other beans.

3. Lock on the lid. Bring to high pressure; cook for 8 minutes. Let the pressure come down naturally. Remove the lid, tilting it away from you.

4. Remove the green bean packet. Carefully open the package and let the beans cool.

5. Taste a few beans from the pot to make sure they are cooked through. If not, lock the lid and return to high pressure; cook for a few minutes longer and release naturally, then carefully remove the lid.

6. Transfer the cooked beans to a large bowl. Remove and discard the bay leaves. Remove the kombu if you like, or leave it in.

7. Combine the mustard, agave, vinegar, and liquid aminos in a small bowl, then add to the mixed beans and toss. Let the beans and dressing cool for 15 to 30 minutes, as they will be quite hot.

8. When the mixed beans are cool, stir in the cooled green beans, scallions, and celery and add the black pepper. Taste and adjust seasonings. Chill or serve at room temperature.

* **Note:** This dish does not freeze well after being dressed. If you want to freeze it, freeze the undressed mixed bean mixture, or a portion of it, without the green beans. To serve, defrost, add the green beans, and dress.

Packet Cooking

When using the pressure cooker, there are techniques to use to keep food from cooking too quickly. What, you say? Don't you want the food to cook quickly? Yes, but sometimes you want to cook faster- and slower-cooking ingredients in the pot at the same time. The four-bean salad is a good illustration of how using a packet enables you to do just that. The packet shields the ingredients within it, slowing the cooking of the green beans in this case, ensuring they don't become overcooked and mushy.

You can use a foil packet. If you are like me and avoid wrapping food in aluminum, you can either make a parchment packet (yes, they hold up to the heat and liquid), or use a parchment packet encased in a foil packet.

I have used this method when adding corn to a dish, without stirring it in at the end of cooking. I suggest limiting the cooking time to 10 minutes or less for the packets. Doing a natural release seems to work well with this method.

Be careful when removing the packet from the pot since it will be hot.

14 minutes high pressure,
natural release

1 cup diced onion

4 cloves garlic, minced

1 teaspoon minced peeled
fresh ginger

1 small hot chile, such as
jalapeño or serrano, or your
favorite dried chile (seeds
included or removed),
minced, optional

1 cup vegetable stock or water

¼ teaspoon ground cardamom

½ teaspoon ground coriander

1 teaspoon ground toasted
cumin

1 teaspoon mustard seeds

2 teaspoons curry powder,
store-bought or homemade
(page 38)

1½ cups dry chickpeas, soaked
and drained

2 tablespoons tomato paste

Salt

¼ cup minced cilantro leaves,
for garnish

Curried Chickpeas

I adore curry of any origin. The appeal, to me, is that you can customize
the blend of spices as you like. Many years ago, I was told that in Indian
households there is no single thing called curry powder, as each family makes
their own; for my version, see page 38. If I don't have any of my own on hand,
I liven up store-bought curry powder by adding chile powder, and cumin.
If you prefer your food less spicy, leave out the hot chile and use less curry
powder, or find a mild one. Alternatively, you can substitute garam masala
(page 39) for the curry powder.

I can eat this dish often, paired with any kind of rice and a side of
vegetables.

SERVES 4 TO 6

1. Heat a stovetop pressure cooker over medium heat or set an
   electric cooker to sauté. Add the onion and dry sauté for 1 to 2
   minutes. Add the garlic, ginger, and chile, if using. Cook 1 minute
   longer, adding 1 to 2 tablespoons of the stock or water if the
   vegetables start to stick. Add the spices and curry powder; cook
   1 minute longer. Add the drained chickpeas and remaining stock or
   water.

2. Lock on the lid. Bring to high pressure; cook for 14 minutes. Let the
   pressure come down naturally. Carefully remove the lid, tilting it
   away from you.

3. Taste a few beans to make sure they are cooked through. If not,
   lock on the lid, return the cooker to high pressure, and cook for
   1 to 2 minutes longer. Again, let the pressure come down naturally
   before carefully removing the lid.

4. Stir the beans, adding the tomato paste and salt to taste. Transfer
   the mixture to a bowl or platter and garnish with the cilantro.

✳ **Note:** The easiest way to have 2 tablespoons of tomato paste
available for this recipe is to spoon 1 tablespoon paste into each
section of an ice cube tray, then freeze the tray until the paste is
solid. Transfer the frozen cubes to a freezer bag and store in the
freezer for up to 3 months.

French Green Lentil Salad

WITH CARROTS AND MINT

The joy of French green lentils is that they hold their shape in cooking, which makes them wonderful for salads. This salad tastes incredibly fresh and can brighten up your menu any time of year, since carrots are always available. You can use dry mint if you don't have any fresh on hand.

SERVES 4 TO 6

1. Heat a stovetop pressure cooker over medium heat or set an electric cooker to sauté. Add the onion and dry sauté for 1 minute. Add the lentils and water.

2. Lock on the lid. Bring to high pressure; cook for 5 minutes. Let the pressure come down naturally. Carefully remove the lid, tilting it away from you.

3. Taste a few lentils to make sure they are cooked through. If not, lock the lid on, return the cooker to high pressure, and cook for 1 minute longer. Again, let the pressure come down naturally before carefully removing the lid.

4. Let the lentils cool a bit. If there is any liquid remaining, drain the lentils. Add the carrots, herbs, lemon zest and juice, and cumin, if using. Sprinkle with a touch of salt and black pepper, if desired. Stir to mix well. Garnish with nuts, if you like.

5. Serve at room temperature or chilled. If you chill, taste again before serving and adjust the seasonings.

5 to 6 minutes high pressure, natural release

1 cup chopped onion

1½ cups French green lentils, rinsed and picked over

1½ cups water or vegetable stock

1½ cups grated or julienned carrots (2 medium)

3 tablespoons chopped fresh mint or 2 teaspoons dried

3 tablespoons chopped fresh flat-leaf parsley

Grated zest and juice of 2 lemons; or 3 to 4 tablespoons red wine or balsamic vinegar

1 teaspoon ground toasted cumin, optional

Salt and freshly ground black pepper

2 to 3 tablespoons toasted pine nuts or slivered almonds, optional

½ cup diced onion

2 to 3 cloves garlic, minced

½ cup diced bell pepper, any color

2 to 3 teaspoons minced hot chile, such as jalapeño or serrano, optional

2 to 3 teaspoons ground toasted cumin

1½ to 2 cups shelled beans (1 to 2 pounds unshelled)

½ to ¾ cup vegetable stock

¼ cup diced tomatillo

½ cup diced tomato

½ cup fresh corn, optional

Chopped fresh herbs, such as parsley or cilantro, for garnish

Fresh Shelling Beans with Summer Vegetables

This dish screams late summer or early fall, which is when fresh shelling beans are in season. Use any variety you can get your hands on. Locally, we get black-eyed peas, Marrowfat, borlotti, and a few others. Here I combine them with tomatillos, tomatoes, and corn, but fresh beans pair well with most other late-summer vegetables. I like to add toasted cumin for the best flavor, although you could use Italian seasonings and add fresh basil or Italian parsley.

The amount of cooking liquid to use here varies. This is because some beans are drier than others. If they are extremely fresh, the beans will need less liquid, so you might find the amount stated to be a little more than you need. Also, different varieties of beans might require slightly different cooking times, generally between 2 and 5 minutes at pressure. Start with 2 minutes and see how well they are cooked. Since so little liquid is used, feel free to do a natural release as the pressure ought to drop quickly. If the pressure is not down in 5 minutes, do a quick release.

SERVES 4

1. Heat a stovetop pressure cooker over medium heat or set an electric cooker to sauté. Add the onion and dry sauté for 2 minutes. Add the garlic, bell pepper, and chile pepper if using; cook for 1 minute longer.

2. Add the cumin, beans, and stock. Lock on the lid. Bring to high pressure; cook for 2 minutes. Let the pressure come down naturally. Carefully remove the lid, tilting it away from you.

3. Taste, and if the beans are not tender yet, bring back to high pressure and cook for 1 to 3 minutes, depending upon how firm the beans are. Carefully remove the lid.

4. Stir in the tomatillo, tomato, and corn, if using. Simmer for 2 to 4 minutes (or replace the lid and let sit for 3 to 5 minutes), until the tomato starts to break down. Remove the lid carefully. Serve garnished with chopped fresh herbs.

Chickpeas and Garlic for Hummus

This recipe is the base for a fantastic hummus (page 276), but also delicious on its own. When cooking chickpeas for hummus, I like to add lots of garlic and cook the beans longer than usual so they are soft and easy to blend. The hummus achieves the creamiest texture when made with warm beans. You don't want to blend them while they are too hot, however, as you could blow the lid off your blender. (This won't happen in the food processor.)

MAKES 4 CUPS, ENOUGH FOR 2 BATCHES OF HUMMUS

1. Combine the chickpeas, water, garlic, and cumin in a pressure cooker. Lock on the lid. Bring to high pressure; cook for 14 minutes. Let the pressure come down naturally. Carefully remove the lid, tilting it away from you.

2. Taste the beans to be sure they are cooked through. If not, lock the lid, return to high pressure, and cook for 1 to 2 minutes longer. Again, let the pressure come down naturally before removing the lid.

3. Let the chickpeas cool until they are just warm, and make hummus according to the directions on page 276.

4. If you won't want to use all the beans at once, freeze any remaining beans for future use.

14 minutes high pressure, natural release

2 cups dry chickpeas, soaked and drained

1½ cups water

6 to 8 cloves garlic, minced

½ teaspoon cumin seeds

10 minutes high pressure,
natural release; 1
minute high pressure,
natural release

1 tablespoon olive oil, optional

1 cup diced yellow onion

½ cup chopped celery

1 tablespoon plus 2 teaspoons ground toasted cumin

1 tablespoon chili powder, or more or less according to your desire for heat

1 cup kidney beans, soaked and drained

¾ cup vegetable stock

1 cup baby carrots or small carrots, sliced

1 cup green beans, cut into 1-inch pieces

1½ cups fresh or frozen (not thawed) corn

¾ cup crushed or diced tomatoes (about half of a 15-ounce can)

Salt and freshly ground black pepper

Chopped mint, for garnish

Graciela's Colombian Beans

Photo, page I-10

Graciela is the beautiful Colombian wife of my husband's friend. At dinner at her house one night, she served this dish as the main course, knowing my vegan and gluten-free dietary preferences. It was mighty tasty and very pretty with the dark beans, carrots, green beans, and yellow corn. Graciela says the key to this dish is fresh, organic ingredients. Did I mention that Graciela is an artist? It shows.

Toast the cumin seeds in a dry pan, then use a blender or spice grinder to grind them into a powder. If you have leftover canned tomatoes, label, date, and freeze them in a jar or plastic zippered bag to use in another recipe.

SERVES 4

1. Heat a stovetop pressure cooker over medium heat or set an electric cooker to sauté. Add the oil, if using. Add the onion and celery and sauté or dry sauté for 2 to 3 minutes. Add the cumin and chili powder and sauté for 1 minute longer. Add the kidney beans and stock.

2. Lock on the lid. Bring to high pressure; cook for 10 minutes. Let the pressure come down naturally. Carefully remove the lid, tilting it away from you.

3. Taste a few beans to make sure they are cooked through. If not, lock the lid, return the cooker to high pressure, and cook for 2 to 3 minutes longer. Again, let the pressure come down naturally before removing the lid. If the pressure has not released after 10 minutes, do a quick release.

4. Add the carrots, green beans, and corn and stir. Put the tomatoes on top but do not stir. Lock the lid on the cooker and either bring to pressure and cook for 1 minute, or let sit with the lid on for 5 minutes without pressure. Carefully open the lid. The beans should be cooked through, and the dish ought to be fairly firm, not soupy.

5. Add salt and pepper to taste and stir the dish to combine everything. Transfer to a platter and garnish with mint.

Greek Stewed Lima Beans

WITH FENNEL AND ARTICHOKES

Fennel and artichokes make a great pair and this brothy, springtime stew brings out the best in all of its vegetables. If you think you don't care for lima beans, this dish may change your mind. It did for me. If you really don't care for them, make this with cannellini beans but add an extra minute to the pressure cooking time.

Serve with a salad and a hunk of hearty bread or spoon over cooked polenta (page 70) for a Mediterranean feast. This dish benefits from using olive oil for sautéing and your best extra virgin olive oil drizzled on top, but you can still leave it out.

SERVES 4

1. Heat a stovetop pressure cooker over medium heat or set an electric cooker to sauté; add the oil. Add the leek and sauté for 1 minute. Add the garlic, carrot, rosemary, and 1 teaspoon of the oregano. Sauté another minute, stirring often. Add a tablespoon of the stock if you get any sticking. Stir well.

2. Add the remaining stock, drained beans, bay leaves, fennel bulb and fronds, and artichoke hearts and stir. Lock on the lid. Bring to high pressure; cook for 6 minutes. Let the pressure come down naturally. Carefully remove the lid, tilting it away from you.

3. Taste a few beans to make sure they are cooked through. If not, lock the lid, return the cooker to high pressure, and cook for 1 to 2 more minutes. Remove the lid carefully.

4. Add the lemon zest and juice and the mint. Taste and add salt and pepper to taste. Add the remaining 1 teaspoon oregano if you want a highly flavored dish. Transfer to a bowl or platter. Drizzle with extra virgin olive oil and serve.

   Greek Stewed Lima Beans with Fennel, Artichokes, and Tomatoes: If you love tomatoes and think that they would make this dish pop for you, feel free to add 1 cup diced tomatoes when you open the pressure cooker. Stir in, lock on the lid, and let sit for 2 minutes.

---

6 minutes high pressure, natural release

1 tablespoon olive oil, optional

1 cup diced leek, mostly the white part

4 cloves garlic, minced

1 cup diced carrot

½ teaspoon crumbled dried rosemary

1 to 2 teaspoons dried oregano

1¼ cups vegetable stock

1 cup baby lima beans, soaked and drained

2 bay leaves

1 cup chopped fennel bulb, cut into 1-inch pieces

¼ cup chopped fennel fronds

½ cup frozen (not thawed) or drained canned artichoke hearts in water

1 teaspoon grated lemon zest

1 to 2 tablespoons fresh lemon juice

½ teaspoon dried or 2 teaspoons chopped fresh mint

Salt and freshly ground black pepper

2 teaspoons extra virgin olive oil, optional

1 cup Rancho Gordo Ayocote negro or other black or dark beans, soaked and drained

1 (3-inch) strip kombu

1½ cups vegetable stock or water or enough to cover the beans, plus ¼ cup or more if needed

Salt and freshly ground black pepper

1 tablespoon neutral oil

½ cup chopped leek

2 cups sliced assorted mushrooms such as oyster or crimini

1 tablespoon tamari

1 teaspoon grated peeled fresh ginger, plus more for after cooking

1 large clove garlic, minced

2 cups kale or collard greens, stemmed and finely sliced

1 tablespoon toasted sesame oil

1 to 2 teaspoons grated tangerine or blood orange zest

3 tablespoons fresh tangerine or blood orange juice

2 scallions, chopped

3 cups salad greens, washed and dried

VEGAN UNDER PRESSURE

110

Large Black Bean, Mushroom, and Greens Salad

*A **wonderful winter salad**,* this combination of beans, mushrooms, and greens will boost your immune system and your spirits. If you can't find Ayocote negro, large, black, meaty-tasting, and firm textured beans, any bean will do. Other good choices would be standard black beans or any large dark heirloom bean (follow the shorter cooking times in Step 1).

SERVES 4 TO 6

1. Combine the beans, kombu, and 1½ cups stock in a pressure cooker. Lock on the lid. Bring to high pressure; cook Ayocote beans for 15 minutes or standard-sized beans for 8 minutes. Let the pressure come down naturally. Carefully remove the lid, tilting it away from you.

2. Taste to be sure the beans are cooked through. If not, lock the lid and return to high pressure; cook for 1 to 2 minutes longer and release naturally, then carefully remove the lid. Remove the kombu and save for another use (or eat) or discard. Transfer the beans to a bowl, sprinkle with salt and pepper to taste, and set aside to cool.

3. While the beans are cooling, rinse the pressure cooker, then heat it over medium heat or set to sauté. Add the oil and allow it to get hot. Add the leek and mushrooms and sauté for 1 to 2 minutes. Add the tamari, ginger, and garlic, then stir. Add the ¼ cup stock.

4. Lock on the lid. Bring to high pressure; cook for 2 minutes. Quick release the pressure. Carefully remove the lid, tilting it away from you.

5. Add the greens and 1 to 3 tablespoons additional stock if the pot looks dry. Lock on the lid and return the pot to high pressure for 1 more minute. Quick release the pressure. Remove the lid, carefully tilting it away from you.

6. Add the mushroom mixture to the beans along with additional ginger, if desired, the sesame oil, citrus zest and juice, and scallions. Taste and adjust seasonings. Serve on top of the salad greens.

Misr Wot (Ethiopian Red Lentil Stew)

This Ethiopian dish is like Indian dal in that it's a mealtime staple. It wasn't until Hanna Asfaw, an Ethiopian caterer (Gursha Catering) and food business colleague, was a guest teacher at one of my Santa Rosa Junior College cooking classes that I realized there is a lot of oil in traditional Ethiopian food. In fact, many Ethiopian recipes start with *niter kibbeh,* which is spiced butter. Olive oil, a less traditional alternative, is what Hanna uses. I've cut the oil considerably; you can eliminate it completely if you like. The dish will still taste good but will have a smoother texture. The flavor of the berbere spice blend is intoxicating. You can make your own or you can purchase it. Serve the stew over rice, millet, or another grain, or with the more traditional injera (fermented flatbread).

SERVES 4 TO 6

1. Heat a stovetop pressure cooker over medium heat or set an electric cooker to sauté. Add the oil, if using. Add the onion and sauté or dry sauté for 3 to 5 minutes, until it begins to soften. Add the garlic and sauté another minute. Add 1 tablespoon of the berbere, along with the tomato, lentils, and stock. Stir well.

2. Lock the lid. Bring to high pressure; cook for 10 minutes. Let the pressure come down naturally. Carefully remove the lid, tilting it away from you.

3. Taste and add the remaining ½ tablespoon berbere, if you like, and salt to taste.

10 minutes high pressure, natural release

1 to 2 tablespoons olive oil, optional

1 cup diced yellow onion

6 cloves garlic, minced

1 to 1½ tablespoons berbere spice powder (not paste), store-bought or homemade (page 36)

1 medium to large tomato, diced; or 1 cup diced canned tomatoes

1 cup red lentils, rinsed and picked over

3 cups vegetable stock or water

1 teaspoon salt, or to taste

BEANS

10 minutes high pressure,
natural release

1 cup adzuki beans

1½ cups water or vegetable
stock

1 (3-inch) piece of kombu

Simple Adzuki Beans

When I open a cooker full of adzuki (also azuki or aduki) beans, the sweet aroma reminds me of Chinatown's sweet red bean buns. The deep red color of the beans gets duller when the beans cool. The somewhat mushy texture is perfect for making burgers or soup. Adzuki beans do not require soaking because they cook so quickly.

SERVES 4

1. Combine the beans, water, and kombu in the pressure cooker. Lock on the lid. Bring to high pressure; cook for 10 minutes. Let the pressure come down naturally. Let the beans sit in the pot for at least 10 minutes. Carefully remove the lid, tilting it away from you.

2. Taste a few beans to make sure they are thoroughly cooked. If not, bring back to pressure, cook for 2 minutes, and let the pressure come down naturally. Carefully remove the lid, remove the kombu (eat, set aside for stock, or compost), and serve.

✳ **Note:** Alternately, you can soak the beans with any method (see page 92) and cook them under pressure for 5 to 9 minutes.

Warming Chickpeas

WITH TURNIPS AND GREENS

This is a simple dish but the warming spices make it quite appealing. Chickpeas pair well with winter vegetables. When you buy turnips, look for small ones (Tokyo white is my favorite) with their greens attached. Separate the greens from the turnips right away so that both parts stay fresher. If you can't find turnips, you can substitute red radishes or daikon radish. Serve over your favorite grain.

SERVES 4 TO 6

1. Heat a stovetop pressure cooker over medium heat, or set an electric cooker to sauté. Add the onion and dry sauté for 2 minutes. Add the carrots, ginger, cinnamon, mustard, and nutmeg and cook for 1 minute longer, adding 1 to 2 tablespoons stock if anything starts to stick.

2. Add the chickpeas, kombu, and stock. Lock on the lid. Bring to high pressure; cook for 12 minutes. Let the pressure come down naturally. Carefully remove the lid, tilting it away from you.

3. Taste a few beans to make sure they are cooked through. If not, lock the lid, return to high pressure, and cook for 2 minutes longer. Carefully remove the lid.

4. Using long tongs, remove the kombu (eat, set aside for stock, or compost). Add the apple and turnips and their greens. Lock the lid on the cooker and bring to high pressure. Cook for 2 minutes. Let the pressure come down naturally for 5 minutes. After 5 minutes, quick release any remaining pressure.

5. Transfer the contents to a bowl or plate. Add salt, pepper, and hot sauce to taste.

1 cup diced onion

1½ cups diced carrots (2 medium)

2 teaspoons grated fresh ginger, or 1 teaspoon powdered ginger

2 teaspoons ground cinnamon

½ teaspoon mustard seeds

¼ teaspoon freshly grated nutmeg

1 cup dry chickpeas, soaked and drained

1 (3-inch) piece kombu

1 cup vegetable stock

½ apple, chopped (½ to ¾ cup)

1 bunch turnips (12 to 16 ounces), roots chopped into 1-inch pieces, greens separated and chopped

Salt and freshly ground black pepper

Hot sauce

BEANS

1 cup organic soybeans,
soaked in 2½ cups water
overnight or for up to
18 hours

2 cups water for cleaning the
blender and pouring through
okara

Homemade Soy Milk

Why make soy milk, you might ask, when you can buy it everywhere these days? I asked myself the same question before I made it for the first time. I think I have the answers: 1) You know how your milk was made, from bean to glass. 2) You can make it as thick or thin as you want by increasing or decreasing the amount of dry beans that you start with, and it tastes much fresher. 3) You can feel like a good do-it-yourselfer. 4) You can put your high-speed blender, which is necessary for this, to great use. And 5) You've finally found a good use for pantyhose or stockings (although they're not essential)!

You also end up with okara, the fiber-rich soybean pulp that is left over after squeezing the milk out of the solids. (For more about using okara, see below). You can also make very tasty chai lattes with the fresh soy milk.

You have the option to make a richer soy milk than what you can buy in the store. The only thing you cannot do with homemade soy milk is make Soy Yogurt (page 266), as it's too pure and pasteurized. You can, however, culture it to make "sour milk," which you can use in a variety of ways; see the variation.

MAKES 1 QUART SOY MILK AND 2 CUPS OKARA

1. Add the soaked soybeans and their soaking water to the pressure cooker. Lock on the lid. Bring to high pressure; cook for 1 minute. Let the pressure come down naturally. Carefully remove the lid, tilting it away from you. Transfer the beans and liquid to a bowl to cool.

2. Once cool, transfer the beans and the liquid to a high-speed blender and blend for at least 30 seconds and up to 2 minutes. The mixture will get frothy and the beans will become smooth.

3. Using a large bowl to catch the milk, pour the soy slush through a double layer of cheesecloth or the foot of an unworn pair of stockings or pantyhose. Turn the cloth and squeeze it hard to squeeze out more liquid into the bowl. (Imagine yourself milking a soy cow.)

4. When the pulp, or okara, feels dry, empty it into another bowl. Repeat the pouring the soy slush and squeezing process until you have strained all the milk out of the beans. Add the okara and the

additional 2 cups water to the blender and repeat the pouring and squeezing until you have dry okara and the milk.

5. You will end up with 1 quart of tasty soy milk. Refrigerate immediately and store for up to 4 days.

Cultured Soy Milk: Culture your soy milk by mixing in 1 tablespoon of homemade soy yogurt (see page 266) or by stirring in 1 opened probiotic capsule. Let sit at room temperature overnight or up to 12 hours. When sour, refrigerate and use as you would buttermilk. Store for up to 4 days.

Okara: Traditional Leftover Soybean Pulp

In Japanese the word *okara* likely means "nutritional powerhouse" as it contains the fiber-rich components of soybeans, the highest protein legume, as well as vitamins, minerals, and important phytochemicals. It's the leftover pulp from making soy milk and there is often a lot of it. It is extremely bland, which makes it very versatile.

When stored fresh in the refrigerator it only lasts a couple of days. That is why it is often dried or frozen for later use. And what are those uses? Up to ½ cup fresh okara can be added to baked goods such as quick breads, crackers, and cookies to give them a lighter texture. The fresh form is also easily incorporated into burgers and loaves, or simply cooked by sautéing it with a touch of sesame oil, vegetables, and tamari. One tablespoon of fresh okara mixed with two tablespoons of water can substitute for one egg in baking.

When dried it can be used instead of nuts in "vegan Parmesan," mixed with nutritional yeast and miso; ½ cup can be added to polenta during cooking; and it can be used instead of protein powder if you are making smoothies. If it is dried and toasted, I have read that it tastes nutty and can be used as a substitute for coconut.

If you enjoy making your own soy milk, you will want to get creative with using okara since you will have plenty with which to experiment.

SIX

Vegetables

Cooking vegetables under pressure brings out their natural flavors.

In Russ Parsons's amazing book, *How to Read a French Fry*, he explains beautifully how and why the pressure cooker has its wonderful way with vegetables—it is by breaking down the cell walls, which allows the liquid to get in and add flavor.

Pressure-cooked vegetables, like other foods, are infused with flavor from the added liquid, herbs, spices, and aromatic vegetables. This doesn't happen with steaming, and when I hear that people are sick of steamed vegetables, I know why: Unless you drizzle steamed vegetables with oil, which some people avoid, and add salt, which many might not use, they simply are not appealing. And getting seasonings to stick is almost impossible.

Of course, I do hear some of you screaming, "They taste so good, just as they are." And, as The Veggie Queen™, I have to say that I love vegetables too. But there is a big difference between broccoli cooked with garlic and ginger in broth and plain steamed broccoli. If you want to steam, please do, but be sure to check out the Toppers chapter (page 252) for some tasty sauces to complement those vegetables.

My goal is to get everyone to eat more vegetables every day. In this chapter, I present a wide array of flavor-infused vegetable dishes and hope to entice you to try a few new ones or some old favorites cooked in new ways. I encourage you to choose the highest quality, preferably organic or sustainably grown, in-season vegetables. Your dishes will never taste better than the ingredients that you start with, and since the flavor of vegetables changes as they age, choose the freshest possible for best results.

One of the best things about the pressure cooker is how it keeps the heat from escaping from the pot into your kitchen. This means that when farm and garden fresh produce is at its peak in the summer, you do not need to heat up your kitchen, but can get incredibly fast cooked dishes.

In the winter, root vegetables and tubers benefit from cooking under pressure, and when cut up, they take just minutes to cook. Eating cooked vegetables has never been faster or more delicious.

Vegetable Cooking Basics

Pressure cooking vegetables that cook quickly requires precision timing to keep them intact. In many recipes containing multiple vegetables, the quick-cooking vegetables are stirred into the hot dish at the last minute to cook in the residual heat. In some instances, the vegetables are stirred in and the lid is locked on for a few minutes to enable the vegetables to fully cook.

If you have a pressure cooker with a low and high setting, using the low setting gives you a bit more leeway when cooking tender vegetables such as broccoli, snow peas, bok choy, and summer squash, allowing you to cook them for twice the time. The time is still short, so don't leave the room, or clip your timer to your shirt, as I do.

Vegetable Cooking Timetable

The chart on page 119 highlights the pressure level, amount of liquid needed, and timing for pressure cooking a wide variety of vegetables. Use it as a quick reference for simple cooking of any vegetable, to adapt one of my recipes to cook a different type of vegetable, or to adapt conventional vegetable recipes. If you choose to use more liquid, or need to use more because of your cooker, be sure to save the leftover cooking liquid and use in any recipe calling for vegetable stock.

Depending on the vegetable, you may not save a lot of time by using the pressure cooker, but hopefully you'll agree that the flavor is unbeatable compared to any other cooking method.

A few quick notes:

* Times will vary according to the age and specific vegetable. Since it's preferable to undercook rather than overcook most vegetables, start by cooking for the minimum time, and return to pressure for another minute or two if needed.

* Cook on high pressure unless otherwise indicated.

* Liquid (such as water, stock, wine, or juice) amounts are for 1 cup of vegetable pieces, or as specified. Larger amounts of vegetables do not necessarily need double, triple, or quadruple the amount of liquid: With watery vegetables like bok choy you may not need to add any more liquid; with a medium-level moisture vegetable like broccoli you may need 50 percent more liquid; with very dry potatoes you may need up to double the amount of water.

Make Friends with Your Freezer

Many of the foods that you cook in your pressure cooker are freezer friendly. I know because I utilize my freezer a lot. The idea is to cook fresh ingredients and store them to enjoy months later when they aren't in season. I am thrilled to search through my freezer in the dead of winter and come upon eggplant, tomato sauce, and tomatoes because I know that an Italian-style dish filled with the flavors of summer is in the immediate future.

I almost always have various beans and grains on hand in the freezer, which makes it easy to pull together complete meals in minutes.

One of the keys to effectively using your freezer is to keep things organized. Put like items with like: beans in one place, grains in another, vegetables somewhere else. Another very important thing is to label and date everything that you put in the freezer. When I am teaching I say, "You want to label your food because when you accidentally put black beans in your morning smoothie instead of blueberries, it might not be the best way to start the day."

"Foraging" in your freezer can be an excellent way to get inspired with new dinner ideas. A recent perusal of my freezer offerings helped me to invent a tasty curry, which I called: Late Winter Eating-Down-the-Freezer Vegetable Curry (page 201).

Vegetable Cooking At-a-Glance

Vegetable (1 cup)	Liquid	Time	Pressure Release
Artichokes, medium (use a rack if desired)	½ cup	6–12 minutes (longer for older artichokes or if you want them very soft)	Either
Artichokes, baby	½ cup	3–4 minutes	Quick
Asparagus	¼ cup or less	1½–2 minutes (or 2 minutes at low pressure)	Quick
Beets, small, whole (in steamer basket)	1 cup	10–12 minutes	Either
Beets, medium to large, whole (in pot or steamer basket)	½–1 cup	12–20 minutes	Either
Beets, cubed or sliced	¼–½ cup	3 minutes	Quick
Broccoli	2–4 tablespoons	1–2 minutes (or 2 minutes at low pressure)	Quick
Brussels sprouts, small, or medium, cut in half	¼–½ cup	1½–2 minutes (or 3–4 minutes at low pressure)	Quick
Brussels sprouts, medium, whole	¼–½ cup	2–3 minutes (or up to 4 minutes at low pressure)	Quick
Cabbage, sliced or shredded	2–4 tablespoons	2–3 minutes	Quick
Carrots, sliced	¼ cup or more	2–3 minutes	Quick
Carrots, whole	½ cup	5–8 minutes	Either
Celery root (celeriac), cut into pieces	⅓–½ cup	3–4 minutes	Either
Corn on the cob (in pot or on rack)	1 cup	3–5 minutes	Quick
Corn kernels	¼ cup	1–2 minutes	Quick
Eggplant, cubed	¼–½ cup	2–3 minutes	Quick
Eggplant, sliced (in pot or steamer basket)	¼–⅓ cup	2–4 minutes	Quick
Green beans	¼ cup	1–3 minutes	Quick
Greens, sturdy, such as kale, collards, turnip	¼ cup or more	2–3 minutes	Quick
Kohlrabi	¼ cup	3–5 minutes	Quick
Leeks, sliced	¼ cup	2–3 minutes	Quick
Mushrooms, sliced	2–4 tablespoons	2–3 minutes	Quick
Mushrooms, whole	¼ cup	2–4 minutes	Quick

— CONTINUED —

Vegetable Cooking At-a-Glance

Vegetable (1 cup)	Liquid	Time	Pressure Release
Okra	¼ cup	2 minutes	Quick
Onions, sliced or chopped	¼ cup	2-3 minutes	Either
Parsnips, sliced	¼ cup	2-3 minutes	Either
Peas, English	¼ cup	1 minute	Quick
Peas, sugar snap or snow	¼ cup	30-60 seconds at low pressure if available	Quick
Peppers, bell or chile, sliced	¼ cup	2 minutes	Quick
Potatoes, medium to large, whole (see page 121 for tips)	½-1 cup	10-14 minutes	Natural
Potatoes, large chunks	¼-½ cup, much more for mashed	4-5 minutes	Quick
Potatoes, small, whole	½ cup	8-10 minutes	Natural
Potatoes, new	¼-½ cup	1-2 minutes	Quick
Potatoes, sliced or diced	¼-½ cup	3 minutes	Quick
Potatoes, sweet, cubed	¼ cup	2-3 minutes	Quick
Potatoes, sweet, small, whole	½ cup	8-12 minutes	Natural
Potatoes, sweet, medium to large, whole	½ cup	10-14 minutes	Natural
Rutabaga, sliced or diced	¼-½ cup	3-5 minutes	Quick
Spinach	3 tablespoons or more	1-2 minutes at low, if available	Quick
Squash, spaghetti, quartered	½ cup	4-5 minutes	Either
Squash, spaghetti, whole	1 cup	6-10 minutes	Either
Squash, winter, halved	½-1 cup	4-10 minutes	Either
Squash, winter, whole (in steamer basket)	1 cup	10-15 minutes	Natural
Squash, winter, quartered	½-1 cup	4-8 minutes	Either
Turnips or radishes, sliced	¼ cup	2-3 minutes	Quick
Turnips, small (2-3 inches), whole	½ cup	4-5 minutes	Quick
Zucchini or other summer squash, sliced	1-2 tablespoons	30-60 seconds (or 1 minute at low pressure)	Quick

Let's Talk Onions

In my first book I wrote a piece called "One Onion." Often a recipe will call for one onion but as you likely know, every onion is different. I have bought some slightly larger than a golf ball and others that are bigger than softballs. So, "1 onion" in an ingredient line doesn't tell you much as a cook. I have now taken to specifying the amount of chopped onion, which makes more sense to me. (I've found that 1 medium onion equals 2 cups chopped.) This matters more in some recipes than others; adding more (or less) onion to soups, stews, and chilis is usually just fine.

The other part of the onion conundrum is what type and color of onion to use. I generally don't give this a whole lot of thought, but a recipe editor once reviewed one of my recipes and wanted to know which color onion I used in the soup. Rather than say that it barely matters, I chose yellow. I probably could have just as easily chosen white or red. The flavors of most onions that are harvested at the same time of year are similar, within reason.

But some can be harsh: I have had fairly recently harvested onions that had me bawling in front of a group at a cooking demonstration. Usually it's the winter, storage onions that do that.

One of my favorite types of onion is the sweet onion. This might be the Vidalia, Maui Sweet, Walla Walla, and there are probably others that don't have the kick white, yellow, and red onions do. They taste great raw and add sweetness to any dish in which they are cooked and can be used instead of yellow or red onions. Due to their higher natural sugar level, though, you must be careful when pressure cooking with them. If they start to stick and burn, be sure to add stock and scrape off any stuck-on bits so that your pot doesn't burn when you turn the heat up to raise the pressure.

Whether you are using Spanish, cipollini, torpedo, sweet, red, yellow, or white onions, count on them to be the backbone of your cooking and for adding to your health.

Cooking Whole Potatoes

I know many of you love your potatoes, whether they be white, gold, purple, or sweet. I do, too. And many people want to know how to "bake" their potatoes in the pressure cooker.

As with other foods, there are a number of ways to do this so that they turn out how you like them.

A popular method is to steam them on a rack over water. Add at least 1 cup water, but be sure that the water remains below the rack. Add unpeeled potatoes to the cooker, which you can fill up to two-thirds full, leaving enough room for the steam to raise the pressure valve. Lock on the lid and cook at high pressure for 10 to 14 minutes, depending upon the size of the potatoes and how many you are cooking. Let the pressure come down naturally. Check to see if all the potatoes are cooked (a knife inserted into the center of a large one should meet no resistance). If not, bring them back to high pressure for another minute or two, or until they are all cooked through.

Alternatively, you can cook whole potatoes directly in water using a similar method as above, but without the rack. Add at least 1 cup water to the cooker, then the potatoes. Bring to high pressure and cook for 10 to 15 minutes. Let the pressure come down naturally. This works for white, russet, Yukon Gold, and all varieties of other potatoes including sweet potatoes. The thinner-skinned potatoes, such as Yukon Golds and Yellow Finns will generally need the shorter cooking times.

Small potatoes, such as new potatoes or fingerlings, may need as little as 6 minutes, or you might end up inadvertently with mashed potatoes.

If you like crispy "baked" potatoes, heat your oven to 400°F 5 minutes after you start cooking your potatoes (or right away if you think you will forget to turn it on). Have a parchment-lined baking sheet handy. When the potatoes are cooked, use a pair of tongs to transfer them to the baking sheet. Bake for 5 to 10 minutes, until the skins crisp.

VEGETABLES

4 medium artichokes

4 cloves garlic, slivered

1 cup vegetable stock or water

2 sprigs fresh thyme, savory, or rosemary

Artichokes in Minutes

Photo, page I-5

Some people use their pressure cookers only for artichokes. They are certainly missing out, but it's understandable, as the time savings with artichokes in the pressure cooker are phenomenal. Medium artichokes work best, or you can cut large artichokes in half. Cooking time for artichokes varies a lot, so start with at least 6 minutes at pressure.

SERVES 4

1. Trim artichokes by cutting off the pointy tips from the leaves and digging inside to clean out the choke. Open up the leaves a bit and insert the garlic slivers between the leaves.

2. Add the stock and herbs to the pressure cooker and place a rack or steamer basket on top.

3. Place the artichokes on the rack, stem side up. Lock on the lid. Bring to high pressure; cook for 6 minutes. Let the pressure come down naturally. Remove the lid carefully, tilting it away from you.

4. Check to see if the artichokes are cooked through by pulling on a center leaf or inserting a knife into the heart. If the leaf pulls out or the knife inserts easily, the artichoke is done. If not, bring back to pressure and cook for 2 minutes or longer. Quick release any pressure and check again.

5. Eat immediately, as they are or with your favorite dipping sauce. Store in the refrigerator for up to 5 days.

Posole Chili, page 207

◀ *opposite*
Farro Salad with Tomatoes and Arugula, page 58, and **4C's Warm Rye Berry Salad,** page 56

previous page
Red Pepper and White Bean Dip, page 278, **Marinated Mushrooms,** page 280,
and **Harissa-Glazed Carrots with Small Green Olives,** page 126

◀ *clockwise from left*
Pear Almond Upside-Down Cake, page 289; **Artichokes in Minutes,** page 122; **Potato Vegetable Salad with Mustard-Tarragon Dressing,** page 140

**Creamy Winter Squash Soup with Toasted
Pumpkin Seed–Apple Topping,** page 173

opposite ▶
Black Bean and Sweet Potato Hash. Make into soft
tacos with (vegan) taco garnishes, page 198

Borscht with a Lemon Twist and Greens, page 164

◀ *opposite*

Gingery Spinach, Scallion, and Sesame Sauce,
page 257. Served over black rice, page 53

clockwise from left ▶
Graciela's Colombian Beans, page 108; **Sassy Sesame Tofu with Sweet Potato, Carrots, and Sugar Snap Peas,** page 211, over **Coconut Pineapple Rice,** page 82; **Red Lentil, Sweet Potato, and Hemp Burgers,** page 244

Shepherd's Pie, page 216

◀ *opposite*
Chickpea Broccoli Salad, page 100

I-13

I-15

Asparagus, Shiitake Mushrooms, and Snow Peas

2 minutes high pressure, quick release; 2 minutes low pressure, quick release

Asparagus and snow and sugar snap peas are in season at the same time. You can use rehydrated dried shiitake mushrooms or fresh ones, depending upon what is available. Shiitakes add bulk and incredible umami flavor, as well as great texture (they also have anti-cancer properties).

This recipe is incredibly fast. You'll get the best results if you start cooking at high pressure and then switch to low pressure so that you don't overcook the more tender vegetables.

SERVES 4

2 teaspoons olive oil, optional

1 cup sliced shiitake or crimini mushrooms; or ½ ounce dried shiitakes, rehydrated in hot water for 30 minutes and drained

2 cloves garlic, minced

¼ cup vegetable or mushroom stock, or mushroom soaking water

½ pound asparagus, bottoms of stalks removed, cut into 1-inch pieces

¼ pound snow or sugar snap peas, strings removed, whole or cut in half on the diagonal

Drizzle of tamari

Sprinkle of toasted sesame seeds, optional

1. Heat a stovetop pressure cooker over medium-high heat, or set an electric pressure cooker to sauté; add the oil, if using. Add the mushrooms and cook for 2 minutes.

2. Add the garlic and cook another minute. Add the stock. Lock on the lid. Bring to high pressure; cook for 2 minutes. Quick release the pressure. Remove the lid, carefully tilting it away from you.

3. Add the asparagus. Lock the lid on the cooker, bring to low pressure, and cook for 2 minutes. Quick release the pressure. (If your stovetop or electric cooker has no low pressure setting, bring it to high pressure and then quick release as soon as the pot reaches pressure.) Remove the lid, carefully tilting it away from you.

4. Stir in the snow peas and lock on the lid. Let sit for 2 minutes. Remove the lid carefully.

5. Drizzle in tamari. Transfer to a bowl, sprinkle with sesame seeds if using, and serve.

Variation: Instead of tamari, top the vegetables with the zest and juice of 1 Meyer or regular lemon.

VEGETABLES

*3 minutes low pressure,
quick release*

1 medium unpeeled apple, cut into bite-sized pieces

2 teaspoons lemon juice

2 teaspoons canola or pure sesame oil, optional

¼ cup finely chopped leek, white part only, or onion

3 cups Brussels sprouts, cut in half or quarters (12 to 16)

1 teaspoon fresh thyme leaves or ½ teaspoon dried thyme

1 tablespoon tamari or Bragg liquid aminos

¼ cup vegetable stock or water

1 to 2 teaspoons balsamic vinegar

Freshly ground black pepper

Chopped fresh flat-leaf parsley and chopped toasted hazelnuts, for garnish, optional

Apple and Herb–Braised Brussels Sprouts with Thyme

Brussels sprouts used to be the butt of jokes, a much maligned vegetable. But more recently they've become a vegetable darling. I have always loved them. This dish is a wonderful combination of sweet, pungent, herbaceous, and tangy. Feel free to add other herbs instead of, or in addition to, the thyme.

SERVES 4

1. Toss the apple with the lemon juice in a small bowl and set aside.

2. Heat a stovetop pressure cooker over medium heat or set an electric pressure cooker to sauté. Add the oil, if using, and then the leek. Sauté or dry sauté the leek for 1 minute, until it starts to soften.

3. Add the apple, Brussels sprouts, and thyme. Stir. Add the tamari and stock. Stir. Lock on the lid. Bring to low pressure; cook for 3 minutes. (If you do not have a low pressure option, bring to high pressure and cook for 2 minutes.) Quick release the pressure. Remove the lid carefully, tilting it away from you.

4. Stir in the balsamic vinegar and pepper. Transfer the vegetables to a bowl or platter. Garnish with parsley and hazelnuts, if desired.

Brussels Sprouts with Maple-Mustard Sauce

I realize that there are people who don't care much for Brussels sprouts. My husband is one of them. When I prepare them this way he will at least eat a few. I gladly eat the rest. They are scrumptious. If you are using small sprouts, do not cut them in half. I prefer my Brussels sprouts al dente, but you can cook them for another minute or two if you prefer them softer. Combined with rice or quinoa and some cooked beans, this is a satisfying fall or winter lunch or dinner.

2 teaspoons pure sesame or sunflower oil, optional

½ cup diced onion

½ cup vegetable stock or water

1½ to 2 tablespoons Dijon mustard

16 medium to large Brussels sprouts (1 to 2 inches in diameter), cut in half or quarters to equal 3 cups

½ to 1 tablespoon maple syrup

Salt and freshly ground black pepper

SERVES 4

1. Heat a stovetop pressure cooker over medium heat or set an electric pressure cooker to sauté; add the oil, if using. Add the onion and sauté or dry sauté for a minute or two, until it starts to soften.

2. Whisk together the stock and mustard in a small bowl or shake in a glass jar. Add the Brussels sprouts to the cooker along with the mustard mixture. Stir. Drizzle the maple syrup over the vegetables but do not stir.

3. Lock the lid on the pressure cooker. Bring to low pressure; cook for 3 minutes. (If you do not have a low pressure option, bring to high pressure and cook for 2 minutes.) Quick release the pressure. Remove the lid, carefully tilting it away from you.

4. Transfer the sprouts to a bowl. Season with salt and pepper, if desired.

2 tablespoons lemon juice

1 to 2 cloves garlic, minced

1 to 2 teaspoons olive oil, optional

2 tablespoons maple syrup

1 to 2 teaspoons Harissa Spice Blend (page 40), plus optional ½ teaspoon for garnish

¼ cup vegetable stock or water

1 pound carrots (6 medium), peeled and sliced on the diagonal

¼ teaspoon cumin seeds, toasted and crushed

Sprinkle of salt

2 to 3 ounces small green olives such as Arbequina or Lucques, pitted or left whole

Harissa-Glazed Carrots with Small Green Olives

Photo, page I-1

This recipe was inspired by an amazing dish of roasted rainbow carrots I sampled at the Purple Café in Seattle. Those carrots were roasted with oil and harissa in a very hot oven. I figured that I could come up with something close in the pressure cooker. If you use oil, you will have something closer to the original, but even without the oil, these are mighty tasty. Serve hot, warm, or at room temperature, as a side dish or an appetizer.

SERVES 4

1. Combine the lemon juice, garlic, olive oil if using, maple syrup, and 1 to 2 teaspoons (to taste) harissa in a small bowl.

2. Add the stock to a 6-quart or smaller pressure cooker, then add the carrots. Drizzle the carrots with the lemon juice mixture. Do not stir.

3. Lock on the lid. Bring to high pressure; cook for 4 minutes. Quick release the pressure. Remove the lid, carefully tilting it away from you. Check to be sure that the carrots are cooked through. If not, bring back to pressure and cook for 1 to 2 minutes, then quick release. Remove the lid, carefully tilting it away from you.

4. Transfer the carrots to a bowl or platter and sprinkle with more harissa if desired, the cumin, and salt. Add the green olives and serve.

Maple and Vinegar–Braised Parsnips

Parsnips look like white carrots but they don't really taste the same. They are starchier and maybe even sweeter in an earthy, nutty way. Most people have tried them in soup, but they are great in this simple sweet-and-sour side dish. Be sure that the parsnips are cooked through, but don't let them get mushy.

SERVES 4

1. Combine the parsnips, stock, and vinegar in a pressure cooker. Lock on the lid, bring to high pressure, and cook for 3 minutes. Quick release the pressure. Remove the lid, carefully tilting it away from you.

2. Check to see that the parsnips are fully tender. If not and they need more liquid, add a few more tablespoons of stock or water. Bring back to high pressure and cook for 1 minute, then quick release. Remove the lid, carefully tilting it away from you.

3. Stir in the maple syrup and season to taste with salt and pepper. Transfer to a bowl and serve.

3 minutes high pressure, quick release

1½ pounds parsnips, all about the same size, peeled and cut into ½-inch slices on the diagonal

¼ cup vegetable stock

3 tablespoons balsamic vinegar

2 tablespoons maple syrup

Salt and freshly ground black pepper

VEGETABLES

127

2 tablespoons mellow white miso

1 large pitted Medjool date, soaked in ¼ cup hot stock or water for 15 minutes

2 to 3 tablespoons lemon juice

½ pound fresh green beans, cut into 1- to 2-inch pieces

¼ cup vegetable stock

Miso-Drizzled Green Beans

You can use this technique with other vegetables such as broccoli, bok choy, cauliflower, and many more. Adjust the cooking time and amount of liquid accordingly, using the chart on page 120.

SERVES 2 TO 4

1. Blend the miso, soaked date and soaking liquid, and lemon juice in a mini food processor or blender until well combined.

2. Combine the green beans and stock in a pressure cooker. Drizzle 1 tablespoon of the miso mixture over the beans.

3. Lock on the lid. Bring to low pressure; cook for 2 minutes. (If you do not have a low pressure option, bring to high pressure and cook for 1 minute.) Quick release the pressure. Remove the lid, carefully tilting it away from you.

4. Check the beans; they should be tender. If not, bring back to low pressure and cook for another minute. Add the remaining miso mixture and toss.

5. Serve right away, at room temperature, or chilled.

Simple Chinese Broccoli and Mushrooms

It fascinates me how just a few ingredients put together in the pressure cooker can make vegetable magic. Voila! This simple combination is full of texture, fresh-tasting and savory, with enough umami flavor to make you want more. Even though this ought to make 4 servings, I will often devour half in one sitting.

SERVES 4

1. Heat a stovetop pressure cooker over medium heat, or set an electric pressure cooker to sauté. Add the onion, garlic, and ginger and dry sauté for 1 minute.

2. Add the mushrooms, broccoli stems, stock, and tamari. Lock the lid on the cooker. Bring to low pressure; cook for 1 minute, then quick release the pressure. (If you don't have a low pressure option, bring to high pressure and release immediately.) Remove the lid, carefully tilting it away from you.

3. Add the broccoli flowers and leaves. Lock on the lid. Bring to low pressure; cook for 2 minutes. (Or 1 minute at high pressure.) Quick release the pressure. Remove the lid, carefully tilting it away from you.

4. Transfer the broccoli and mushrooms to a bowl, garnish with sesame seeds, and serve.

1 minute low pressure, quick release; 2 minutes low pressure, quick release

¼ cup diced onion

3 cloves garlic, minced

1 teaspoon minced fresh ginger

8 ounces crimini or oyster mushrooms, sliced

1 pound Chinese broccoli, stems chopped, flowers and leaves sliced and kept separate

2 tablespoons vegetable stock

2 tablespoons tamari

1 to 2 tablespoons toasted sesame seeds, for garnish

1 cup diced spring or other
onions

¼ cup diced green garlic; or
3 cloves garlic, minced

⅓ cup vegetable stock

2 baby bok choy, sliced

1 cup broccoli florets

1 cup chopped asparagus

1 cup sliced stemmed kale

½ cup diced peeled daikon or
other radish

2 teaspoons toasted sesame
seeds

2 to 3 teaspoons ume vinegar
or tamari, optional

Clean Spring Greens

After a long winter, spring greens are a welcome addition to our diet. This refreshing blend of broccoli, bok choy, kale, and daikon helps purify your blood, which ought to make you feel a bit lighter, and asparagus is one of my favorite spring treats. This tastes best served over brown rice or your favorite grain. Adding Sesame Tempeh Sticks (page 220) makes it a complete meal.

SERVES 4

1. Heat a stovetop pressure cooker over medium heat, or set an electric pressure cooker to sauté. Dry sauté the onion for 1 minute. Add the garlic and cook 30 seconds more.

2. Add the stock, bok choy, broccoli, asparagus, kale, and daikon and stir. Lock on the lid. Bring to low pressure; cook for 3 minutes. (If you don't have a low pressure option, cook for 2 minutes at high pressure.) Quick release the pressure. Remove the lid, carefully tilting it away from you.

3. Transfer the vegetables to a bowl or platter, sprinkle with the toasted sesame seeds, and add a drizzle of ume vinegar or tamari, if desired.

Greens with Turmeric, Ginger, and Garlic

We should ideally eat greens daily for good health, and this everyday recipe is a perfect way to do that. The tahini adds richness, but you can leave it out if you prefer.

SERVES 4

1. Heat a stovetop pressure cooker over medium heat, or set an electric pressure cooker to sauté; add the oil, if using. Add the garlic, ginger, and turmeric and cook for 1 minute. Add the greens, ¼ cup stock, adding more if your greens are very thick or tough, and sesame oil, if using.

2. Lock the lid on the pressure cooker. Bring to high pressure; cook for 3 minutes. Quick release the pressure. Remove the lid, carefully tilting it away from you.

3. Using tongs, stir the greens. Add the tahini and pepper to taste. Drizzle with soy sauce, if using, and the vinegar and serve.

1 teaspoon neutral oil, optional

4 cloves garlic

1 inch fresh ginger, peeled and grated or minced

1½- to 1-inch piece turmeric root, grated or minced, or 1 teaspoon ground turmeric

1 large bunch greens such as kale, collards, turnip greens, or Swiss chard, thick stems removed, sliced to equal 8 cups

¼ cup or more vegetable stock

2 teaspoons toasted sesame oil, optional

1 to 2 tablespoons tahini

Freshly ground black pepper or crushed red pepper flakes

1 to 2 teaspoons soy sauce or tamari, optional

Drizzle of balsamic vinegar

VEGETABLES

1 minute high pressure,
quick release; 2 minutes
high pressure,
quick release

1 tablespoon olive or vegetable
oil, optional

1 cup diced onion

4 cloves garlic, minced

1 teaspoon minced fresh
ginger

1 teaspoon ground turmeric

½ teaspoon ground fenugreek,
optional

1½ cups vegetable stock

1¼ pounds Yukon Gold potatoes,
cut into eighths (3 cups)

2 medium carrots, peeled and
cut into ¾- to 1-inch pieces

4 cups sliced green cabbage
(about ¼ head)

½ teaspoon salt

Freshly ground black pepper

Hot sauce, optional

Atakilt Wat

(ETHIOPIAN CABBAGE, CARROTS, AND POTATOES)

I see this vegetable combination as the "holy trinity" of Ethiopian cuisine. The potatoes are usually peeled, but when using thin-skinned potatoes, such as Yukon Golds, I don't bother. Why waste time peeling off what's good to eat? Usually this dish has a lot of fat in it, but here it has little or even none.

This dish can accompany Misr Wot (page 111) and Gomen (page 133) to form a typical Ethiopian spread, and also makes an excellent side dish in many other meals.

SERVES 4 TO 6

1. Heat a stovetop pressure cooker over medium heat, or set an electric pressure cooker to sauté; add the oil, if using. Add the onion and cook for 2 minutes. Add the garlic, ginger, turmeric, and fenugreek, if using, and cook 1 more minute, adding a tablespoon or two of the stock if anything starts to stick.

2. Add the potatoes and remaining stock. Lock on the lid. Bring to high pressure; cook for 1 minute. Quick release the pressure. Remove the lid, carefully tilting it away from you.

3. Add the carrots, cabbage, and salt. Lock on the lid, bring to high pressure, and cook for 2 minutes. Quick release the pressure. Remove the lid, carefully tilting it away from you.

4. If the carrots and potatoes are not tender enough, lock on the lid and let sit for 2 to 5 minutes.

5. Add freshly ground black pepper and hot sauce, if desired, and serve.

Gomen

(ETHIOPIAN COLLARD GREENS)

I have a fondness for Ethiopian food, and these greens are no exception. They are traditionally made with collards, but lacinato (dinosaur or black) kale, or even Swiss chard, can stand in. Most Ethiopian recipes call for a flavored butter called *niter kibbeh,* but this tastes just wonderful without the added fat.

I grind fenugreek seeds in my spice grinder. If you can't find the seeds or ground fenugreek, leave it out. I haven't used any hot chiles in this dish but if you are a hot head, feel free to slice up a couple of jalapeño or serrano peppers with the bell pepper. Remember that you can always add more heat but it's hard to take it out.

SERVES 4 TO 6

1. Heat a stovetop pressure cooker over medium heat, or set an electric pressure cooker to sauté; add the oil, if using. Add the onion and cook for 1 minute. Add the bell pepper, garlic, and spices. Cook another 30 seconds. Add the stock and stir the bottom of the cooker to be sure that nothing is sticking.

2. Add the greens and lock on the lid. Bring to low pressure; cook for 10 minutes. (If you don't have a low pressure option, cook at high pressure for 5 minutes.) Quick release the pressure. Remove the lid, carefully tilting it away from you.

3. Add salt and pepper to taste and serve.

1 tablespoon olive oil, optional

½ cup diced red onion

½ cup diced red, yellow, orange, or green bell pepper

3 cloves garlic, minced

½ teaspoon ground fenugreek

1 to 1½ teaspoons berbere spice blend, store-bought or homemade (page 36)

¾ cup vegetable stock

1 large bunch collards, lacinato kale, or chard, stems removed and sliced (6 cups)

Salt and freshly ground black pepper

VEGETABLES

7 minutes high pressure,
quick release; 4 minutes
high pressure,
quick release

1 tablespoon neutral or pure sesame oil, optional

2 cups finely chopped onion

1 medium carrot, peeled and diced

6 cloves garlic, minced

1 medium hot chile, such as jalapeño or serrano, minced

½-inch piece fresh ginger, minced or grated to equal at least 2 teaspoons

1 teaspoon cumin seeds

1 pound greens, such as kale, collards, Swiss chard, or a combination, chopped very fine (like you often find in chopped frozen spinach)

¼ cup red lentils

1¼ cups vegetable stock

1 cup diced tomatoes, fresh or canned

1 medium zucchini or other summer squash, cut into ¼-inch cubes, optional

2 teaspoons garam masala, store-bought or homemade (page 39)

1 teaspoon ground turmeric

Salt

Sai Bhaaji

(PAKISTANI GREENS)

I want to thank Stefan at plantbasedonabudget.com for this recipe, which I have adapted for the pressure cooker. It was originally billed as "slow cooked greens." This is not the case anymore, since the original 2-hour cook time is now less than 15 minutes. To make it my own, I've simplified the cooking process, which originally involved three stages, used red lentils instead of split peas, and used garam masala as the seasoning instead of individual spices.

It's still a dish based on cooked and seasoned greens. I'd never eaten this dish prior to making it, but it's now a favorite. To simplify the recipe even more, use a 16-ounce bag of washed chopped greens, making sure to remove any thick stems from the mix. If you make this with Swiss chard, include the stems, finely chopped, which will make it both colorful and tasty. Definitely include the summer squash when it's in season, but it can be omitted if not available.

SERVES 4 TO 6

1. Heat a stovetop pressure cooker over medium heat, or set an electric pressure cooker to sauté. Add the oil, if using. Add the onion and cook for 1 minute. Add the carrot, garlic, chile, ginger, and cumin seeds. Cook for another 30 seconds.

2. Add the greens, lentils, and stock. Lock on the lid, bring to high pressure, and cook for 7 minutes. Quick release the pressure. Remove the lid, carefully tilting it away from you.

3. Add the tomatoes, zucchini, garam masala, and turmeric. Lock the lid back on the cooker. Bring to high pressure; cook for 4 minutes. Quick release the pressure. Remove the lid carefully, tilting it away from you.

4. Stir well. Add salt, if desired. Transfer to a bowl and serve.

Herbed Summer Squash with Walnuts

This recipe—so easy to put together—transforms summer squash from boring vegetable to delectable dish. The sweet pepper brings flavor and bright color and the toasted walnuts add a bit of allure. If you are not fond of walnuts, you can use any other toasted nuts or seeds.

Do not think that the addition of a minute amount of liquid is a mistake: The small amount deglazes the cooker, but keeps the squash from drowning in its own juices. Summer squash has a very high water content and it's low in calories, so eat as much as you want.

SERVES 4

1. Heat a stovetop pressure cooker over medium heat or set an electric pressure cooker to sauté; add the oil, if using. Add the garlic and cook for 15 seconds, stirring occasionally to prevent sticking. Add the bell pepper and herbs and sauté for another 15 seconds. (Turn off the sauté function if using electric.)

2. Add the stock and stir well to loosen any stuck bits. Add the squash; do not stir.

3. Lock on the lid. Bring to low pressure if using a stovetop cooker (or high if you have no other option), or set to 0 on an electric cooker. Thirty seconds later, quick release the pressure. Remove the lid, carefully tilting it away from you.

4. Transfer the contents to a bowl. Sprinkle with salt and pepper to taste, garnish with nuts, and serve.

Mexican-Spiced Summer Squash with Pumpkin Seeds: Omit the basil and parsley and add 1 teaspoon ground cumin, ½ teaspoon dried or 1 teaspoon fresh oregano, and 1½ teaspoons chili or chipotle powder when you add the garlic. Garnish with toasted pumpkin seeds instead of walnuts.

30 seconds low pressure, quick release

1 tablespoon olive oil, optional

2 large cloves garlic, minced

¼ cup diced red, yellow, or orange bell pepper

2 tablespoons chopped fresh flat-leaf parsley

2 tablespoons chopped fresh basil

1 to 2 tablespoons vegetable stock or water

1 pound zucchini or other summer squash, sliced into thin ¼-inch rounds or half rounds (about 3 cups)

Salt and freshly ground black pepper

3 tablespoons chopped toasted walnuts

VEGETABLES

135

4 cups plum tomatoes, cut into quarters

3 cloves garlic

¼ cup chopped fresh basil

2 tablespoons chopped fresh flat-leaf parsley

1 to 3 teaspoons Italian seasoning, store-bought or homemade (page 41), to taste

1 cup finely chopped onion

1 spaghetti squash, about 2½ pounds, cut into quarters and seeds removed

Salt and freshly ground black pepper

Spaghetti Squash with Tomato Sauce

Don't let the simplicity of this dish fool you into thinking that it can't be that good, because it is. It's fast, too. Choose your spaghetti squash wisely: A medium sized one that is 2½ to 3 pounds works best. Carefully cut it into quarters and scoop out the seeds. I like to clean the seeds off and roast them in the oven.

It's amazing that you can cook both the sauce and the squash in the cooker at one time, making this a simple one-pot meal. Serve with a sprinkling of nutritional yeast or nondairy cheese, if desired.

SERVES 4 TO 6

1. Briefly pulse the tomatoes, garlic, basil, and parsley in a blender or food processor. Stir in the Italian seasoning.

2. Heat a stovetop pressure cooker over medium heat or set an electric cooker to sauté. Add the onion and dry sauté for 3 to 4 minutes. Add the blended tomatoes; do not stir.

3. Put the spaghetti squash quarters into the pressure cooker with the stem and bottom ends down in the tomatoes, and the cut ends up. Lock the lid on the pressure cooker. Bring to high pressure; cook for 4 minutes. Let the pressure come down naturally. Remove the lid carefully, tilting it away from you.

4. Check to be sure that the squash is thoroughly cooked. If so, remove it with tongs and transfer to a large bowl. If not, lock on the lid, bring the cooker to high pressure, and cook for 1 to 2 minutes longer. This time, you can do a quick release.

5. Using a fork or spoon, scoop out the squash strands into a bowl. Add salt and pepper to taste and spoon the tomato sauce over the squash.

Cooking Whole Winter Squash

Just knowing that you can cook a whole butternut or acorn squash in the pressure cooker ought to intrigue you enough to try it. However, because each winter squash is a bit different in size, and even the same squash has different thicknesses, it's not always possible to determine exactly how long to cook it. The general rule of thumb for a squash that is 2 pounds or larger is to add 1 cup water or stock to the cooker and set in a rack or basket, if you want. No need to poke holes in the squash, peel it, or cut it, unless you want to. Cook for at least 10 minutes at high pressure, then release naturally. Test for doneness in a few places: If a knife or fork inserted goes through without resistance, the squash is cooked. If not, it needs more time, usually an additional 2 to 5 minutes. Use tongs to remove the squash and be prepared for it to be falling apart.

A 3-pound kabocha with 1 cup water usually cooks in 12 to 15 minutes at high pressure. A buttercup-type squash (which is similar to a kabocha but not as meaty or dense) of about 2 pounds, cut in half, takes approximately 11 minutes at high pressure with a natural release.

Sometimes different parts of the squash cook at different rates. On one attempt, the thinner part of the squash was thoroughly cooked at 7 minutes at high pressure but the other parts were not close to done, so the squash went back into the cooker for 4 more minutes. Then it was "just right."

A whole small squash, such as delicata, with its thin skin, takes only 4 to 5 minutes at pressure with a quick or natural pressure release. When cut into pieces, it takes only 3 minutes at pressure with a quick release. I often don't bother peeling the delicata, which just adds to the appeal.

The skin on delicata and kabocha are edible while the skin on butternut, acorn, and many other squash is generally too tough to eat or be enjoyable, but it can be easily removed after cooking. The squash "meat" easily pulls away from the skin.

My best trick for cutting squash is to use a Halloween pumpkin carving knife. It's not sharp like a paring or carving knife, but is serrated and so easily cuts through squash.

3 cloves garlic, minced

1 tablespoon curry powder,
store-bought or homemade
(page 38), optional

¼ cup vegetable stock

4 cups cauliflower florets
(1 small head)

1 cup 2-inch diced peeled
celery root (also called
celeriac)

½ cup nondairy milk

¼ cup coconut milk or
additional nondairy milk

1 tablespoon unsweetened
flaked or shredded coconut

2 teaspoons coconut extract, if
not using coconut milk

Salt and freshly ground black
pepper

Coconut Cauliflower Mash

I want to thank CJ Bruce, the Vegetarian Dude, for the inspiration to make this dish. Cauliflower is a vegetable chameleon, and low in calories, too. The celery root adds to the depth of flavor. The coconut milk and coconut add richness and boost the flavor tremendously. If you don't want to use coconut milk, use nondairy milk and add coconut extract. If you love curry, use your favorite curry powder. This recipe is versatile and a great option for people who want to avoid potatoes. That wouldn't be me, yet I still adore the mash.

SERVES 4 TO 6

1. Heat a stovetop pressure cooker over medium heat, or set an electric pressure cooker to sauté. Add the garlic and curry powder, if using, and dry sauté for 15 to 30 seconds.

2. Add the stock and stir well, making sure that anything stuck on the bottom of the cooker is incorporated into the liquid.

3. Add the cauliflower, celery root, milks, and flaked coconut. Lock the lid on the pressure cooker. Bring to high pressure; cook for 4 minutes. Quick release the pressure. Remove the lid carefully, tilting it away from you.

4. Check to be sure that the cauliflower and celery root are tender. If not, bring back to pressure and cook for 1 minute, then quick release. Add the coconut extract, if using.

5. Using a handheld potato masher or an immersion blender, blend the mixture until smooth or to your desired texture. Transfer to a dish. Add salt and pepper to taste, and serve.

Curried Coconut-Spinach Cauliflower Mash: Use the curry powder, and add 1 cup frozen spinach when you add the cauliflower. (You can also omit the curry powder and add ¼ teaspoon grated nutmeg with the spinach.) If you like a cheesy flavor with your spinach, add a tablespoon or two of nutritional yeast.

Romanesco and Cauliflower

WITH LEEKS AND LEMON-MUSTARD CASHEW-CREAM SAUCE

Braising generally involves fat and liquid. In this case, the vegetables cook in stock and finish with a lemony cashew-cream sauce. If you cannot find cashew meal, grind raw cashew pieces in a blender or spice grinder. (Do not grind too long or you will end up with cashew butter.)

Romanesco is a kind of green cauliflower. If you can find it—or cheddar (orange) or purple cauliflower—you will end up with a spectacular looking dish. If not, it will still taste amazing.

SERVES 4

1. Add the cauliflower and Romanesco to a pressure cooker along with the leek.

2. Add the stock and lock on the lid. Bring to low pressure; cook for 3 minutes. (If you don't have a low pressure setting, cook for 2 minutes at high pressure.) Quick release the pressure. Carefully open the lid, tilting it away from you.

3. Add the cashew meal, mustard, lemon juice, and a few tablespoons more stock if the mixture seems too dry. Stir over medium heat or using the sauté function until the cashews form a creamy sauce-like consistency. Add freshly ground black pepper to taste and serve.

3 minutes low pressure, quick release

4 cups assorted chopped cauliflower and Romanesco, cut into similar-sized pieces

1 cup chopped leek

⅓ cup vegetable stock, plus more as needed

¼ cup powdered cashew meal or flour

1 tablespoon Dijon mustard

1 tablespoon lemon juice

Freshly ground black pepper

1 medium onion, sliced into
¼-inch-thick half rounds

1½ pounds fingerling or other
small potatoes, cut into
2-inch pieces

¾ cup vegetable stock

1 cup fresh or frozen (not
thawed) corn kernels

3 tablespoons fresh lemon
juice

1 tablespoon olive oil, plain or
lemon flavored

2 teaspoons Dijon mustard

1 tablespoon rice, champagne,
or white wine vinegar

2 tablespoons cashew butter,
tahini, or olive oil

1 to 2 tablespoons chopped
fresh tarragon

1 cup cherry tomatoes, cut in
half

Salt and freshly ground black
pepper

1 to 2 tablespoons chopped
fresh flat-leaf parsley, for
garnish

Potato Vegetable Salad

WITH MUSTARD-TARRAGON DRESSING

Photo, page I-5

Adding corn and tomatoes to potato salad makes it something special—
colorful and bright—as does the tarragon dressing. If you can get potatoes in
different colors, it makes this dish even more impressive.

SERVES 4 TO 6

1. Heat a stovetop pressure cooker over medium heat, or set an
   electric cooker to sauté. Add the onion and dry sauté for 2 minutes.
   Add the potatoes and stock. Lock on the lid, bring to high pressure,
   and cook for 3 minutes. Quick release the pressure. Remove the lid,
   carefully tilting it away from you.

2. Add the corn, lock the lid on the cooker, and let sit for 1 minute.
   Transfer everything to a bowl and cool for at least 15 minutes.

3. While the potatoes are cooling, combine the lemon juice, olive oil,
   mustard, vinegar, and cashew butter in a bowl and whisk well. Stir
   in the tarragon.

4. Add the cherry tomatoes to the potatoes and then add the
   dressing. Season with salt and pepper to taste.

5. Let the potatoes sit for another few minutes for flavors to blend.
   Garnish with parsley and serve.

Mediterranean Potatoes

This is an almost creamy casserole, because the potatoes get meltingly soft. The other ingredients add texture and the whole thing is served over arugula, which gives it a little bite. Very tasty, if I do say so myself. You need a glass or metal casserole dish or bowl that fits easily into your pressure cooker. I use a 1½- to 2-quart glass or CorningWare-type bowl.

SERVES 4 TO 6

1. Layer half of the potatoes in a casserole dish (see headnote). Top with a layer of half the artichokes and leeks and half of the sun-dried tomatoes. Sprinkle with 1 teaspoon of the seasoning and some black pepper and tuck a bay leaf and the sprig of rosemary into the potatoes.

2. Pour ½ cup of the stock on top of this. Add the remaining potatoes in a layer, followed by the remaining artichokes, leeks, sun-dried tomatoes, 2 bay leaves, more black pepper, and 2 tablespoons of the olives. Drizzle with the olive oil, if using. Pour the remaining ½ cup stock over the mixture. Cover the dish with a heatproof cover or with foil.

3. Add 1 cup water to the bottom of a pressure cooker. Add a trivet or rack to elevate the dish above the water (see page 14). Create a set of helper handles (see page 15) to enable you to remove the casserole, and set on the trivet. Place the covered casserole on top.

4. Lock on the lid. Bring to high pressure; cook for 5 minutes. Quick release the pressure. Carefully remove the lid, tilting it away from you.

5. Remove the foil or cover. Insert a knife into the potatoes; it should meet no resistance, indicating they are cooked through. If the potatoes need more time, bring the pot to high pressure and cook for another 1 to 2 minutes. Quick release. Remove the lid, tilting it away from you.

6. Carefully remove the casserole. Remove the cover, and discard the bay leaves. Sprinkle with the remaining 2 tablespoons olives.

7. To serve, arrange arugula on each plate and top with a serving of the potatoes.

5 minutes high pressure, quick release

2 pounds thin-skinned potatoes, such as Yukon Gold, Yellow Finn, or red, thinly sliced

1 cup frozen artichoke hearts, thawed

1 cup thinly sliced leeks or onion

½ cup sliced sun-dried tomatoes, not oil-packed

2 teaspoons of your favorite herb and garlic seasoning (store-bought or see page 55 for other ideas)

Freshly ground black pepper

3 bay leaves

1 small sprig fresh rosemary

1 cup vegetable stock

¼ cup sliced pitted kalamata olives

2 teaspoons olive oil, optional

2 to 3 cups arugula or spinach

VEGETABLES

1 medium onion, sliced

2 teaspoons minced fresh ginger

3 garlic cloves, minced

1 medium hot chile, such as jalapeño or serrano, seeded and finely chopped

¾ cup vegetable stock

1 pound Yukon Gold or other thin-skinned potatoes, cut into ½-inch slices

1 pound sweet potatoes, peeled and sliced ½ inch thick

Grated zest and juice of 1 lemon

½ cup nondairy yogurt, optional

1 tablespoon tamarind paste

Salt and freshly ground black pepper

4 scallions, sliced

Spicy White and Sweet Potatoes

This side dish can turn up the heat at any meal. If you are a potato lover as I am and like savory and spicy dishes, you will fall in love with this one. The heat of the ginger, garlic, and chile gets balanced with the tartness of lemon juice, yogurt, and tamarind. The combo takes potatoes to a new level. Serve alongside your favorite cooked beans and vegetables.

SERVES 4 TO 6

1. Heat a stovetop pressure cooker over medium heat or set an electric cooker to sauté. Add the onion and dry sauté for 3 minutes.

2. Add the ginger, garlic, and chile and sauté another minute.

3. Add the stock and Yukon Gold and sweet potatoes. Lock the lid on the cooker. Bring to low pressure; cook for 5 minutes. (If you don't have a low pressure option, bring to high pressure and cook for 3 minutes.) Quick release the pressure. Remove the lid, carefully tilting it away from you.

4. Transfer the potatoes to a dish.

5. In a small bowl, whisk together the lemon zest and juice, yogurt, if using, and tamarind paste. Drizzle over the potatoes. Add salt and pepper to taste, sprinkle with the scallions, and serve.

Spiced Sweet Potatoes and Apples

This amazing and quick side dish is perfect for fall and winter holidays, especially the times when the oven is in use for many other dishes. Use the rum and apple cider if they are available. Tone down the black pepper and avoid the rum if children are being served.

SERVES 4 TO 6

1. Heat a stovetop pressure cooker over medium heat or set an electric cooker to sauté. Add the onion and dry sauté for 2 minutes. Add all the spices and sauté for 1 minute longer.

2. Add the sweet potatoes, apples, stock, cider, and rum. Lock the lid on the pressure cooker. Bring to high pressure; cook for 3 minutes. Quick release the pressure. Remove the lid, carefully tilting it away from you.

3. Add the lemon zest and juice. Transfer to a dish. Garnish with the toasted nuts if desired and serve.

1½ cups sliced onion

1 teaspoon ground cinnamon

½ teaspoon ground toasted coriander seeds

¼ teaspoon freshly ground nutmeg

⅛ to ¼ teaspoon freshly ground black pepper

Pinch of cardamom

4 cups diced sweet potatoes (1½ pounds or 2 medium)

1½ cups diced unpeeled tart-sweet firm apples, such as Granny Smith, Jonathan, or Stayman, thinly sliced (1 to 2 medium)

½ cup vegetable stock

¼ cup apple cider or juice

2 tablespoons dark rum or additional vegetable stock

1 teaspoon grated lemon zest

1 tablespoon lemon juice

Chopped toasted pecans or walnuts, optional

VEGETABLES

2 medium rutabagas, peeled
and cut into 1½-inch dice
(3 to 3½ cups)

2 teaspoons grated fresh
ginger root

2 teaspoons grated orange
zest

Juice of 2 sweet oranges,
such as Cara Cara

Vegetable stock to equal a
total of ¾ cup liquid when
combined with the juice

Freshly ground black pepper

Rutabaga with Ginger and Orange

If you live in the middle of the country, you are likely more familiar with rutabaga than those who live on the coasts. Or at least that's how it seems to me. I only started eating rutabaga in the past few years when they began showing up at the farmers' market with their beautiful tops attached. Rutabaga taste like starchy turnips, almost potato-like, but still part of the cruciferous vegetable family. This firm-textured, mildly sweet dish can stand alongside many other dishes. This treatment also works well with other root vegetables.

If you prefer a mash, add ¼ cup more orange juice or stock and cook for an extra minute or two, then use your potato masher or immersion blender and mash to your desired smoothness.

SERVES 4

1. Combine all the ingredients in a pressure cooker. Lock on the lid. Bring to high pressure; cook for 4 minutes. Quick release the pressure. Remove the lid, tilting it away from you.

2. Insert a knife into the rutabaga to see if it is cooked through; it should meet no resistance. If done, transfer to a bowl. If not, either bring back to high pressure and cook for 1 minute and quick release, or lock the lid on and let sit for 3 to 5 minutes.

3. Add freshly ground black pepper to taste and serve.

Mustard-Parsley Kohlrabi

Kohlrabi is an underappreciated cruciferous vegetable that is most often seen in the fall and winter. It looks a bit strange, a bulbous green or purple ball. The skin is tough, so peel it well. The flavor is akin to a mild turnip (a cousin) or broccoli stems. I want to thank Sue Ferguson, one of my recipe testers, for the inspiration for this dish. She had never tried kohlrabi prior but thought this treatment would make it appealing. I agree. It's like eating German potato salad without the potatoes.

SERVES 4

1. Combine the kohlrabi, ½ cup of the stock, 1 tablespoon of the vinegar, and some pepper in a pressure cooker. Lock on the lid. Bring to high pressure; cook 5 minutes. Let the pressure come down naturally.

2. Make the dressing while the kohlrabi is cooking: Combine the remaining 2 tablespoons stock, remaining 1 tablespoon vinegar, the parsley, and Dijon mustard to taste in a mini food processor. Process until almost smooth, with flecks of the parsley evident.

3. When the pressure is down, remove the lid, carefully tilting it away from you. Transfer the kohlrabi to a dish.

4. Stir the mustard seeds and red onion into the kohlrabi. Add the dressing and stir well. Season with freshly ground black pepper and salt to taste.

1 medium kohlrabi, about 1 pound, peeled and cut into ½- to 1-inch cubes (2 to 3 cups)

½ cup plus 2 tablespoons vegetable stock

2 tablespoons apple cider vinegar

Freshly ground black pepper

¼ cup packed fresh flat-leaf parsley

1 to 2 teaspoons Dijon, yellow, or brown mustard

1 teaspoon yellow or black mustard seeds

¼ cup diced red onion

Salt

VEGETABLES

1½ pounds beets (about
    6 medium)

3 large strips orange peel and
    2 teaspoons grated zest,
    plus ½ cup freshly squeezed
    orange juice (1 to 2 oranges)

2 tablespoons cider vinegar

2 tablespoons Sucanat or
    brown sugar

2 teaspoons Dijon mustard

2 scallions, sliced

2 cups spicy greens, such as
    arugula, mustard greens, or a
    mix, washed and dried

Orange-Scented Beet Salad

Cooking beets has never been easier. They become so tender in the pressure cooker that you don't even need to peel them if you don't want to. It's best to use young beets that are no more than 3 or 4 inches in diameter as they are most tender and even the skin becomes edible in the pressure cooker.

SERVES 4

1. Scrub the beets. Remove the stems and tails and cut in half. Lay cut-side down and cut into ¼-inch slices.

2. Combine the orange zest strips, orange juice, and vinegar in a pressure cooker. Add the beets. Lock on the lid. Bring to high pressure; cook for 3 minutes. Let the pressure come down naturally for 7 minutes, then release any remaining pressure. Remove the lid carefully, tilting it away from you.

3. Remove and discard the zest strips. Stir the Sucanat and mustard into the beets.

4. Remove the beets from the cooking liquid and transfer to a bowl. Let cool for at least 5 minutes. (At this point, you may chill the beets in their liquid for a day or two; mix in the grated zest and scallions just before serving.)

5. Mix the grated orange zest and scallions into the beets. Pour the liquid from the cooker over the beets.

6. Divide the greens among 4 salad plates, spoon the beet salad over the greens, and serve.

The Lowdown on Beets

The pressure cooker seems to be tailor-made for cooking beets. I have cooked all manner of beets, from teeny tiny ones to whole, very large beets. What I have learned is that the cooking time depends as much on the particular beet as the size of the beet. Even some freshly dug beets take longer than others because they are more mature when the farmer harvested them, which you have no way of knowing when you buy them.

Before cooking beets, I often cut off the entire top stem to just above the round part, leaving just a little bit of the bottom tail intact, and the skins on. If the beets are well cooked, the skins will often peel right off without a vegetable peeler—a sharp knife will do, if you choose to peel them. I prefer eating the skin.

I also like to cook my beets directly in the cooker rather than on a rack as I think that they taste better that way (as do many other vegetables). They absorb the cooking liquid, which improves the flavor and texture. But feel free to steam them on a rack, above at least 1 cup of water, if you like.

You can do either a quick or natural release when cooking beets. To check doneness, stick a knife into the beets to determine if they are cooked to your liking, which is another part of beet cooking I cannot account for. I might like my beets firmer than you like yours. The more resistance, the firmer the beets will be.

How well cooked you want your beets also depends upon how you intend to use them. Will you be using them in a salad or blending them into a dip? Beets for salads can be more firm; for a dip you want them extremely tender.

Here are the times that I have determined for cooking beets at high pressure:

- Small whole: 10 to 12 minutes

- Medium to large whole: 12 to 20 minutes

- Beets cut into cubes or slices: 3 minutes

Did you know that you can freeze cooked beets? I found this out when I bought half of a 9-pound beet. Yes, *a 9-pound beet*. The 4½ pounds that I had were delicious but I couldn't eat it all so I froze it. It was just as tasty once defrosted and made into beet salad.

2 cups finely chopped onion

1 pound fresh okra

3 cups fresh (or canned if you must) diced tomatoes with their juice

1 tablespoon grated fresh ginger

Pinch of cayenne or a minced small fresh hot chile, such as serrano, optional

Salt and freshly ground black pepper

Okra with Ginger and Tomatoes

Okra is considered a "love it or hate it" vegetable because it tends to get slimy, but I find it only does so when overcooked. I think that it has a welcome viscosity, in the same way as eggplant, which some people also don't like. Most people who like okra tend to be from America's deep South or India, where the vegetable is popular. Here you can prepare okra quickly and easily with or without curry and warm spices; it's delicious either way.

When buying okra, look for pods of uniform size, about 3 to 4 inches long, that have some give and don't feel tough. Cut the okra right before cooking since the longer it sits, the more viscous it gets.

SERVES 4

1. Heat a stovetop pressure cooker over medium heat, or set an electric cooker to sauté. Add the onion and dry sauté for 2 to 3 minutes.

2. While the onions are cooking, slice the okra ½ inch thick.

3. If using an electric cooker, turn off the sauté function. Add the okra, tomatoes, ginger, and cayenne or chile, if using. Lock the lid on the cooker. Bring to high pressure; cook for 2 minutes. Quick release the pressure. Remove the lid, tilting it away from you.

4. Transfer the vegetables to a plate, season with salt and pepper, and serve.

Indian-Style Okra with Ginger and Tomatoes: Add 1 teaspoon mustard seeds when sautéing the onion. Just before adding the vegetables, stir in 2 to 3 teaspoons curry powder, store-bought or homemade (page 38).

Summer Southern Trio: Okra, Corn, and Tomatoes

This resembles succotash in some ways. If you are afraid to cook okra, give this a try, as you'll find that the sliminess associated with okra is diminished by cooking in the pressure cooker. Dry sautéing them before adding the tomatoes seems to help as well. If you want to spice this up, add ½ teaspoon smoked paprika and 1 teaspoon chopped hot chile before cooking. Garnish with fresh chopped herbs if you like. Let the flavor of summer shine through.

SERVES 4

1. Heat a stovetop pressure cooker over medium heat or set an electric cooker to sauté. Add the onion and dry sauté for 2 minutes.

2. Add the okra and cook for 30 seconds. Add the corn and stock and stir. Lay the tomatoes on top of the other vegetables. Do not stir.

3. Lock the lid on the cooker. Bring to high pressure; cook for 2 minutes. Quick release the pressure. Remove the lid, tilting it away from you.

4. Transfer the vegetables to a bowl. Season with salt and pepper and garnish with fresh herbs, if desired.

2 minutes high pressure, quick release

1 cup diced onion

½ pound okra, medium pods, cut into 1- to 2-inch pieces

1 large ear corn or 2 small ears, kernels removed to equal 1½ cups

¼ cup vegetable stock

1 pound heirloom or other ripe tomatoes, diced to equal 2 cups

Salt and freshly ground black pepper

2 to 3 tablespoons chopped fresh flat-leaf parsley or cilantro, for garnish

3 minutes low pressure,
quick release; 3 minutes
low pressure,
quick release

1 to 2 tablespoons olive oil,
plus more if desired

2 medium red, yellow, or
orange bell peppers, cored,
seeded, and diced

2 cups finely chopped red
onion

10 to 12 cloves garlic, minced

⅓ cup vegetable stock

2 medium eggplants, about
1 pound each, peeled, if
desired, and cubed

1 medium zucchini, cut into
1- to 2-inch chunks

2 small yellow squash, cut into
1- to 2-inch chunks

8 plum tomatoes or 3 ripe
globe tomatoes, seeded and
diced

½ cup fresh basil, finely
chopped

¼ cup fresh flat-leaf parsley,
finely chopped

2 tablespoons balsamic vinegar

1 tablespoon chopped capers

1 teaspoon coriander seeds,
crushed lightly

Salt and freshly ground black
pepper

Ratatouille

Ratatouille comes together so easily in the pressure cooker. The key is to have everything ready and to get it in and out quickly. Remember that eggplant, summer squash, and tomatoes all exude water, so don't add too much liquid when cooking. Follow the directions. This might not be the most flavorful ratatouille that you've ever had (that would be my grilled ratatouille), but it's a fine stand-in and pressure cooking is a perfect way to avoid heating up the kitchen or standing over a hot grill in the summer when ratatouille ingredients are at their peak. If you have a low pressure setting, use it here. Otherwise, see the alternate directions.

SERVES 4 TO 6

1. Heat a stovetop pressure cooker over medium heat, or set an electric pressure cooker to sauté. Add 1 to 2 tablespoons olive oil, or more to taste, and let it get hot. Add the peppers and onion and sauté for 2 minutes. Add half of the garlic and sauté another minute.

2. Add the stock and stir. Lock on the lid. Bring to low pressure; cook for 3 minutes. (If you don't have a low pressure setting, bring to high pressure and cook for 2 minutes.) Quick release the pressure. Remove the lid, carefully tilting it away from you.

3. Add the eggplant, zucchini, and squash. Stir. Lay the tomatoes on top. Do not stir. Lock the lid back on the cooker. Bring to low pressure; cook for 3 minutes. (Or at high pressure for 2 minutes.) Quick release the pressure. Remove the lid, carefully tilting it away from you.

4. Check to be sure the eggplant is cooked through. If not, lock the lid back on and let the pot sit for 2 minutes.

5. Transfer the ratatouille to a bowl or platter, using a slotted spoon if there is a lot of liquid (leave that behind and save for another use).

6. Add the remaining garlic, the basil, parsley, vinegar, capers, coriander, and 1 to 3 tablespoons olive oil, if desired. Add salt and pepper to taste and serve.

Mixed Vegetables with Peanut Sauce

This recipe is all about the sauce. Who can resist peanut butter, fresh ginger, and garlic? Vary the recipe by using 4 cups of any fresh seasonal vegetables, adjusting the cooking time (see Vegetable Cooking At-a-Glance, page 119). If you want to add tofu, tempeh, or seitan pieces, this becomes a main dish when served over cooked rice or quinoa.

SERVES 4

1. Mix the peanut sauce ingredients and set aside.

2. To cook the vegetables: Heat a stovetop pressure cooker over medium heat or set an electric pressure cooker to sauté. Add the onion and dry sauté for 2 minutes.

3. Add the sweet potato, carrot, and ⅓ cup stock. Lock the lid on the cooker. Bring to high pressure; cook for 2 minutes. Quick release the pressure. Remove the lid, carefully tilting it away from you.

4. Add the broccoli and ¼ cup more stock if there is no liquid left in the cooker. Stir. Lock on the lid. Bring to low pressure; cook for 2 minutes. (If you only have a high pressure option, bring to high pressure and cook for 1 minute.) Quick release the pressure. Remove the lid, carefully turning it away from you.

5. Stir in the peanut sauce. Transfer the vegetable mixture to a plate. Garnish with cilantro and serve.

Sweet and Tangy Vegetables with Peanut Sauce: Use pineapple juice instead of stock and add a teaspoon of Dijon mustard to the sauce.

2 minutes high pressure, quick release; 2 minutes low pressure, quick release

Peanut Sauce

3 tablespoons peanut butter

1 tablespoon balsamic vinegar

1 tablespoon maple syrup

1 tablespoon tamari

2 teaspoons grated or minced fresh ginger

2 to 3 cloves garlic, minced

Pinch of crushed red pepper flakes, or ½ teaspoon Chinese chili paste with garlic, optional

Vegetables

1 cup sliced onion (cut from top to bottom)

1 cup diced sweet potato

1 cup ½-inch sliced carrot (cut on the diagonal)

⅓ cup vegetable stock or water, plus an additional ¼ cup if needed

1½ cups broccoli florets

Chopped cilantro, for garnish

VEGETABLES

151

1 cup sliced onion

3 cloves garlic, minced

1 teaspoon or more minced hot chile, such as jalapeño; or ½ teaspoon crushed red pepper

½ cup chana dal or split red lentils

2 pieces dried galangal slices

2 kaffir lime leaves

1¾ cups vegetable stock

½ cup regular or light coconut milk

2 teaspoons Thai red curry paste

4 to 5 cups (or more) peeled cubed winter squash, such as butternut, kabocha, or acorn (1 pound)

4 ounces oyster mushrooms, sliced

1 cup broccoli florets; or 2 cups thinly sliced kale, collard greens, or Swiss chard

1 to 2 tablespoons lime juice

Chopped cilantro, for garnish

Thai Red Curry

WITH WINTER SQUASH, MUSHROOMS, AND BROCCOLI

Photo, page I-16

I am wowed by the flavor of this fusion-style dish, where winter squash pairs very well with Thai curry. The mushrooms add earthiness and a lot of texture, while the broccoli (or greens) adds freshness.

If you are not familiar with lime leaves, you will likely recognize the flavor if you've eaten Thai food. Store the leaves in your freezer so that they are available when you need them. Galangal is a root, similar to ginger, that is used in Thai cooking. Chana dal is split chickpeas, which are used often in Indian cooking. If you can't find them, split red lentils stand in easily.

This is a perfect winter dish.

SERVES 4 TO 6

1. Heat a stovetop pressure cooker over medium heat or set an electric cooker to sauté. Add the onion and dry sauté for 1 minute. Add the garlic and chile and cook 1 minute longer.

2. Add the chana dal, galangal, lime leaves, ¾ cup of the stock, the coconut milk, and curry paste. Lock the lid on the cooker. Bring to high pressure; cook for 3 minutes. Let the pressure come down naturally. Remove the lid, carefully tilting it away from you.

3. Add the squash, mushrooms, and remaining 1 cup stock. Lock the lid back on the cooker. Bring to high pressure; cook for 3 minutes. Quick release the pressure. Remove the lid, carefully tilting it away from you.

4. Stir in the broccoli. Lock the lid back on and let sit for 2 minutes. Carefully open the lid. Remove the galangal slices.

5. Transfer the contents to a large bowl. Add lime juice to taste, sprinkle with cilantro, and serve.

Mirepoix of Winter Vegetables and Greens

A farmers' market–inspired dish you can take in multiple directions. The leek, carrot, and celery root combo is a takeoff on the traditional *mirepoix* of onion, carrot, and celery. The mushrooms add depth. I season this with Asian flavors, but you could use traditional French herbs such as thyme, parsley, and tarragon (leave out the tamari, ginger, and sesame oil and substitute salt and a drizzle of olive oil at the end).

SERVES 4

1. Heat a stovetop pressure cooker over medium heat or set an electric cooker to sauté. Add the leek and carrots and dry sauté for 1 minute. Add the mushrooms, ginger, garlic, and tamari and cook for 1 minute longer.

2. Add the celery root and stock. Lock the lid on the cooker. Bring to high pressure; cook for 2 minutes. Quick release the pressure. Remove the lid, carefully tilting it away from you.

3. Add the radish and bok choy. Lock the lid on the cooker. Bring to high pressure; cook for 1 minute. Quick release the pressure. Remove the lid, carefully tilting it away from you.

4. Transfer the vegetables to a plate, bowl, or platter. Drizzle with sesame oil or olive oil, if desired, and serve.

2 minutes high pressure, quick release; 1 minute high pressure, quick release

1 medium leek, sliced into thin rings to equal 1 cup

2 medium carrots, peeled and sliced on the diagonal

3 medium to large crimini or white button mushrooms, thinly sliced

2 teaspoons minced fresh ginger

2 to 3 cloves garlic, minced

1 tablespoon tamari; or ½ to 1 teaspoon salt

½ medium celery root (also called celeriac), peeled and cut into thin strips to equal 1 cup

¼ cup vegetable stock or water

½ cup watermelon or daikon radish, peeled and cut into thin strips

1 to 1½ cups chopped bok choy, stems and leaves separated

1 to 2 teaspoons toasted sesame oil or extra virgin olive oil, optional

VEGETABLES

SEVEN

Soups

Soup is one of my favorite foods. You don't need a lot of ingredients to make soup taste great, although having a stocked pantry can make the difference between good and great soup.

Soup cooked in a standard pot on the stovetop cannot compare to what you can make in the pressure cooker. The heat and pressure infuse the soup with so much flavor—and quickly. All of these soups take less than 30 minutes at pressure and have great next-day taste right away.

And a stock from the pressure cooker assures a great base for soup. In addition to my Simple Vegetable Stock, I also make stock specifically for different soups by adding some of the soup ingredients to the stock. You'll find my favorite mushroom stock here, and a recipe for corn stock within the Sweet Summer Corn Chowder recipe (page 188).

One soup base can often make many different types of soup, depending upon the seasonings that you choose. Shane's Fabulous Lentil Soup (page 181), for example, can have herbes de Provence, curry powder, or berbere added to spice it up. Cooking soup allows a lot of experimentation and I encourage you to embellish these simple recipes in ways that warm your heart and soul. Nothing says love to me more than a steaming hot bowl of soup.

Taking Stock of Stock

Before I had my pressure cooker, I often found it easier to grab the aseptic box or can of broth off the store shelf than to take the time to make stock. Now, I save suitable vegetable scraps, put them in a plastic bag, and store in the refrigerator or freezer so they are ready when inspiration strikes. Some situations make it easy to keep stock making in mind.

A stock doesn't have to be made from root vegetables. You can use whatever you have on hand, using the lists in Vegetables (and Other Ingredients) for Stock (page 158) as a guide. You can also choose vegetables with flavors that will complement your soup. If I have asparagus or mushrooms, which can be overpowering, I save those stems separately for soups that will benefit from their flavors. I use only members of the onion family for Allium Broth (page 161). I can make bright springtime broth with just asparagus ends, green garlic, and a few herbs, or a broth from peas (either English, snow, or sugar snap). In the summer, I make sweet corn stock with the cobs left after removing the kernels.

As far as seasoning, usually I add a Mediterranean bay leaf (not California, which is not truly a culinary herb and can be overpowering), some peppercorns, and a few sprigs of fresh cut herbs such as thyme or savory. I'll use ginger for an Asian flair. What stays out of the pot are any cruciferous vegetables (think broccoli, cauliflower, cabbage) as their taste gets concentrated and becomes overpowering. Also, avoid intensely colored vegetables such as beets or purple carrots unless you want an odd-colored stock. Stick with what you know works or be bold and experiment.

If you like a richer-flavored stock, you can take larger pieces of vegetables, rather than scraps, coat them with a tablespoon of oil, and roast on a baking sheet in a 450°F oven for about 30 minutes. The vegetables caramelize, adding flavor depth and sweetness to the stock.

The possibilities are endless and healthy without all the sodium found in boxed and canned stocks and broths. My stocks reflect the flavors I seek. Let yours do the same.

Hot Food and Your Blender

Having seen a few too many students add hot liquid to a blender with less than desirable results—as in hot liquid spewing out of the blender top, causing danger to the user and others nearby—I would like to instruct you on the best way to handle hot food in a blender.

Remember that pressure-cooked food is much hotter than food that has been cooked on the stovetop. Safety in the kitchen is a top priority, so take precautions and use caution when blending hot food. **There are 4 steps to safety:**

- Fill the blender only halfway with hot food.

- Put a piece of plastic wrap on top of the blender, put the lid on.

- If your blender lid has a center piece, remove it as it helps keep hot steam from getting trapped.

- Put a towel over the blender lid and process. Repeat with the rest of your food.

It is easier to blend your food with an immersion blender, which can be put right into your pot, although often you will not get the smooth creaminess that results from using a blender, especially a high-speed blender.

When using the food processor, be careful as some tend to develop leaks around the top where the two pieces fit together. Wrapping a kitchen towel around the place where the lid and base join might be helpful.

Simple Vegetable Stock

If you've never made stock before, you'll be surprised at the rich flavor of homemade stock, which adds body to any soup or stew. Giving up canned and boxed stock is easy when you can make your own so quickly in your pressure cooker. When you're cooking with fresh vegetables, save the scraps, ends, and pieces and use them to make great stock—see the list of the best options on page 158.

It's great to have homemade stock on hand: I will often double the recipe and freeze half in zippered bags, freezer containers, or ice cube trays. The stock cubes are great when you just need a couple of tablespoons for a recipe.

I prefer not to salt my stock, instead adding salt to taste when using it in cooking. Do remember to do this, as unsalted stock is bland compared to canned stock, where usually the main flavor is salt.

MAKES 8 CUPS

1. Put all the ingredients in a pressure cooker. Lock the lid in place. Bring to high pressure; cook 5 minutes. Let the pressure come down naturally. Remove the lid, tilting it away from you.

2. Allow the stock to cool slightly. Strain by pouring through a strainer and pressing on the solids with a spoon to extract all the liquid and flavor. Cool and refrigerate for a few days, or keep in the freezer for up to 3 months.

Variations: Instead of making stock from purchased vegetables, you can make stock scraps by saving ends and pieces as instructed on page 156. And you can season your stock with a tablespoon of ginger, 4 to 6 cloves garlic, and 4 dried shiitake mushrooms for an Asian flair; or add 4 sun-dried tomatoes, 6 cloves garlic, 2 teaspoons rosemary, and an extra bay leaf for a Mediterranean stock.

5 minutes high pressure, natural release

1 onion, peeled and quartered

2 cups roughly chopped leek leaves

3 to 4 garlic cloves, optional

3 carrots, cut into chunks

3 stalks celery, cut into pieces

2 bay leaves (true bay, not California bay, which can be overpowering)

A few peppercorns, or up to 1 teaspoon

2 sprigs fresh thyme or savory, or other herbs of your choosing (beware of using rosemary as it can be overpowering)

1 (3-inch) piece of kombu, optional

10 to 12 cups pure (non-chlorinated) water, depending upon the size of your cooker (don't fill it more than three-fourths full)

Vegetables (and Other Ingredients) for Stock

The Best	Use with Caution	Exclude or Use Only in Small Amounts
• All alliums: onions, garlic, leeks, shallots, scallions, chives	• Roots: Limited amounts of potato, sweet potato, or winter squash peelings, as they make stock cloudy	• Artichokes
• Celery, including leaves		• Chile peppers
• Roots: carrots, celery root (but not much of the tops which get bitter), parsley root, parsnips	• Lettuce, summer squash, or tomatoes (but not good for storing for "scrap" stock)	• Cruciferous vegetables, which tend to get more bitter as they cook: bok choy, broccoli, Brussels sprouts, cabbage, cauliflower, greens (such as kale, collards), horseradish, kohlrabi, radish, tastoi, turnips, rutabaga, watercress
• Green leafy herbs and their stems: parsley and cilantro (for Asian-inspired stock)	• Bell peppers: Limited amounts as the flavor can become overpowering (and not good for storing for scrap as they tend to get slimy when stored)	
• Mushrooms, fresh or dried		
• Peas: English pea shells, snow peas, or sugar snap peas	• Fennel	• Eggplant
• Green beans	• Strong herbs: basil, dill, marjoram, oregano, rosemary, sage, and savory	• Endive and other bitter greens such as radicchio and arugula
• Asparagus ends, in season (to make asparagus soup)	• Dark colored vegetables such as purple carrots and beets	• Okra
• Corn cobs, in season (see Sweet Summer Corn Chowder, page 188)	• Ginger root peel or whole root, unless you are making Asian-inspired stock	• Spinach
• Kombu seaweed: 1 to 2 (3-inch) pieces is sufficient for 1 pot of stock	• Turmeric root due to its color, unless you want yellow stock with a bitter edge	• Swiss chard
• Black peppercorns		

Dark Vegetable Stock

Use this stock any time you want an extremely rich soup or stew. It works well with many fall and winter dishes, but can easily overpower a delicate summer soup.

You can roast the stock ingredients in the oven but why bother turning it on when you can brown them in your pressure cooker? Browning the vegetables is easiest to do if you use oil, but the choice is yours. Without oil, you have to pay more attention to be sure that the vegetables do not burn. To alleviate this, always be sure to stir the bottom of the cooker to dislodge food particles that stick.

Don't buy shiitake mushrooms just for this stock; save the stems each time you use them in other recipes. If you don't have enough, add a few dried shiitakes.

MAKES 2 QUARTS

1. Heat a stovetop pressure cooker over medium heat or set an electric cooker to sauté; add the oil, if using. Add the onions and cook for 4 minutes. Add the garlic and cook 6 minutes longer, until the onions start turning brown. Add all the remaining ingredients except the salt.

2. Lock the lid on the cooker and bring to high pressure; cook for 10 minutes. Let the pressure come down naturally. Remove the lid, carefully tilting it away from you.

3. Strain the stock by pouring through a strainer and pressing on the solids with a spoon to extract all the liquid and flavor. Add the salt to the stock.

4. The stock will keep for a week in the refrigerator or 3 months in the freezer.

1 tablespoon oil, optional

2 red onions, peeled and quartered

3 cloves garlic, smashed

2 carrots, peeled and coarsely chopped

½ cup shiitake mushroom stems, or 4 whole dried shiitake mushrooms

6 ounces crimini or shiitake mushrooms, sliced

2 celery stalks with leaves, chopped

8 cups water

1 sprig rosemary

3 sprigs thyme

2 bay leaves

¼ teaspoon whole black peppercorns

½ teaspoon salt

SOUPS

2 cups finely chopped onion or
leeks (white and light green
parts)

6 ounces crimini mushrooms,
diced

8 to 12 dried shiitake
mushrooms, plus any
additional fresh mushroom
stems you may have on hand

½ ounce dried wild mushroom
mix

8 cups water

2 tablespoons porcini powder
(see Note)

2 bay leaves

1 teaspoon black peppercorns

1 teaspoon fresh thyme,
optional

Mushroom Stock

When you want to kick up the flavor of any mushroom soup, stew, or sauce, use this extremely fragrant stock as your liquid base. The best part is that you use both fresh and dried mushrooms to make it. Rehydrated dried mushrooms intensifies the mushroom flavor.

If you are a mushroom lover, as I am, you will appreciate having this stock on hand. Freeze any you don't immediately use in ice cube trays and add a bit whenever you cook with mushrooms.

MAKES 6 TO 8 CUPS

1. Heat a stovetop pressure cooker over medium heat or set an electric cooker to sauté. Add the onion and fresh mushrooms and dry sauté for 3 to 5 minutes. Add the remaining ingredients.

2. Lock the lid on the pressure cooker. Bring to high pressure; cook 5 minutes. Let the pressure come down naturally. Remove the lid, carefully tilting it away from you.

3. Carefully strain the stock through a fine mesh strainer, pressing on the solids to extract more liquid and flavor, if desired. (Compost the solids.) Put into jars and use within 5 days, or freeze for up to 3 months.

✱ **Note:** You can buy porcini or shiitake mushroom powder (see Resources, page 304) or make your own by grinding dried mushrooms in a spice grinder until smooth.

Allium Broth

This flavorful stock makes an amazing base for any spring or early summer soup, which is when fresh alliums are at their peak. If you find that you have scallions, shallots, green garlic, or garlic scapes handy, add those to the allium mixture used here.

MAKES 7 TO 8 CUPS

1. Heat a stovetop pressure cooker over medium heat or set an electric cooker to sauté. Spray with cooking spray or add the oil. Add the onion, leek, and garlic and sauté for 2 to 3 minutes. Add 8 cups water, the herbs, and the peppercorns.

2. Lock on the lid. Bring to high pressure; cook for 5 minutes. Let the pressure release naturally.

3. Carefully remove the lid, tilting it away from you. Strain the stock and season to taste with salt and pepper. This will keep in the refrigerator for 4 to 5 days, or it may be frozen.

Vegetable cooking spray or 1 teaspoon oil

1 medium onion, chopped

1 leek, cleaned well and sliced

2 tablespoons minced garlic (1 large or 2 small heads)

1 sprig fresh sage or 1 teaspoon dried

3 sprigs flat-leaf parsley

1 sprig fresh thyme

2 teaspoons black peppercorns

Salt and ground black pepper

SOUPS

10 minutes high pressure, natural release; 5 minutes high pressure, natural release

1 tablespoon olive oil, optional

2 cups finely chopped onion

2 to 3 tablespoons minced garlic

2 bay leaves

2 tablespoons Italian seasoning, store-bought or homemade (page 41)

1½ cups dried white beans (cannellini preferred, but Great Northern, navy, or other beans are fine), soaked and drained

¼ cup finely chopped sun-dried tomatoes

3 cups vegetable stock

½ medium green cabbage, cut into 1- to 2-inch pieces (6 cups or more)

1 (15-ounce) can tomatoes, diced, crushed or stewed; or 1½ cups diced fresh tomatoes

Salt to taste or a splash of vinegar, optional

Pesto (recipe follows), for garnish

Chopped fresh basil leaves, if available

Cabbage, White Bean, and Tomato Soup

WITH PESTO

Cabbage ought to be a staple in your kitchen as it is so versatile and good for your health. It's also fairly inexpensive and available year-round, although the flavor tends to be best when the weather is cool. This soup is thick and hearty, with most of the liquid coming from the cabbage and tomatoes. The pesto adds a bright note. If you don't want to add salt, add a splash of balsamic or red wine vinegar. The soup freezes well.

SERVES 6 TO 8

1. Heat a stovetop pressure cooker over medium heat or set an electric cooker to sauté; add the oil, if using. Add the onion and sauté or dry sauté for 2 minutes. Add 1 to 2 tablespoons of the garlic (to taste), the bay leaves, and Italian seasoning and sauté 1 minute longer. (If using an electric cooker, turn off sauté now.) Add the beans, sun-dried tomatoes, and stock.

2. Lock on the lid and bring to high pressure; cook for 10 minutes. Let the pressure come down naturally. Carefully remove the lid, tilting it away from you.

3. Add the cabbage, tomatoes, and remaining 1 tablespoon garlic. Lock on the lid and bring to high pressure; cook for 5 minutes. Let the pressure release naturally. Remove the lid carefully, tilting it away from you.

4. Remove and discard the bay leaves with tongs. Add the salt or vinegar to the soup, if you like, and garnish each bowl with a spoonful of pesto and a few chopped basil leaves, if you have them.

The Veggie Queen's Oil-Free Pesto

This slightly chunky pesto delights everyone who tries it with its brightness and umami flavor. I developed the recipe years ago when teaching a low-fat cooking class. You can choose to mix it with blended silken tofu to make it creamy to top pasta, cooked polenta, grains, or beans. If you have any leftover (without tofu), it freezes well. Freezing it in ice cube trays allows you to use a couple of tablespoons at a time.

MAKES ABOUT ¾ CUP

In a food processor or high-speed blender, combine all the ingredients except the water. Pulse until finely minced. With the machine running, slowly add the water until the pesto reaches the desired consistency. Scrape down the sides of the processor or blender, if necessary.

3 to 4 cloves garlic, minced

3 cups chopped fresh basil leaves (removed from stems)

1 cup chopped fresh flat-leaf parsley

2 to 3 tablespoons pine (or other) nuts

1 slice gluten-free or other white or sourdough bread; or ¼ cup dry bread crumbs; or ¼ cup cooked white beans

1 to 2 tablespoons light miso

2 tablespoons nutritional yeast

¼ to ⅓ cup water or vegetable stock

1 cup diced red onion

2 medium carrots, diced equal to about 1 cup

½ teaspoon dill

½ teaspoon caraway seeds

2 bay leaves

5 cups finely sliced red cabbage (about ½ medium head)

1 pound beets (2 to 3 medium), ideally with their greens, washed well, roots chopped

½ cup red lentils, rinsed and picked over

4 cups vegetable stock

Grated zest and juice of 1 lemon

1 teaspoon smoked or regular salt, optional

2 to 3 cups finely chopped beet greens or Swiss chard

Finely chopped fresh flat-leaf parsley, chives, or dill, for garnish

Nondairy yogurt, for garnish

Borscht with a Lemon Twist and Greens

Photo, page I-9

I cannot claim that it was my idea to add red lentils to this beautiful red beet soup. Christy Morgan, author of *Blissful Bites,* gave me the idea. I love how it gives the soup more body. Get the freshest beets you can find, ideally with the greens on, which you should cut off immediately and reserve to include in the soup. Both the root and greens stay freshest when stored separately.

If you can't find beets with greens, substitute Swiss chard for the greens. (You can also substitute green cabbage for the red cabbage, though the red has more potent antioxidants and looks nicer.) I add the finely diced beet greens to the bowls first and pour the hot soup over to slightly wilt them, but you could also just stir the greens into the hot soup.

A dollop of nondairy yogurt adds to the allure, as does lemon zest and juice and smoked salt. You decide how pureed you like this soup. I prefer mine a bit chunky. It's not necessary to peel the beets, as they will puree well either way. This soup freezes well but add the yogurt right before serving.

SERVES 6 TO 8

1. Heat a stovetop pressure cooker over medium heat or set an electric cooker to sauté. Add the onion and carrots and dry sauté for 2 to 3 minutes. Add the dill, caraway, bay leaves, cabbage, beet roots, lentils, and stock.

2. Lock the lid on the cooker. Bring to high pressure; cook for 8 minutes. Let the pressure come down naturally. Remove the lid, carefully tilting it away from you.

3. Using a pair of tongs, carefully remove and discard the bay leaves. Using an immersion blender if you have one, puree the soup in the pot to the consistency that you like. (If you don't have an immersion blender, carefully blend in batches in a regular blender.) Add the lemon zest and juice and smoked salt, if using.

4. Add the beet greens or chard to the soup; or add to individual serving bowls. Spoon the hot soup over the greens. Garnish with herbs and a dollop of nondairy yogurt.

Lemongrass Cabbage Soup

Hearty cabbage combined with the lightness of lemongrass yields a sunny, refreshing soup—and you can eat a lot of it without feeling stuffed. The potatoes add a little body. If you prefer sweet potatoes, use them instead of Yukon Golds. The soup freezes well.

SERVES 4 TO 6

1. Heat a stovetop pressure cooker over medium heat or set an electric cooker to sauté; add the oil, if using. Add the onion and cook for 1 to 2 minutes, until no longer raw. Add the chile, if using, the lemongrass, garlic, and ginger, and cook another minute or two, until the onion is just beginning to soften.

2. Add the sliced cabbage and potato, along with the stock and coconut milk. Lock on the lid. Bring to high pressure; cook for 4 minutes. Let the pressure come down naturally. After 10 minutes, quick release any remaining pressure. Carefully remove the lid, tilting it away from you.

3. Using tongs, remove and discard the dried chile, if using, along with the ginger and lemongrass pieces.

4. Add lime zest and juice to taste and season with salt and pepper and grated ginger, if you like. Garnish with cilantro and serve.

2 teaspoons canola oil, optional

1 cup diced onion

1 hot chile, such as ripe jalapeño or serrano, either dried and left whole or fresh and minced, optional

1 lemongrass stalk, hard outer leaves discarded, stalk trimmed, cut into 2-inch pieces, and bruised with the back of a knife

1 garlic clove, minced

2 thin slices fresh ginger, about the size of a quarter, plus more for grating

½ medium to large cabbage, thinly sliced to equal at least 6 cups

1 medium Yukon Gold or other potato, sliced to equal about 1 cup

4 cups vegetable stock

½ cup coconut milk, coconut water, or coconut beverage, or a few drops coconut extract mixed with water or stock

Grated zest and juice of 1 lime

Salt and freshly ground black pepper

Fresh chopped cilantro, for garnish

SOUPS

1 to 2 tablespoons olive oil

1 cup diced onion

Salt

6 cloves garlic, minced to equal
at least 1 tablespoon

1 to 2 teaspoons smoked
paprika

Pinch of cayenne, optional

2 cups diced potatoes, peeled
if russets, but unpeeled if
Yukon Golds

1½ cups dried white beans of
any kind, soaked and drained

4 to 6 cups vegetable stock

1 large bunch Portuguese
kale or collard greens, ribs
removed and sliced in small
shreds as thin as possible to
equal at least 6 cups

4 to 6 ounces Beef-Style Seitan
(page 213) or store-bought
seitan, finely chopped,
optional

Freshly ground black pepper

Caldo Verde
(PORTUGUESE KALE SOUP)

The first time I encountered Portuguese kale at the farmers' market, I mistook it for collard greens, as it looks incredibly similar, but kale has a thicker mid-rib. Will, the farmer, explained what Portuguese kale was and told me that the greens are traditionally used in soup with white beans and chorizo. In this version, seitan stands in for chorizo, with smoked paprika adding the smoky note of sausage.

Despite what Will told me, it turns out that the traditional soup contains only potatoes and not white beans, unless you are from the Azores. Since I am a bean lover, I've added them to make a heartier soup. Be sure to remove the thick ribs from the kale and slice the leaves as thinly as possible. If you want to make the soup more authentic and don't mind "fake meat," use soy chorizo instead of paprika and seitan, browning it first, setting it aside, and then adding it at the end of cooking. The smoky, hearty soup is satisfying even without any sausage substitute.

SERVES 4 TO 6

1. Heat a stovetop pressure cooker over medium heat or set an electric cooker to sauté; add the oil. Add the onion and a pinch of salt and sauté for at least 5 minutes, until translucent. Add a bit of stock if they start to stick. Let the stock evaporate, add the garlic, and cook for 2 minutes longer.

2. Add smoked paprika (to taste), the cayenne, if using, the potatoes, beans, and 4 cups of stock. Lock the lid on the cooker and bring to high pressure; cook for 8 minutes. Let the pressure come down naturally. Remove the lid, carefully tilting it away from you.

3. Using an immersion blender if you have one, puree the soup in the pot to your desired thickness; I like to leave some chunks of potato and beans. (If you don't have an immersion blender, carefully use a food processor or blender to blend.)

4. Add the kale and seitan, if using. Lock on the lid and let the pot sit, covered, for 5 minutes. Release any remaining pressure. Stir in more stock if the soup is too thick. Add salt and pepper to taste.

Cold Curried Mostly Green Vegetable Soup

Hot summer days call for cold soups, ideally made in the pressure cooker to minimize time heating up the kitchen. This smooth soup, full of bright flavor, comes together quickly. Feel free to add any extra produce you have around. Be sure to taste the soup before serving as chilling tends to mute the flavors. If you like a little heat, add a little chopped hot chile when cooking or after blending.

SERVES 4 TO 6

1. Heat a stovetop pressure cooker over medium heat or set an electric cooker to sauté; add the oil, if using. Add the onion, garlic, celery, and bell pepper and cook for 2 to 3 minutes, until they start to soften. Add curry powder to taste and cook for 30 seconds.

2. Add the stock and lock the lid on the pressure cooker. Bring to low pressure; cook for 4 minutes. (If you don't have a low pressure option, bring to high pressure and cook for 3 minutes.) Quick release the pressure and remove the lid, carefully tilting it away from you.

3. Add the broccoli and cucumber and bring to high pressure; cook for 1 minute. Quick release the pressure. Remove the lid, carefully tilting it away from you.

4. Blend the soup carefully in a high-speed blender for the creamiest result, or use an immersion blender, regular blender, or food processor, adding the herbs and vinegar while you blend. Add salt and pepper to taste. Chill soup for at least 4 hours or overnight.

5. When ready to serve, taste the soup and adjust seasonings. Serve, garnished with diced avocado and colored peppers, if using.

1 to 2 tablespoons olive oil, optional

1 cup diced onion

3 cloves garlic, minced

2 stalks celery, diced

½ yellow, orange, or green bell pepper, cored, seeded, and chopped

1 to 2 teaspoons curry powder, store-bought or homemade (page 38)

3 cups vegetable stock

1 cup broccoli florets

½ large cucumber, chopped to equal 2 cups

¼ to ½ cup chopped fresh green herbs such as flat-leaf parsley, basil, or cilantro

1 to 2 teaspoons vinegar of your choice

Salt and generous amount of cracked white or black pepper

1 avocado, diced, for garnish

Additional chopped bell pepper, optional, for garnish

SOUPS

3 minutes high pressure,
quick release

1 tablespoon olive oil, optional

2 large leeks (white and pale green parts only), chopped to equal at least 3 cups

2 cups vegetable stock

2 teaspoons curry powder, store-bought or homemade (page 38); or Thai curry paste, color of your choice

2 small white potatoes, peeled and cut into ½-inch pieces to make about 1¼ cups

½ teaspoon salt, plus more to taste

1 large bunch spinach, trimmed of any stems, washed well, and chopped (8 to 10 cups); or 1 (16-ounce) bag frozen (not thawed) chopped spinach

1 cup nondairy milk

1 (15-ounce) can light coconut milk

1 teaspoon Sucanat or coconut palm sugar

Freshly ground black pepper

½ cup plain unsweetened nondairy yogurt (to make your own, see page 266)

¼ cup chopped fresh cilantro

Creamy Curried Spinach Soup

Spinach lovers go crazy over this soup, especially in spring when the vegetable is at its best. But you can use this recipe as a model for other creamy curried vegetable soups. Try broccoli, cauliflower, green beans, sweet potatoes, or winter squash (leave out the white potato with these), and plenty of others.

SERVES 4 TO 6

1. Heat a stovetop pressure cooker over medium heat or set an electric cooker to sauté; add the oil, if using. Add the leeks and cook for 2 minutes. Add some stock, 1 tablespoon at a time, if they start to stick. Add the curry powder or paste and stir 30 seconds. Add the remaining stock, the potatoes, and salt.

2. Lock the lid on the cooker and bring to high pressure; cook for 3 minutes. Quick release the pressure. Remove the lid, carefully tilting it away from you.

3. Stir in the spinach. Lock the lid on the cooker and let sit for 2 minutes. Remove the lid, tilting it away from you.

4. Puree the soup with an immersion blender until almost smooth. (If you don't have an immersion blender, carefully use a food processor or blender to blend.) Add the nondairy and coconut milk and sweetener. Season to taste with salt and pepper.

5. Ladle the soup into 4 or 6 bowls. Whisk the yogurt until smooth. Swirl 2 tablespoons yogurt into each bowl. Sprinkle with cilantro and serve.

Creamy Broccoli (or Any Vegetable) Soup

3 minutes high pressure, quick release; 1 minute low pressure, quick release

This "cream soup" uses cooked potato blended with silken tofu and nondairy milk to add a creamy mouthfeel. The technique works with almost any vegetable. If you don't want to add potatoes, add ½ cup baby oats (also called "quick oats," but not instant oats) or ⅓ cup white rice with the stock. Still use the tofu and nondairy milk mixture to add creaminess. Add herbs in season, such as thyme, lemon thyme, tarragon, or another favorite for even more flavor.

SERVES 4

1. Remove any stems from the broccoli; peel and cut them into small pieces. Cut the rest of the head into florets.

2. Heat a stovetop pressure cooker over medium heat or set an electric cooker to sauté. Add the onion and dry sauté for about 2 minutes. Add the broccoli stems, potatoes, and stock. Lock on the lid. Bring to high pressure; cook for 3 minutes. Quick release the pressure. Remove the lid, carefully tilting it away from you.

3. Add the broccoli florets and lock the lid back on the cooker. Bring to low pressure; cook for 1 minute. (If you do not have a low pressure option, lock the lid on the cooker and let sit for 3 minutes.) Quick release the pressure. Remove the lid carefully.

4. Test to be sure that the florets are cooked through. (If not, lock on the lid and let sit for a minute or two until they are cooked.) Remove some florets and reserve for garnish.

5. Puree the tofu and nondairy milk in a food processor or blender until perfectly creamy.

6. Using an immersion blender if you have one, puree the soup mixture in the pot until almost smooth. (If you don't have an immersion blender, carefully use a food processor or blender to blend.) Stir the tofu puree into the soup.

7. Return the pot if necessary to heat briefly on the stovetop or using the sauté function, but do not allow to boil or the tofu mixture will curdle. Season to taste with salt and pepper. Garnish with reserved broccoli florets and parsley or chives and their flowers.

- 1 head broccoli, or 4 to 5 cups of any chopped vegetable

- 2 cups chopped onion

- 2 medium thin-skinned potatoes, such as Yukon Gold, cut into eighths

- 3 cups vegetable stock or water

- ½ (12.3-ounce) box Mori-Nu firm silken tofu or 6 ounces refrigerated silken tofu, drained

- ½ cup nondairy milk

  Salt and freshly ground black pepper

- 1 tablespoon chopped fresh flat-leaf parsley or chives and their flowers, or other herbs, for garnish

SOUPS

5 minutes high pressure, quick release

1 tablespoon olive oil, optional

1 large sweet onion, such as Vidalia or Walla Walla, cut in half and sliced into half rounds to equal about 1½ cups

1 bay leaf

3¼ to 3½ cups vegetable stock

1 to 3 teaspoons maple syrup

Freshly ground black pepper

1 medium leek (white part only) or yellow or white onion, diced to equal 1 cup

1 to 2 teaspoons ground cardamom

1 pound parsnips, peeled and chopped into ½- to 1-inch pieces

1 small to medium celery root (also called celeriac), peeled and chopped into ½- to 1-inch pieces

1 small kohlrabi, peeled and chopped into ½- to 1-inch pieces

1 small to medium Japanese white sweet potato, peeled and diced to equal 1 to 1½ cups

1 cup unsweetened nondairy milk, such as almond milk

Creamy White Root Soup
WITH CARAMELIZED ONIONS AND CARDAMOM

Cardamom, which imparts a flowery, spicy, elusive flavor to this soup, is one of my favorite spices. It's like a hidden gem that provides intrigue in recipes. It tastes best when you open the pods and freshly grind the seeds in your spice grinder, since the oils are very volatile.

When parsnips are in season, I use them often. Here they join celery root, kohlrabi, and white sweet potato to produce a creamy white soup, made creamier with almond—or your favorite nondairy—milk. If you can't get all these vegetables, be sure to include at least the parsnips and white sweet potato (often called Japanese sweet potato).

I caramelize the onions first, rinse the pressure cooker, and then proceed. To save time, you could sauté the onions in a separate pan while the soup cooks, but I often don't want to dirty one more pot or pan.

SERVES 6 TO 8

1. Heat a stovetop pressure cooker or a skillet over medium heat; or set an electric cooker to sauté. Add the oil, if using. Add the sweet onion and bay leaf and cook for about 5 minutes, stirring occasionally. If the onion starts to stick, add ¼ to ½ cup of the stock, 1 tablespoon at a time. You want the onion to be soft and sweet, but not quite brown. Continue to cook over medium heat until the onion is very soft. This might take 15 to 20 minutes. When the onion is soft, add maple syrup, a teaspoon at a time, until the onion tastes sweet to you. Remove and discard the bay leaf. Season with freshly ground black pepper. Set aside. Rinse and dry the pressure cooker if needed.

2. Heat the stovetop pressure cooker over medium heat or set the electric cooker to sauté. Add the leek and 1 teaspoon cardamom and dry sauté for 2 to 3 minutes. The leek does not need to become translucent. Add the parsnips, celery root, kohlrabi, sweet potato, and remaining 3 cups stock.

3. Lock the lid on the pressure cooker and bring to high pressure; cook for 5 minutes. Quick release the pressure. Remove the lid, carefully tilting it away from you.

4. Check to be sure that the vegetables are very soft. If not, put the lid back on, bring to high pressure, and cook for 2 minutes longer. Quick release the pressure.

5. Add the nondairy milk and blend the soup with an immersion blender until smooth; or puree the soup in batches in a blender. Season with salt and pepper, adding more ground cardamom, if desired. Serve garnished with the caramelized onion, and the parsley, if you like.

Salt

2 tablespoons finely chopped fresh flat-leaf parsley, for garnish, optional

2 tablespoons finely chopped fresh flat-leaf parsley, for garnish, optional

2 cups finely chopped onion

3 cloves garlic, minced

4 cups zucchini or summer
squash of any kind, cut into
2-inch chunks

¼ cup ground red lentils

¼ cup almond flour or meal

2 cups vegetable stock

¼ cup nutritional yeast

Salt and freshly ground black
pepper

¼ cup minced fresh basil, for
garnish

Creamy Dreamy Zucchini Chowder

Summer is when you're looking for ways to use up your bounty, which often means zucchini and other summer squash. This screams summertime to me, with a few simple additions to add body and flavor: ground red lentils (grind in your spice grinder or the blender), almond flour (or meal), and nutritional yeast. Oh so yummy and not too heavy for lighter summer fare. Turn it into dinner by serving with a large salad and a hunk of hearty bread.

SERVES 4

1. Heat a stovetop pressure cooker over medium heat or set an electric cooker to sauté. Add the onion and dry sauté for 1 minute. Add the garlic and sauté another minute. Add the squash, lentils, almond flour, and stock.

2. Lock on the lid. Bring the cooker to high pressure. Cook for 4 minutes. Let the pressure come down naturally. Remove the lid, carefully tilting it away from you.

3. Stir in the nutritional yeast. Using an immersion blender, blender, or food processor, blend soup until creamy.

4. Add salt and pepper to taste. Pour into bowls and serve, garnished with basil.

Creamy Winter Squash Soup

WITH TOASTED PUMPKIN SEED–APPLE TOPPING
Photo, page I-6

I must make winter squash soup at least twenty different ways, depending upon the type of squash and how I season it. This soup has double apple flavoring and a touch of curry powder. The addition of coconut milk makes it rich, while using coconut water adds flavor but keeps the soup lighter.

The topping takes it a big step beyond ordinary. If you like this soup and want to vary the topping, try the Apple and Squash Relish (page 282) or Apple Chutney (page 279).

SERVES 6 TO 8

1. To make the topping: Mix the chopped apple, orange juice, lemon or lime zest and juice, and cardamom in a small bowl. Cover and set aside. Keep the cilantro and pumpkin seeds separate.

2. To make the soup: Heat a stovetop pressure cooker over medium heat or set an electric cooker to sauté. Add the onion and dry sauté for 3 minutes. Add the curry powder, squash, diced apple, stock, coconut milk, and salt.

3. Lock the lid on the cooker. Bring to high pressure; cook for 4 minutes. Let the pressure come down naturally. Remove the lid, carefully tilting it away from you.

4. Using an immersion blender, blender, or food processor, blend the soup until it is smooth and creamy. Add freshly ground black pepper to taste.

5. Just before serving, top each bowl with apple topping, cilantro, and pumpkin seeds.

✱ Note: Want to gild the lily? Toast the pumpkin seeds by tossing them with 2 teaspoons maple syrup, ¼ teaspoon ground cinnamon, ⅛ teaspoon grated nutmeg, and a pinch of salt. Put in a nonstick pan over medium-high heat for 3 to 5 minutes, until they smell toasty. Alternatively, toast coated seeds on a parchment-lined baking sheet in a 400°F oven for 5 to 8 minutes, paying close attention.

I recommend making a double or triple batch of these as you might eat more than a few after they are toasted.

4 minutes high pressure,
natural release

Topping

1 red tart sweet apple such as Gala or Pink Lady, cored and finely chopped

1 tablespoon orange juice

½ teaspoon grated lime or lemon zest

2 teaspoons fresh lime or lemon juice

Pinch of ground cardamom

2 tablespoons chopped cilantro or flat-leaf parsley

¼ cup pumpkin seeds (pepitas), toasted (see Note)

Soup

2 cups finely chopped onion

2 to 3 teaspoons (or more) curry powder

1 medium to large kabocha-type or butternut squash, peeled, seeded, and cubed to equal at least 5 cups

1 apple (any kind), peeled and diced

4 cups vegetable stock

1½ cups coconut milk or coconut water

½ teaspoon salt

Freshly ground black pepper

SOUPS

3 cups sliced crimini
mushrooms

½ medium onion or leek, diced

2 bay leaves

3 cups mushroom or vegetable
stock

2 tablespoons porcini
mushroom powder (see Note,
page 32) or ground dried
shiitake mushrooms

1 cup diced peeled winter
squash, optional

½ cup cashew meal; or ½ cup
cashews, soaked for at least
2 hours and drained

Salt and freshly ground black
pepper

3 tablespoons chopped fresh
flat-leaf parsley or minced
chives

Creamy Mushroom Soup

This is as pure a mushroom soup as you can get. If you want to add more body, include the optional squash. Poor mushroom soup just doesn't have a lot of color appeal, so it's garnished with chopped herbs.

SERVES 4 TO 6

1. Heat a stovetop pressure cooker over medium heat or set an electric cooker to sauté. Add the mushrooms and onion and dry sauté for 3 minutes, until the mushrooms start to get firmer and smaller. Add the bay leaves, stock, porcini powder, squash, if using, and cashew meal or drained cashews.

2. Lock on the lid. Bring to high pressure; cook for 5 minutes. Quick release the pressure. Remove the lid, carefully tilting it away from you.

3. Remove and discard the bay leaves. Using an immersion blender if you have one, blend the soup to your desired consistency. (If you don't have an immersion blender, pour the soup into a high-speed blender in batches; let cool for a few minutes and carefully blend until smooth.)

4. Add salt and pepper to taste. Garnish with parsley.

Chestnut Mushroom Soup

Wild mushrooms and chestnuts are abundant around the same time of year—the fall—where I live in Northern California. In fact, Jim and Dave, two characters from Cazadero, up in the redwoods, sell both. They actually harvest chanterelle mushrooms from under their chestnut trees. So this is a natural pairing where one ingredient enhances the other: The sweetness and creaminess of the chestnuts play off the earthy flavor and texture of the mushrooms. You can use already peeled chestnuts or fresh ones.

SERVES 4 TO 6

1. Heat a stovetop pressure cooker over medium heat or set an electric cooker to sauté; add the oil, if using. Add the leek and cook for 1 to 2 minutes. Add the mushrooms, garlic, and thyme and cook for another few minutes.

2. Add the chestnuts and stock and bring to high pressure; cook for 5 minutes. Let the pressure come down naturally for 10 minutes, then quick release any remaining pressure. Remove the lid, carefully tilting it away from you.

3. Add mushroom powder to taste. Using an immersion blender, blend the soup to the desired consistency, from chunky to very smooth. (If you don't have an immersion blender, carefully use a food processor or blender to blend.) Add salt and pepper to taste.

4. Divide the soup into bowls and serve garnished with a dollop of nondairy yogurt. If you want to go fancy, add the yogurt in the middle of each bowl and use a knife to pull it through the yogurt to make a star shape in your soup.

5 minutes high pressure, natural release

1 tablespoon oil, optional

1 cup finely sliced leek

1 pound crimini or any wild mushroom, such as shiitake, oyster, chanterelle, or porcini, cleaned and thinly sliced

2 cloves garlic, minced

1 teaspoon dried thyme

1 cup chopped shelled chestnuts

4 cups dark mushroom stock or vegetable stock

1 to 2 tablespoons porcini powder (see page 32)

Salt and freshly ground black pepper

¼ cup nondairy yogurt (to make your own, see page 266)

SOUPS

1 tablespoon oil, optional

2 cups diced onion

1 teaspoon minced peeled
fresh ginger

½ cup sliced crimini or oyster
mushrooms

2 or 3 potatoes (¾ to 1 pound),
sliced

1 to 2 teaspoons red (or your
favorite color) Thai curry
paste

3 cups vegetable stock

1 cup coconut water or
coconut milk

1 to 2 medium summer squash,
sliced to equal 1½ cups

4 to 8 ounces seitan, store-
bought or homemade (page
212 or 213), sliced or cubed

1 to 2 tablespoons lime juice

1 tablespoon Bragg liquid
aminos or tamari

1 to 2 tablespoons chopped
cilantro

Easy Thai Summer (or Winter) Vegetable Soup with Seitan

Using red curry paste and coconut water or milk along with some lime juice adds simple Thai flavor to this easy soup starring almost any vegetables. It can be made any time of year; see the winter ingredient swaps in the Variation. Feel free to add other vegetables to this aromatic and flexible soup.

SERVES 4 TO 6

1. Heat a stovetop pressure cooker over medium heat or set an electric cooker to sauté; add the oil, if using. Add the onion, ginger, and mushrooms and cook for 2 to 3 minutes. Add the potatoes, curry paste to taste, vegetable stock, and coconut water.

2. Lock the lid on the cooker. Bring to high pressure; cook for 3 minutes. Quick release the pressure. Carefully remove the lid, tilting it away from you.

3. Add the summer squash and seitan. Lock on the lid. Let sit for 1 minute. Carefully remove the lid, tilting it away from you.

4. Add lime juice to taste and the aminos. Taste and adjust seasonings. Garnish with chopped cilantro and serve.

Variation: In the winter, use peeled, cubed winter squash and add it at the same times as the potatoes. Add chopped greens—such as spinach, chard, or finely chopped kale—with the seitan after releasing the pressure.

Hearty Healing Sweet Potato Soup

I had my tooth pulled and could only eat purely pureed or soft foods for three days, which to me is not really eating. I realized that I would need something beyond drinking a green smoothie to satisfy my taste buds and keep my belly full. This soup was both tasty and filling, thick and creamy, and probably even good for me. You don't have to have a tooth pulled to enjoy this anytime.

Stir the miso in just before serving to preserve its probiotic qualities.

SERVES 2 TO 4

1. Heat a stovetop pressure cooker over medium heat or set an electric cooker to sauté. Add the onion, garlic, and ginger and dry sauté for 2 minutes. Add the sweet potato, carrot, spinach, chickpeas, stock, and curry powder.

2. Lock the lid on the cooker. Bring to high pressure; cook for 4 minutes. Let the pressure come down naturally. Remove the lid, tilting it away from you.

3. Add the cilantro. Using an immersion blender (or your blender in batches), puree the soup until smooth. Stir in the miso right before serving.

2 cups finely chopped onion

1 clove garlic, cut in half

1 (½-inch) piece fresh ginger, peeled and cut in half

1 medium sweet potato, peeled and cut into 2-inch chunks

½ medium carrot, cut into 1-inch pieces

1 cup chopped fresh spinach

½ cup cooked chickpeas, white beans, or baby lima beans

3 cups vegetable stock

1 to 2 teaspoons curry powder

¼ cup packed chopped cilantro

1 tablespoon or more mellow white miso, or your favorite miso

SOUPS

8 minutes high pressure, natural release; 2 minutes high pressure, natural release

Soup

2 cups finely chopped onion

4 to 6 cloves garlic, minced

¼ cup cacao (not cocoa) powder

2 tablespoons cacao nibs, ground in a spice grinder until fine; or additional 2 tablespoons cacao powder

1 hot chile, such as a jalapeño or serrano, minced

1 tablespoon mild chili powder

1 teaspoon dried oregano

1 stick cinnamon

1 teaspoon ground cinnamon

1 teaspoon ground cumin

½ teaspoon dried thyme

4 cups vegetable stock

2 cups dried black beans, soaked and drained

¼ cup raisins

2 dates, pitted and soaked in ¼ cup water for at least 30 minutes

2 to 3 tablespoons peanut butter

1 (15-ounce) can fire roasted tomatoes with chilies

Holy Mole Black Bean Soup

Don't let the long list of ingredients keep you from making this wonderful dish—an elevated black bean soup made with typical mole ingredients. You'll be happy you took the plunge.

Once you have cacao powder (which is less processed and contains more fiber and fat than cocoa powder) on hand, you'll probably look for other ways to use it. (Try the Moist Chocolate Cake on page 288.) Cacao nibs also add to the deep, dark flavor; buy them in bulk, if you can. Grinding cacao nibs enhances the character of the soup more than cacao powder alone, but even without them, you will likely find this soup exotic and intoxicating. This recipe takes a bit longer to make than a simple black bean soup, so prepare it only when time allows.

SERVES 6 TO 8

1. Heat a stovetop pressure cooker over medium heat or set an electric cooker to sauté. Add the onion and dry sauté for 3 to 4 minutes. Turn off sauté if using an electric cooker. Add the garlic, cacao powder, cacao nibs, chile, chili powder, oregano, cinnamon stick, ground cinnamon, cumin, and thyme. Stir to combine.

2. Add the stock and stir well, making sure nothing is sticking to the bottom of the cooker. Next, add the beans, raisins, and dates, plus the date-soaking water.

3. Lock the lid on the cooker. Bring to high pressure; cook for 8 minutes. Let the pressure come down naturally, releasing any remaining pressure after 15 minutes. Carefully remove the lid, tilting it away from you.

4. Add peanut butter to taste and the fire roasted tomatoes. Do **not** stir. Lock the lid on the cooker and bring back to high pressure; cook for 2 minutes longer. Let the pressure come down naturally for 10 minutes, then release any remaining pressure. Carefully remove the lid, tilting it away from you.

5. Using a pair of tongs, remove and discard the cinnamon stick. Transfer half the soup to a blender or food processor and carefully blend. (Or remove half the soup and use an immersion blender to puree the soup remaining in the pot.) Return the soup to the cooker or transfer all to a bowl or tureen.

6. In a small bowl, combine the roasted chopped peanuts, avocado, lime juice, and cilantro to form a salsa. Divide the soup among bowls and garnish with the salsa and a sprinkle of smoked salt.

Salsa Garnish

3 tablespoons roasted peanuts, chopped

½ avocado, cut into chunks

2 teaspoons lime juice

2 tablespoons chopped cilantro

Smoked or regular salt

10 minutes high pressure, natural release; 2 minutes high pressure, natural release

2 tablespoons olive oil, optional

2 cups finely chopped Spanish onion

½ cup dried chickpeas, soaked overnight and drained

4 cups vegetable stock

2½ cups chopped carrots (about 2 large)

1½ cups diced potatoes

4 cloves garlic, minced

½ teaspoon ground red pepper or cayenne powder

1 teaspoon coriander seeds, toasted and ground

2 large tomatoes, chopped; or 2 (15-ounce) cans diced tomatoes

2 (14-ounce) cans artichoke hearts in water, drained, or 2 (9- to 14-ounce) packages frozen artichoke hearts, cut in halves or quarters

3 cups fresh chopped greens, such as nettles, chard, kale, or collards

Grated zest and juice of 1 lemon

Salt

¼ cup chopped fresh flat-leaf parsley

2 lemons, cut into wedges

Lebanese Vegetable Soup

This flavorful vegetable and bean soup is bright, lemony, and just a little bit spicy. It came about because a friend asked me to adapt a recipe from *Sundays at Moosewood Restaurant* for the pressure cooker. The original recipe uses canned beans and since dried beans cook so quickly in the pressure cooker, that was the first step in my adaptation. If you don't like heat, leave out the red pepper or cayenne. If it's the spring and you can find fresh nettles, use them. If not, any leafy green will do.

SERVES 6 TO 8

1. Heat a stovetop pressure cooker over medium heat or set an electric cooker to sauté; add the oil, if using. Add the onion and cook for 2 to 3 minutes. Add the chickpeas and 1 cup of the stock.

2. Lock on the lid. Bring to high pressure; cook for 10 minutes. Let the pressure come down naturally. Remove the lid, carefully tilting it away from you.

3. Add the carrots, potatoes, garlic, red pepper, and coriander. Add the remaining 3 cups stock. Lock on the lid. Bring to high pressure; cook for 2 minutes. Let the pressure come down naturally. Remove the lid, carefully tilting it away from you.

4. Add the tomatoes, artichoke hearts, and greens. Lock on the lid and let sit for 5 minutes. Carefully remove the lid.

5. Add the lemon zest and juice and stir. Taste and add salt, if needed. Serve garnished with parsley and lemon wedges.

Shane's Fabulous Lentil Soup

This is named for my son Shane, whose favorite dinner when he was 4 years old was my lentil soup. He brought the soup in for a kindergarten class project that he created about lentils and all the kids enjoyed it. It is easy to make, extremely nutritious, and keeps well in the freezer for up to 4 months. It has become my most loved and requested recipe. I don't use oil but you can sauté the onions in a couple of teaspoons, if you prefer.

Although I didn't do this for Shane, I have since spiced up the soup by adding a few teaspoons, or more, of spice blends, such as herbes de Provence, curry powder, or berbere (pages 38 and 36). Choose your favorite or eat it Shane's way.

SERVES 4 TO 6

1. Heat a stovetop pressure cooker over medium heat or set an electric cooker to sauté. Add the onion and dry sauté for about 2 minutes, until no longer raw. Add a tablespoon of water if sticking occurs. Add the carrots and sauté for another minute. Add the bay leaves, thyme, stock, lentils, and potato. Stir well.

2. Lock the lid in place. Bring to high pressure and cook for 6 minutes. Let the pressure come down naturally. Remove the lid, tilting it away from you.

3. Remove and discard the bay leaves and thyme stems with a pair of tongs. Add the salt and pepper to taste.

Variation: Add 1 cup corn when you remove the pressure cooker lid. Stir in, lock on the lid, and let sit for 2 minutes. You can also do the same with chopped spinach or other greens.

6 minutes high pressure, natural release

2 cups chopped onion

2 carrots, chopped

2 bay leaves

2 sprigs fresh thyme

6 cups vegetable stock or water

1½ cups green or brown lentils, rinsed and picked over

½ cup red lentils, rinsed and picked over

1 medium potato, peeled if desired and diced

1 teaspoon salt

Freshly ground black pepper

6 cups vegetable stock

2 cups dried chickpeas, soaked and drained

1 large unpeeled potato, diced

½ cup grated onion

½ cup chopped fresh flat-leaf parsley

2 teaspoons ground cumin

1 teaspoon ground coriander

½ teaspoon ground turmeric

¼ teaspoon saffron threads, soaked in 1 tablespoon hot water for at least 5 minutes

½ teaspoon salt

2 cups diced fresh or canned plum tomatoes

2 tablespoons fresh lemon juice

Pinch of cayenne

½ teaspoon ground sumac, optional

Salt and freshly ground black pepper

¼ cup chopped cilantro, for garnish

Middle Eastern Chickpea and Tomato Soup

Chickpeas might just be my favorite bean. Their flavor is so rich and nutty, probably due to the slightly higher fat content. Here they are combined with bright spices—including saffron, which adds beautiful color and flavor, and sumac, which lends its exotic lemony flavor—to make a delicious soup that freezes well.

SERVES 4 TO 6

1. In a pressure cooker, combine the stock, chickpeas, potato, onion, parsley, cumin, coriander, turmeric, saffron with its soaking water, and salt.

2. Lock the lid on. Bring to high pressure; cook for 14 minutes. Let the pressure come down naturally. Carefully remove the lid, tilting it away from you.

3. Transfer 2 cups of the chickpea mixture to a blender and add 1 cup of the tomatoes. Carefully puree until blended, then return to the pot along with the remaining tomatoes.

4. Cook for about 3 minutes over medium heat on the stovetop or, if you have an electric cooker or don't want to heat again, lock the lid on and let sit for 5 minutes, until the flavors are combined.

5. Add the lemon juice, cayenne, and sumac, if using, and stir well. Taste and adjust seasonings with salt and pepper. Serve, garnished with cilantro.

The Veggie Queen's Immune Boosting Bowl

This is not party fare; this is what you need when you've had too much people contact and want to nourish yourself in a deep way. If there are two of you who need nourishing, double the recipe. I often make this when I am feeling the first signs of being chased by a nasty virus. But I don't consider this "sick food" because it contains so many flavorful ingredients with immune-boosting properties which appeal to me.

My favorite miso comes from South River Miso in Massachusetts. If I have it, I use their Garlic Red Pepper flavor for this, but any type or brand will do.

SERVES 1

1. If you are using dried mushrooms, drain them and reserve the soaking water. Slice the mushrooms thinly, reserving any stems for stock.

2. Drain the sea vegetables, remove any hard stems, and cut the remainder into small pieces.

3. Add the mushroom soaking water (or the stock), reserved mushrooms, sea vegetables, and chopped greens to the pressure cooker. Bring to high pressure; cook for 2 minutes. Quick release the pressure. Remove the lid, carefully tilting it away from you.

4. Stir in the miso and garlic and/or ginger, along with the chile and ume paste, if using. Top with the scallions and sesame seeds.

5. Breathe in the steam from the soup and then enjoy.

6 large dried shiitake mushrooms, soaked in 2 cups hot water for 30 minutes (save the water); or 2 cups mushroom stock

¼ ounce dried arame, dulse, or wakame sea vegetables, soaked in hot water for 30 minutes

2 cups chopped greens, such as kale, chard, collards, or spinach

2 tablespoons miso paste

1 clove garlic, minced, and/or ¼ teaspoon grated fresh ginger

¼ to ½ teaspoon minced hot chile, such as jalapeño or serrano, optional

1 teaspoon ume plum paste or ume plum vinegar, optional

1 to 2 scallions, sliced

Sprinkling of toasted sesame seeds

1 tablespoon olive oil

1½ cups finely chopped onion

½ cup diced celery

1 cup diced carrot

4 cloves garlic, minced

1 bay leaf

2 to 3 teaspoons Cajun seasoning, store-bought or homemade (page 37), or other spice blend

1 pound (2½ to 3 cups) mixed bean soup mix, soaked and drained

5 cups vegetable stock

1 (14- to 15-ounce) can diced fire-roasted (or other) tomatoes

Salt and freshly ground black pepper

2 Bean Sausages (page 98), or your favorite vegan sausages, cut into 8 to 12 pieces, at room temperature or heated through

¼ cup chopped fresh flat-leaf parsley, for garnish

Multi-Bean Soup
WITH BEAN SAUSAGES

Here is a stick-to-your-ribs soup: a vegan version of bean and sausage soup, using a mix of beans.

You can start with a purchased dried bean soup mix, which is what I often do. The key to cooking a blend of different beans in the pressure cooker is to cook them for the time required to get the longest-cooking bean cooked. With most bean mixes, 8 minutes at pressure ought to be just fine. But if your mix contains chickpeas or pearled barley, then you should cook for at least 14 minutes at pressure. Refer to Bean Cooking At-a-Glance on page 95 for times.

SERVES 6 TO 8

1. Heat a stovetop pressure cooker over medium heat or set an electric cooker to sauté; add the oil. Add the onion, celery, and carrot and sauté for 2 to 3 minutes. Add the garlic, bay leaf, and Cajun seasoning and sauté 30 seconds longer.

2. Add the drained beans and stock. Lock on the lid. Bring to high pressure; cook for 8 minutes. Let the pressure come down naturally. Remove the lid, carefully tilting it away from you.

3. Test some beans to be sure that they are cooked through. If not, lock on the lid, bring back to pressure, and cook for 1 minute longer. Let the pressure release naturally again; after 10 minutes, quick release any remaining pressure.

4. Add the tomatoes. Lock on the lid and let sit for 3 minutes. Remove the lid carefully.

5. Remove and discard the bay leaves. Season the soup with salt and pepper to taste. To serve, divide among bowls, add the bean sausages, and garnish with parsley.

Oat Berry, Adzuki, and Squash Soup

This is a hearty and tasty combination made with whole oats, perfect for winter. If you eat gluten-containing grains, you can use wheat, rye, spelt, Kamut, or farro instead of oats, with good results. If you prefer mung beans to adzuki beans, you can substitute them although you won't get that pretty red color.

SERVES 4 TO 6

1. Heat a stovetop pressure cooker over medium heat or set an electric cooker to sauté; add the oil, if using. Add the onion, garlic, and celery and cook for a minute or two. Add the oat groats, beans, squash, bay leaves, oregano, and stock.

2. Lock the lid on the cooker and bring to high pressure; cook for 20 minutes. Let the pressure come down naturally. Remove the lid, carefully tilting it away from you.

3. Using tongs, carefully remove and discard the bay leaves. Stir in the orange zest and juice. Season to taste with salt and pepper and serve.

1 tablespoon olive oil, optional

2 cups finely chopped onion

3 cloves garlic, minced

2 stalks celery, diced

2 cups oat groats (also known as oat berries), soaked and drained

¾ cup dried adzuki beans

2 cups diced peeled winter squash, such as butternut, acorn, or kabocha

2 bay leaves

1 tablespoon dried oregano or thyme

6 cups vegetable stock, or a combination of water and stock

1 teaspoon grated orange zest

3 to 4 tablespoons fresh orange juice

Salt and freshly ground black pepper

SOUPS

185

1½ cups finely chopped onion

4 cloves garlic, minced

¼ to ½ teaspoon smoked paprika, or 1 teaspoon sweet paprika

2 bay leaves

¼ teaspoon saffron threads, soaked in 2 tablespoons hot stock for at least 10 minutes

2 to 3 large red bell peppers, cored, seeded, and diced to equal 3 cups or more

½ cup raw cashews, soaked in ¾ cup water for at least 4 hours

3½ cups vegetable stock

Salt and freshly ground black pepper

2 to 3 tablespoons nondairy yogurt, for garnish

Red Pepper Bisque

This smooth, easy-to-prepare soup is full of the sweetness of ripe red peppers. There is also a subtle flavor of saffron and a hint of smoked paprika. Cashews thicken the soup and provide some richness; and a dollop of nondairy yogurt makes it look nice and provides a tangy contrast.

If you prefer a more highly seasoned soup, add a small chopped chile before cooking, or stir in 2 to 3 teaspoons toasted ground cumin.

SERVES 4 TO 6

1. Heat a stovetop pressure cooker over medium heat or set an electric cooker to sauté. Add the onion and dry sauté for 2 minutes. Add the garlic and smoked paprika and sauté another minute.

2. Turn off sauté if using an electric cooker. Add the bay leaves, saffron and its soaking liquid, bell peppers, cashews and their soaking water, and the stock.

3. Lock the lid on the cooker and bring to high pressure; cook for 5 minutes. Let the pressure come down naturally. If it takes more than 10 minutes, quick release the remaining pressure. Carefully remove the lid, tilting it away from you.

4. Use a pair of tongs to carefully remove and discard the bay leaves. Blend the soup with an immersion blender right in the pot. For a smoother soup, or if you don't have an immersion blender, blend in a high-speed blender in batches, being careful to cover the lid with a towel to prevent explosions.

5. Season to taste with salt and pepper. Divide the soup among bowls and serve garnished with a dollop of yogurt.

Spicy Brown Rice and Bean Soup

WITH CILANTRO AND LIME

This standby soup can be made from pantry ingredients combined with a few fresh vegetables. Even better, if you have cooked brown rice and beans stashed in your freezer, you can make the soup in just 5 minutes at pressure. You can even add frozen corn at the end. Here, I start from scratch with dried beans and rice. Any way that you make it, this soup is seasoned to appeal to most palates.

SERVES 4 TO 6

1. Heat a stovetop pressure cooker over medium heat or set an electric cooker to sauté; add the oil, if using. Add the onion and cook for 2 minutes. Add the garlic, chile, if using, cumin, and paprika and cook for 1 minute. Add the bay leaf, rice, beans, and stock.

2. Lock the lid on the pressure cooker and bring to high pressure; cook for 25 minutes. Let the pressure come down naturally. Remove the lid, carefully tilting it away from you.

3. With tongs, remove and discard the bay leaf. Add the summer squash or other vegetables. If using a stovetop cooker, lock the lid on the cooker, bring back to high pressure, and cook for 1 minute. If using an electric cooker, simply lock the lid on and let sit for 5 minutes. Quick release any pressure and remove the lid carefully.

4. Add the lime juice and cilantro. Taste and adjust seasonings with salt and pepper.

25 minutes high pressure, natural release; 1 minute high pressure, quick release

1 tablespoon olive oil, optional

1 cup diced onion

4 cloves garlic, minced

1 medium-hot chile, such as Anaheim or jalapeño, chopped, optional

1 tablespoon ground cumin

1 tablespoon paprika

1 bay leaf

¾ cup brown rice

¾ cup unsoaked dried pinto beans

¾ cup unsoaked dried black beans

5 cups vegetable stock

1 to 2 cups chopped summer squash, broccoli, green beans, corn, or any greens, or a combination

3 tablespoons fresh lime juice (about 2 limes)

2 tablespoons cilantro, or more (as much as you like)

Salt and freshly ground black pepper

SOUPS

Corn Stock

5 to 6 ears fresh corn (possibly fewer), frozen will not work

6 or more cups water

Chowder

1 tablespoon olive oil, optional

2 cups finely chopped onion

2 teaspoons minced fresh thyme

Salt and freshly ground black pepper

2 tablespoons brown rice flour, all-purpose flour, or other flour

¾ pound unpeeled red potatoes, cut into ½-inch pieces

½ cup plain (not vanilla) unsweetened or sweetened nondairy milk of your choice

Pinch to 1 tablespoon Sucanat or coconut palm sugar, optional

3 tablespoons chopped fresh basil or flat-leaf parsley, or sprinkle of chipotle powder

Sweet Summer Corn Chowder

This recipe was adapted from the TV show *America's Test Kitchen.* The big difference is that I make the corn stock right away in the pressure cooker, in just a few minutes. This gives a wonderful underlying corn flavor to the soup. Freeze any leftover corn stock for other uses, such as Yellow Summer Squash Chowder (page 193).

You must use the freshest and sweetest corn that you can get. Frozen corn will not work. While there are a number of steps, they all lead to an incredible soup, deeply rich with layers of corn flavor.

SERVES 4 TO 6

1. To make the stock: Using a chef's knife or corn stripper, cut the kernels off the corn cobs, making sure that you don't cut too deep because you are going to squeeze the milk out of the cobs. Also, if you cut the kernels too deep they get tough and fibrous at the bottom. (You should have 5 to 6 cups kernels.) Transfer the kernels to a bowl and set aside.

2. Holding the cobs over a second medium bowl lined with a clean kitchen towel or piece of cheesecloth, use the back of a butter knife or a vegetable peeler to scrape the remaining pulp and milk out of the cobs into the cloth (you should have 1½ to 2 cups of this fibrous milky stuff).

3. Wrap the towel tightly around the pulp and squeeze until dry. (Instead of using a towel or cheesecloth you can push the pulp through a fine mesh strainer, or just squeeze with your hands.) Add the pulp in the towel to the corn kernels, and set aside the corn juice in the bowl (you should have about ⅔ cup juice).

4. Put the scraped corn cobs into a pressure cooker with 6 or more cups water, enough to cover the cobs but no more than two-thirds full. Lock the lid on and bring to high pressure; cook for 5 minutes. Let the pressure come down naturally. Remove the lid carefully. Strain and reserve 4 cups of this stock for the soup.

5. To make the chowder: Heat a stovetop pressure cooker over medium heat or set an electric cooker to sauté; add the oil, if using. Add the onion, thyme, 2 teaspoons salt, and 1 teaspoon pepper. Cook, stirring frequently, until the onion is softened and edges are just beginning to brown, 5 to 6 minutes. Stir in the flour and cook, stirring constantly, for 2 minutes. Whisking constantly, gradually add the 4 cups reserved corn stock, making sure to scrape any stuck bits off the bottom of the cooker. Add the reserved corn kernels and pulp and potatoes.

6. Lock on the lid. Bring to high pressure; cook for 4 minutes. Quick release the pressure. Remove the lid carefully, tilting it away from you.

7. Remove 2 cups of the chowder and puree in a blender, carefully, until the mixture is very smooth. Depending upon your blender, it could take up to 2 minutes.

8. Return the puree to the chowder and add the nondairy milk. Remove the pot from the heat and stir in the reserved corn juice. Season to taste with salt, pepper, and Sucanat or sugar (add a pinch or up to 1 tablespoon, depending on how sweet your corn was and milk is). Serve, sprinkled with chopped basil or chipotle powder.

1 tablespoon oil, optional

2 cups coarsely chopped onion
or leek

2 carrots, peeled and diced

2 large stalks celery, diced

6 cups water or vegetable
stock, or a combination

2 cups yellow or green split
peas, picked over and rinsed

1 piece smoked or regular
dulse, or ¼ to ½ teaspoon
dulse granules

2 large bay leaves

½ to 1 teaspoon dried thyme,
optional

½ cup fresh English peas or
frozen (not thawed) peas

Juice of 1 lemon

Sprinkle of smoked or regular
salt, optional

Spring Split Pea Soup

Making split pea soup in the pressure cooker is a breeze. Either green
or yellow split peas will work here; the addition of fresh peas at the end of
cooking makes it special.

Split pea soup can be spiced any way that you like. If you like Indian
spices, by all means add them: Use 1 to 3 teaspoons curry powder or garam
masala or your favorite spices, such as cumin, coriander, and turmeric.
Otherwise, add 1 to 2 tablespoons herbes de Provence or Italian seasoning
(page 41), or your favorite all-purpose blend.

All pressure cooker manufacturers warn you to use oil when cooking
split peas to control foaming, but I have made this without oil with positive
results. Use a 6-quart or larger pressure cooker as a precaution.

SERVES 6

1. Heat a 6-quart or larger stovetop pressure cooker over medium
   heat or set an electric cooker to sauté; add the oil, if using. Add
   the onion, carrot, and celery and cook for a minute or two. Add the
   water or stock, split peas, dulse, and bay leaves.

2. Lock the lid in place. Bring to high pressure; cook for 10 minutes.
   Allow the pressure to come down naturally. Remove the lid, tilting
   it away from you.

3. With long tongs, remove and discard the bay leaves. Add the
   thyme, if using, and simmer over medium heat or using the sauté
   function, for 1 to 2 minutes, until the thyme flavor pervades the
   soup. Stir well, taking care to blend in the peas that have sunk to
   the bottom of the cooker.

4. Add the fresh peas. Lock the lid on the cooker and let sit for
   5 minutes. Remove the lid carefully. Add the lemon juice and
   season with salt to taste (as much as 1 teaspoon), if desired.

Thai Rice Noodle Soup with Seitan

The aroma of Thai soup is so intoxicating: the coconut, lemongrass, ginger, lime leaves, red curry, basil, and cilantro—Oh, boy. That the soup typically includes rice noodles makes it even easier to enjoy if you don't eat gluten. This recipe uses thin rice noodles. If you use thicker ones, such as those used for pad Thai, add at least a minute to the cooking time. If time is up and the noodles don't seem as cooked as you'd like, just lock the lid on the cooker, wait a minute, and check again.

You can easily add other vegetables to this soup, such as sliced red pepper, green beans, summer squash, or hot chiles. It's an easy-to-like, easy-to-digest meal-in-a-bowl.

———

SERVES 4

1. Heat a stovetop pressure cooker over medium heat or set an electric cooker to sauté. Add the mushrooms, half the scallions, the carrot, seitan, and 2 tablespoons of the coconut milk. Dry sauté for 2 minutes. Add the curry paste, ginger or galangal, lemongrass, and lime leaves. Cook for another minute. Add the stock and rice noodles.

2. Lock the lid on the cooker and bring to low pressure; cook for 2 minutes. (If you don't have a low pressure option, bring to high pressure and cook for 1 minute.) Carefully quick release the pressure in short bursts to avoid having hot liquid spew out the vent. Remove the lid, carefully tilting it away from you.

3. Using long tongs, remove and discard the lemongrass, ginger or galangal, and lime leaves. Add the remaining scallions, the basil, cilantro, and lime zest and juice. Taste and adjust the seasoning with salt, tamari, or liquid aminos, if desired.

2 minutes low pressure, quick release in short bursts

1 cup thinly sliced crimini mushrooms

1 bunch scallions, sliced

1 medium carrot, peeled and sliced on the diagonal into ½-inch pieces to equal 1 cup

4 to 8 ounces seitan (store-bought or homemade, page 212 or 213) or extra firm tofu, diced

1 (14-ounce) can coconut milk or coconut water

2 to 3 teaspoons red Thai curry paste, depending upon desired heat

1 (2-inch) piece fresh ginger or galangal, sliced (no need to peel), or 2 slices dried galangal

1 stalk lemongrass, bruised with the back of a knife and cut into 2-inch pieces

3 kaffir lime leaves

4 cups vegetable stock

4 ounces thin rice noodles

¼ cup Thai or regular basil leaves, minced

¼ cup chopped cilantro

Grated zest and juice of 1 lime

Salt, tamari, or Bragg liquid aminos, optional

1 tablespoon oil

2 cups finely chopped onion

3 cloves garlic, minced

2 stalks celery, diced

1 bay leaf

2 medium purple potatoes, diced

1 medium parsnip, peeled and diced to equal 1 cup

½ cup diced peeled celery root (also called celeriac)

1 medium carrot, peeled and diced

½ cup dried cranberry beans, soaked and drained (soaked are best but unsoaked will work)

⅔ cup wild rice

6 cups vegetable stock

1 to 2 tablespoons your favorite herb or spice blend, such as herbes de Provence or Italian seasoning, store-bought or homemade (see page 41)

1½ cups diced peeled winter squash

Salt and freshly ground black pepper

3 to 4 tablespoons chopped fresh flat-leaf parsley, cilantro, or chives for garnish, optional

Wild Rice, Cranberry Bean, and Winter Vegetable Soup

This is a highly adaptable soup. Use what you like and leave out what you don't. The wild rice and cranberry beans provide the bulk of the soup for a hearty meal.

My winter vegetable larder often contains the same things: potatoes, parsnips, celery root, and carrots. If you have any fresh green herbs such as parsley, cilantro, or chives, sprinkle them on as garnish to make this soup look and taste even better than it already is.

SERVES 6 TO 8

1. Heat a stovetop pressure cooker over medium heat or set an electric cooker to sauté; add the oil. Add the onion and sauté for a minute or two. Add the garlic and celery and sauté another minute. Add the bay leaf, potatoes, parsnip, celery root, carrot, beans, wild rice, stock, and herb blend.

2. Lock the lid on the pressure cooker. Bring to high pressure; cook for 22 minutes. Let the pressure come down naturally. Remove the lid carefully, tilting it away from you.

3. Add the squash, and salt and pepper to taste. Do not stir. Lock the lid back on the cooker and bring to high pressure; cook for another 3 minutes. Quick release the pressure. Carefully remove the lid, tilting it away from you.

4. Remove and discard the bay leaf with a pair of tongs. If you find the soup too thick, add more water or stock. Serve hot, garnished with herbs, if you like.

Sopa de Calabacitas

(YELLOW SUMMER SQUASH CHOWDER)

When summer squash is abundant, there are rarely too many ways to serve it. Although my husband is not a summer squash lover, he enjoys this soup. It is easy to make and tasty because you're serving up the freshness of summer in a bowl. It can be served hot, warm, or chilled. If you chill it, be sure to adjust the seasoning before serving as chilling tends to mute flavors. You can toast the cumin and coriander together or spend a few minutes one day toasting a good amount of each to use regularly. A wonderful addition to the soup would be ½ to 1 cup leftover cooked pinto, kidney, or Anasazi beans, heated for a few minutes.

SERVES 4 TO 6

1. Heat a stovetop pressure cooker over medium heat or set an electric cooker to sauté; add the oil, if using. Add the leek and cook for 1 minute. Add the garlic, cumin, coriander, and chile and cook 1 minute longer. Add the stock and scrape the bottom of the pot to be sure that nothing is sticking.

2. Add the squash and lock the lid on the cooker. Bring to high pressure and immediately quick release the pressure. Remove the lid, carefully tilting it away from you.

3. Using an immersion blender, puree the squash. (If you don't have an immersion blender, carefully use a food processor or blender to puree the soup in batches and return to the cooker.) Add the corn, green chiles, and nondairy milk.

4. Lock the lid back on the cooker and bring to high pressure; cook for 1 minute. Quick release the pressure. Remove the lid, carefully tilting it away from you.

5. If serving hot, transfer the soup to a large bowl or tureen, or spoon into individual bowls. If not, let cool and refrigerate for a few hours or overnight. Serve with a squeeze of lime juice if you like, and any or all of the suggested garnishes.

High pressure, immediate quick release; 1 minute high pressure, quick release

- 1 tablespoon olive oil, optional

- 1 cup diced leek (white part only) or onion

- 1 tablespoon or more minced garlic

- 1 teaspoon ground toasted cumin

- ½ teaspoon ground toasted coriander seeds

- ½ small hot chile, such as jalapeño or serrano, minced; or ½ teaspoon chili or chipotle powder

- 2 cups vegetable stock or corn stock (see page 188)

- 2 to 3 medium yellow summer squash, diced to equal 4 cups

- 2 ears corn, kernels removed to equal at least 1½ cups

- ¼ cup roasted green chiles, canned or fresh

- 1 cup unsweetened nondairy milk of your choice

- Squeeze of fresh lime, optional

- Garnishes: chopped scallions (or cilantro or parsley), avocado, sweet red pepper, and/or baked corn tortilla strips

SOUPS

EIGHT

Main Courses

The pressure cooker truly shines when it comes to main course dishes. The range of dinners that can be produced in the pressure cooker is amazing, since any dish that requires long cooking on the stovetop or in the oven can be easily adapted for the pressure cooker (as long as there is liquid involved in the cooking process).

You can cook stews, chilies and other bean dishes, and grain dishes directly in the pot, or you can use the steam heat of the pot to cook savory pies and stuffed greens.

Keep in mind that dishes with ingredients that cook for different times must stay under pressure for the amount of time it takes for the longest-cooking ingredient to be thoroughly cooked. Due to this, most bean dishes, of which you'll find many here, use a two-step cooking process: The beans are cooked with other longer-cooking ingredients, and then the shorter-cooking food is added to cook while the beans finish. But remember, if you keep a stash of cooked beans in the freezer, you can use them in many of the recipes for even quicker dinner prep. Just note that it will require decreasing the amount of added liquid and adjusting the cooking time.

Most of these mixed dishes can easily be varied by substituting a different grain or bean. Once you start experimenting with combinations of food, you will be amazed by what you can do in your pressure cooker.

A reminder about seasoning: In general, the heat of the pressure cooker tends to dull spices, so you should increase the amount you use compared to stovetop cooking (except for chile peppers or crushed red pepper flakes, which become more intense under pressure). You can always add more spices at the end of cooking, but once you've overspiced your dish, it's hard to make adjustments. And while I prefer highly seasoned dishes, I have tempered the heat in recipes that have any. Please don't hesitate to amp up the heat if you're so inclined.

1 cup diced onion

1 cup ½-inch-thick sliced carrot

½ cup sliced peeled parsnip
(about 1 medium)

4 cloves garlic, minced

1½ tablespoons Italian
seasoning, store-bought or
homemade (page 41)

2 bay leaves

1 cup Anasazi beans, soaked
and drained

1½ cups vegetable stock

1½ cups diced peeled rutabaga
or unpeeled small turnips

1¼ cups diced peeled butternut
or other winter squash

1 (15-ounce) can diced
tomatoes or fire roasted
tomatoes; or 1½ cups diced
fresh tomatoes

1 cup finely sliced kale leaves
or baby spinach

Salt and freshly ground black
pepper

¼ cup chopped fresh flat-leaf
parsley, for garnish

Anasazi Bean and Winter Vegetable Stew

This is a hearty, thick stew that is filling and perfect for winter eating. I originally made this stew with black beans and I can honestly tell you that even though it tasted very good, the color of the black vegetables was so off-putting that another bean had to come to the rescue. I have fallen in love with Anasazi beans, but if you cannot get them substitute pinto or kidney beans.

SERVES 4

1. Heat a stovetop pressure cooker over medium heat or set an electric cooker to sauté. Add the onion and dry sauté for 2 minutes. Add the carrot, parsnip, and garlic and cook another minute. Add the seasoning, bay leaves, beans, and stock.

2. Lock the lid on the cooker, bring to high pressure, and cook for 6 minutes. Let the pressure come down naturally. Remove the lid, carefully tilting it away from you.

3. Add the rutabaga and squash. Lock on the lid and bring the cooker back to high pressure; cook for 3 minutes. Quick release the pressure. Remove the lid carefully.

4. Add the tomatoes and greens. Stir. Lock the lid on the pot and let sit for 2 minutes. Remove the lid carefully. Remove and discard the bay leaves. Add salt and pepper to taste, garnish with the parsley, and serve.

Arroz non Pollo

This is my adaptation of a Peruvian dish I found on a Facebook pressure cooking group, posted by Silvana Arevalo O'Brien, who was sharing her mother's recipe. Here's my version. The key to making this taste great is to use lots of cilantro. If you don't care for it, you can substitute parsley but it won't taste as traditional. I wish that I could have tasted Silvana's mother's version of this dish. Since we missed that meal, we have to make it.

───────

SERVES 4

1. Blend the stock with the cilantro in a blender until smooth.

2. Heat a stovetop pressure cooker over medium heat or set an electric cooker to sauté. Add the mushrooms and dry sauté for 3 minutes. Add the carrot, garlic, turmeric, cayenne, and red pepper, stir well, and cook for 1 more minute. Add the blended cilantro, brown rice, and drained beans. Stir.

3. Lock the lid on the pressure cooker. Bring to high pressure; cook for 20 minutes. Let the pressure come down naturally. Remove the lid, carefully tilting it away from you.

4. Add the bell pepper, peas, and corn. Lock the lid on the cooker and let sit for 5 minutes.

5. Remove the lid carefully and add salt and pepper to taste. Transfer to a platter and serve.

20 minutes high pressure, natural release

2¾ cups vegetable stock

1 bunch cilantro

1 cup sliced crimini or shiitake mushrooms

1 cup carrot quartered lengthwise and chopped

3 cloves garlic, minced

1 teaspoon turmeric or a pinch of saffron

Pinch of cayenne

Pinch of crushed red pepper flakes

2 cups brown rice

½ cup Peruano (aka Mayocoba) or pinto beans, soaked and drained

½ cup diced red bell pepper

½ cup frozen peas

½ cup fresh or frozen corn kernels

Salt and freshly ground black pepper

1 tablespoon oil, optional

1 cup chopped onion

1 to 2 cloves garlic, minced

2 cups chopped peeled sweet
potatoes, about 2 small or
medium

2 teaspoons mild or hot chili
powder

⅓ cup vegetable stock

1 cup cooked black beans (see
Bean Cooking At-a-Glance,
page 95)

¼ cup scallions, chopped

¼ teaspoon salt

Splash of hot sauce, optional

Chopped cilantro, for garnish

Black Bean and Sweet Potato Hash

Photo, page I-7

This is an ideal breakfast food for me, but others will probably like it for lunch or a light dinner. It can be served simply as a side dish, spooned over brown rice or quinoa, wrapped in a whole wheat tortilla, or made into soft tacos, garnished with avocado, cilantro, and your other favorite taco toppings as featured in the photo.

SERVES 4

1. Heat a stovetop pressure cooker over medium heat or set an electric cooker to sauté; add the oil, if using. Add the onion and cook for 2 to 3 minutes. Add the garlic and stir. Add the sweet potatoes and chili powder. Stir to coat the sweet potatoes with chili. Add the stock and stir.

2. Lock the lid on the pressure cooker. Bring to high pressure; cook for 3 minutes. Quick release the pressure. Remove the lid, tilting it away from you.

3. Add the black beans, scallions, and salt. Cook another minute or two, or lock on the lid for 3 minutes, until the beans are heated through.

4. Add hot sauce, if desired. Taste and add more salt, if you like. Top with chopped cilantro and serve.

Cajun Tofu with Eggplant, Okra, and Summer Squash

Tofu firms up in the pressure cooker. Here it is coated and marinated with Cajun seasoning, tamari, and vinegar for at least 15 minutes before it is pressure cooked. The squash exudes liquid and so does the eggplant, so use less liquid than you think you need: Don't add extra unless you want your food swimming in liquid.

SERVES 4

1. Put the tofu in a bowl or container that can be covered and sprinkle with the spice mix. Drizzle on 1 tablespoon of the tamari and the vinegar. Stir so that all of the tofu is covered with seasoning. Cover and let sit for at least 15 minutes, or up to 30 minutes.

2. Heat a stovetop pressure cooker over medium heat or set an electric cooker to sauté. Add the onion and celery and dry sauté for 2 minutes. Add the bell pepper, chile pepper, if using, and garlic and sauté 1 minute longer. Add the tofu and stir. Add the eggplant, okra, and summer squash; do not stir.

3. Pour in the stock and lock on the lid. Bring to high pressure; cook for 3 minutes. Quick release the pressure. Remove the lid carefully by tilting it away from you.

4. Transfer to a bowl or platter. Drizzle with the remaining 1 tablespoon tamari and garnish with parsley.

Curried Tofu: Use 1 tablespoon curry powder (page 38) instead of the Cajun seasoning.

Italian Tofu: Use 1 to 2 tablespoons Italian seasoning (page 41) instead of the Cajun seasoning in the marinade. Omit the hot pepper and use tomatoes instead of okra.

3 minutes high pressure, quick release

- 1 pound extra firm vacuum packed tofu, drained and cubed

- 1 to 2 tablespoons Cajun seasoning blend (store-bought or homemade, see page 37), Creole blend, or your favorite hot blend

- 2 tablespoons tamari or Bragg liquid aminos

- 1 tablespoon red wine vinegar

- 1 cup diced onion

- ½ cup diced celery

- ½ cup diced red bell pepper

- 1 small chile pepper, such as jalapeño or serrano, minced, optional

- 1 tablespoon minced garlic

- 1 cup diced eggplant (I used 2 small slender white eggplant)

- 1 cup sliced okra (about 10 pods)

- 1 cup diced summer squash, any color

- ¼ cup vegetable stock

- Chopped fresh flat-leaf parsley, for garnish

MAIN COURSES

10 or more large collard leaves (1 to 2 bunches), stems removed, finely chopped, and reserved

1 cup diced crimini or shiitake mushrooms

¾ cup sliced leek, mostly the white part

3 cloves garlic, minced

2 to 3 teaspoons Italian seasoning, store-bought or homemade (page 41)

1 cup oat groats, soaked and drained

2 cups vegetable stock

1 (8-ounce) can organic tomato sauce

½ cup water

Collard Rolls
WITH OAT GROATS AND MUSHROOMS

I have a fondness for stuffed food, so was pleased to discover that large collard greens make amazing wrappers—and are easier to handle than cabbage. You could also use Swiss chard but it's a bit more delicate. The nice part about this dish is that all parts are cooked in the pressure cooker. If gluten is not an issue for you, you can use any other brown whole grain—barley, rye, farro—instead of the oats; they are tasty either way, with or without gluten.

SERVES 4 TO 6

1. Heat a stovetop pressure cooker over medium heat or set an electric cooker to sauté. Add the collard stems, mushrooms, and leek and dry sauté for 3 minutes. Add the garlic and Italian seasoning and cook 1 minute longer. Add the drained oat groats and stock.

2. Lock the lid on the cooker. Bring to high pressure; cook for 20 minutes. Let the pressure come down naturally. Remove the lid carefully, tilting it away from you. Transfer the contents to a large bowl; let the filling sit until it's cool enough to handle.

3. Wash the pressure cooker. Add 1 cup water and a trivet or rack to elevate the dish above the water (see page 14). Create a helper handle (see page 15) and place it on top of the trivet.

4. When you are able to handle the filling, lay out a collard leaf and add about ½ cup filling. Roll the sides in and roll up like a spring roll. Put the completed roll into a lidded dish that fits inside the pressure cooker. Repeat with the remaining filling and the leaves, fitting each new roll snugly into the dish.

5. Combine the tomato sauce and ½ cup water. Pour over the collard rolls. Place a lid on the dish and lower into the pressure cooker.

6. Lock the lid on the cooker. Bring to high pressure; cook for 3 minutes. Let the pressure come down naturally for 10 minutes, then quick release any remaining pressure.

7. Using the helper handle, carefully lift the casserole dish out of the cooker. Remove the cover and serve.

Late Winter Eating-Down-the-Freezer Vegetable Curry

One cold day, I was hungry and decided to see what I might find in my freezer to add some sunshine to my dreary day. Finding beans, eggplant, and tomatoes, I created a dish that made me appreciate how I use my freezer as part of my pantry. For me, there's nothing like frozen eggplant and pre-chopped tomatoes to brighten a winter's day. Root around in your freezer and refrigerator and see what kind of crazy curry you can make.

SERVES 4 TO 6

1. Heat a stovetop pressure cooker over medium heat or set an electric cooker to sauté. Add the onion and dry sauté for 3 minutes. Add the garlic, curry powder, cumin, and cinnamon and cook for 2 minutes longer, adding some of the stock, a tablespoon at a time, if anything starts to stick. Add the stock, beans, eggplant, tomatoes, and date.

2. Lock the lid on the cooker. Bring to high pressure; cook for 2 minutes. Quick release the pressure. Carefully remove the lid, tilting it away from you.

3. Add the tomato paste and greens. Do not stir. Lock the lid back on, bring to high pressure, and cook for 1 minute. Quick release the pressure. Remove the lid carefully.

4. Stir contents and add the orange juice. Transfer to a bowl. Serve garnished with cilantro or parsley, if available.

2 minutes high pressure, quick release; 1 minute high pressure, quick release

2 cups finely chopped onion

3 cloves garlic, minced

2 teaspoons curry powder

2 teaspoons ground toasted cumin

½ teaspoon ground cinnamon

½ cup vegetable stock

2 cups cooked white or other beans (see Bean Cooking At-a-Glance, page 95)

1 cup chopped frozen cooked eggplant, thawed

1 cup frozen chopped (or canned diced) tomatoes

1 large Medjool date, cut up

2 to 3 tablespoons tomato paste

2 cups chopped greens, such as turnip, mustard, or kale

3 tablespoon fresh orange juice

2 to 3 tablespoons chopped fresh cilantro or parsley, optional

2 cups finely chopped onion

1 cup diced crimini mushrooms

1 cup diced carrot

4 cloves garlic, minced

1 small chile pepper, such as jalapeño or serrano, seeded (or not, if you prefer more heat) and minced

1 tablespoon paprika or mild chili powder

½ to 1½ teaspoons ancho or other chili powder (with heat)

1½ cups brown, green, black, or French green lentils, rinsed and picked over

½ cup split red lentils, rinsed and picked over

1½ cups diced peeled winter squash

2 cups vegetable stock

1 (15-ounce) can diced fire roasted tomatoes

2 tablespoons tomato paste

Salt and freshly ground black pepper

Hot sauce, optional

Lentil, Winter Squash, and Mushroom Chili

I love chili, especially ones that cook quickly. To a base of lentils, I add carrots and squash for sweetness and mushrooms for texture and a little umami flavor. Make it as mild or as spicy as you like. You know what I'll likely be doing, but the directions are for mild chili. You can use any type of lentils that you like, but I include red lentils for creaminess (as I do in Shane's Fabulous Lentil Soup, page 181).

SERVES 4 TO 6

1. Heat a stovetop pressure cooker over medium heat or set an electric cooker to sauté. Add the onion, mushrooms, and carrot and dry sauté for 2 minutes. Add the garlic, chile pepper, paprika, and chili powder and cook 1 minute longer. Add both kinds of lentils, the winter squash, and stock. Stir once.

2. Lock the lid on the pressure cooker. Bring to high pressure; cook for 6 minutes. Let the pressure come down naturally. Remove the lid, carefully tiilting it away from you.

3. Add the diced tomatoes and tomato paste. Stir. Lock the lid on the cooker and let sit for 3 to 5 minutes. Remove the lid carefully.

4. Add salt and pepper to taste. Transfer to a serving dish and serve with hot sauce, if desired.

Mediterranean Tofu with Bell Pepper Sauce

This dish comes together easily and the taste truly belies the simplicity. Get the ripest peppers that you can; a mix of colors is nice but all red is wonderful, too.

You can cut the tofu into slabs, or sticks, or cubes, depending upon how you want to serve it: As slabs, I would serve it over cooked grains or atop a beautiful salad. Sticks can be served in a similar way and cubes would be wonderful with pasta. No matter how you serve it, it turns tofu from boring to exciting.

SERVES 4

1. Heat a stovetop pressure cooker over medium heat or set an electric cooker to sauté; add the olive oil, if using. Add the onion and peppers and cook for 3 minutes. Add the garlic, rosemary, and bay leaves and cook another 30 seconds.

2. Add the vinegar and tofu and stir. Add the stock and stir again. Spoon the tomato paste over the top of the other ingredients but do not stir.

3. Lock the lid on the pressure cooker. Bring to high pressure; cook for 3 minutes. Quick release the pressure. Remove the lid, carefully tilting it away from you.

4. Stir in the olives and chopped herbs. Put the lid back on the cooker and let sit for 3 minutes.

5. Remove and discard the bay leaves. Season with salt and pepper to taste, transfer to a platter, and serve.

3 minutes high pressure, quick release

- 1 tablespoon olive oil, optional
- 1 cup diced red onion
- 2 red, yellow, or orange bell peppers, cored, seeded, and sliced into pieces up to 1½ inches long
- 3 cloves garlic, minced
- ½ to 1 teaspoon fresh rosemary leaves, finely chopped
- 2 bay leaves
- 2 tablespoons red wine vinegar or sherry vinegar
- 1 pound tofu, cut into 4 or 8 slabs, into sticks, or cubed
- ½ cup vegetable stock
- 1 tablespoon tomato paste
- 10 to 15 small black olives, such as Kalamata or Niçoise, pitted and chopped to equal ¼ cup
- 2 to 3 tablespoons chopped fresh flat-leaf parsley or basil
- Salt and freshly ground black pepper

Crust

¾ cup rolled oats

½ cup walnuts

3 tablespoons vegetable stock

2 teaspoons tahini

Vegetable cooking spray

Filling

1 cup diced red onion

1½ cups sliced crimini and/or oyster mushrooms

6 to 7 tablespoons vegetable broth

3 cups packed sliced greens, such as kale or Swiss chard

1 (12.3-ounce) package Mori-Nu firm or extra firm silken tofu; or 12 ounces silken tofu, drained

3 cloves garlic, minced

¼ cup packed fresh flat-leaf parsley

1 tablespoon mellow white miso paste

1 tablespoon arrowroot powder

2 teaspoons salt-free spicy mix (page 45) or your favorite all-purpose seasoning blend

Cracked black pepper, optional

Mushroom and Greens Quiche

WITH OAT WALNUT CRUST

Sometimes you just want something creamy and satisfying. This dish, perfect for brunch, is easy to make once you get the initial work out of the way. While it is cooking, you can make a big green salad to go with it.

MAKES 1 QUICHE, 4 GOOD-SIZED SERVINGS

1. To make the crust: Combine the oats, walnuts, stock, and tahini in a mini food processor. Pulse until combined. The dough can be a bit crumbly.

2. Spray a 7- or 8-inch pie plate that fits into the pressure cooker with vegetable cooking spray (or use a 1- or 2-quart casserole dish). Press the dough onto the bottom (and up the sides if there is enough crust) of the pie plate.

3. To make the filling: Heat a stovetop pressure cooker over medium heat or set an electric cooker to sauté. Add the onion and mushrooms and dry sauté for 3 minutes, adding 2 to 3 tablespoons stock if anything starts to stick. Add the greens and ¼ cup stock.

4. Lock the lid on the cooker. Bring to high pressure; cook for 1 minute. Quick release the pressure. Carefully remove the lid, tilting it away from you. Transfer the vegetables to a small bowl to cool for a few minutes.

5. Clean the pressure cooker. Add 1 cup water to the cooker, along with a trivet onto which you will place the pie plate. Have a set of helper handles (see page 15) nearby if you need it to remove the pie plate.

6. While the vegetables are cooling, combine the tofu, garlic, and parsley in a blender and blend until smooth, scraping the contents down, if necessary. Add the cooked vegetables, miso, arrowroot, and seasoning and blend until smooth.

7. Pour the filling into the prepared crust. Smooth the top. Sprinkle with cracked black pepper, if desired.

8. Cover the pie plate or casserole dish with foil or the lid. Lower into the cooker, using the helper handle, if you need it. Lock the lid on the cooker. Bring to high pressure; cook for 20 minutes. Let the pressure come down naturally. Remove the lid carefully.

9. Remove the dish from the cooker. Carefully remove the lid, being careful not to get water onto the quiche. Let cool for a few minutes. Slice and serve.

2 teaspoons olive oil, optional

2 medium leeks, washed well, sliced into ½-inch pieces to equal at least 2 cups

2 cloves garlic, minced

½ teaspoon ground caraway seeds

1 teaspoon ground toasted cumin

¼ teaspoon crushed red pepper

2 teaspoons Harissa Spice Blend (page 40)

1 or 2 bay leaves

1 cup dried chickpeas, soaked

3 to 3½ cups vegetable stock

1 cup diced peeled sweet potato

2 cups diced butternut or other winter squash

2 medium carrots, sliced into ½-inch-thick pieces

1 cup diced peeled celery root

1 cup turnips (peeled if large) cut in 1 to ½-inch pieces

1 cup peeled and diced kohlrabi

1 cup peeled and diced rutabaga

2 tablespoons tomato paste

Salt and freshly ground black pepper

¼ cup chopped fresh flat-leaf parsley

Lemon wedges, for garnish

Moroccan Chickpea Stew

What I like most about this stew, other than its beauty, is that it shows off the abundance of winter vegetables such as kohlrabi, celery root, turnips, and winter squash. The sweet and spicy stew has a kick, so if you prefer less spice, tone down the red pepper and harissa.

Don't let the long list of ingredients deter you from making this, but do note that it's not a weeknight meal, unless you have the time or have previously prepped the veggies.

SERVES 6 TO 8

1. Heat a stovetop pressure cooker over medium heat or set an electric cooker to sauté; add the oil, if using. Add the leeks and cook for 2 minutes, adding a tablespoon or two of the stock if the leeks start sticking. Add the garlic, spices, and bay leaves and cook for another minute, stirring often. Add the drained chickpeas and 3 cups of the stock.

2. Lock the lid on the cooker. Bring to high pressure; cook for 12 minutes. Let the pressure come down naturally. If the pressure has not released after 15 minutes, quick release any remaining pressure. Carefully remove the lid, tilting it away from you.

3. Add the sweet potato, squash, carrots, celery root, turnips, kohlrabi, and rutabaga. Lock on the lid, bring back to high pressure, and cook for 3 minutes. Quick release the pressure. Remove the lid, carefully tilting it away from you.

4. Remove and discard the bay leaves with long tongs. Stir in the tomato paste, along with the remaining stock if the veggies seem too dry. Transfer the stew to a large bowl or platter. Season with salt and pepper, garnish with the parsley, and serve with lemon wedges on the side.

Posole Chili

(JAZZED-UP HOMINY)

Photo, page I-3

"What?" you say, "posole chili?" Well, I warned you early on that my recipes often depart from traditional ingredient combinations and draw from multiple cuisines with which I have no ties. Here I combine canned hominy (you could also easily cook dry hominy in the pressure cooker) with soaked beans to come up with a hearty chili. Many years ago I went to an in-the-field dinner event at Tierra Vegetables, a local farm known for its smoked, fresh, and dried chiles. Chef Eric Tucker of San Francisco's Millennium Restaurant made vegan hominy; another chef made a meat version. People went back for second helpings of Tucker's. This dish, inspired by his hominy, won't be quite the same but I hope that you will enjoy it.

SERVES 4 TO 6

1. Heat a stovetop pressure cooker over medium heat or set an electric cooker to sauté; add the olive oil. Add the onion and sauté for 3 minutes. Add the garlic, chili powder, cumin, and paprika and sauté another minute. Add the hominy, drained beans, and stock.

2. Lock the lid on. Bring to high pressure; cook for 8 minutes. Let the pressure come down naturally. Remove the lid, carefully tilting it away from you.

3. Add the tomatoes, tomato sauce, tomato paste, and corn. Stir once. Lock the lid on the cooker and let sit for 3 minutes. Remove the lid.

4. Transfer the chili to a large bowl. Add the scallions, cilantro, and lime juice. Add salt to taste and serve.

8 minutes high pressure, natural release

- 1 tablespoon olive oil
- 2 cups finely chopped onion
- 4 cloves garlic, minced
- 2 tablespoons mild or hot chili powder
- 2 to 3 teaspoons ground toasted cumin
- ½ teaspoon smoked paprika
- 1 (15-ounce) can hominy, rinsed and drained
- 1 cup dried black beans, soaked and drained
- 1 cup dried pinto beans, soaked and drained
- 1¼ cups vegetable stock
- 1 (15-ounce) can diced fire roasted tomatoes with chilies, or regular canned diced tomatoes
- 1 (8-ounce) box or can tomato sauce
- 3 tablespoons tomato paste
- 1 cup fresh or frozen corn kernels
- ½ cup chopped scallions
- ¼ cup chopped cilantro
- 2 tablespoons lime juice
- Salt

1 cup sliced leek or onion

¼ to ½ cup thinly sliced shiitake
or oyster mushrooms

2 cloves garlic, minced

1 cup millet, rinsed

½ cup French green lentils,
rinsed and picked over

2¼ cups vegetable stock

½ cup thinly sliced bok choy

1 cup sliced snow or sugar
snap peas

1 cup asparagus, cut into 1-inch
pieces

¼ cup chopped fresh herbs,
such as parsley mixed with
chives and garlic chives

Drizzle of lemon juice

Gomasio (sesame salt), for
garnish

Millet and Lentils
WITH MUSHROOMS AND SEASONAL VEGETABLES

Millet is one of my go-to grains, especially now that the price of quinoa is skyrocketing. Use whatever vegetables are in season. I first made this in the spring with bok choy, snow peas, and asparagus. In the summer you could use green beans and summer squash. Adding fresh herbs and lemon juice at the end always lends a bright flavor note and lots of antioxidants.

Gomasio is a blend of ground, toasted sesame seeds and salt. If you don't have it, just sprinkle on toasted sesame seeds and salt to taste.

SERVES 4 TO 6

1. Heat a stovetop pressure cooker over medium heat or set an electric cooker to sauté. Add the leek, mushrooms, and garlic and dry sauté for 2 minutes. Add the millet and lentils and toast for 1 minute. Add the stock.

2. Lock the lid on the pressure cooker. Bring to high pressure; cook for 10 minutes. Let the pressure come down naturally. Remove the lid, carefully tilting it away from you.

3. Add the bok choy, peas, and asparagus. Replace the lid and let sit for 2 to 3 minutes. Check to be sure that the millet is cooked through; it should be bright yellow. If not, lock on the lid and let sit for another minute or two.

4. Stir, add the fresh herbs, and transfer to a bowl. Add the lemon juice and gomasio right before serving.

Kitchidi

(ALSO CALLED KITCHARI)

As this dish was cooking, my husband said he recognized the smell, which is like a mild curry. After it was fully cooked, with the lid off, he told me he wanted this for lunch instead of what I had already given him. Traditionally a food served in India to people who are healing or sick, kitchidi is a mild, easy-to-digest rice and bean dish that can be dressed up in a variety of ways. I don't want to be sick but love to eat this—morning, noon, or night.

SERVES 4 TO 6

1. Heat a stovetop pressure cooker over medium heat or set an electric cooker to sauté. Toast the cumin and mustard seeds in the dry cooker until they smell toasty, 3 to 5 minutes. Add the turmeric, beans, rice, and stock.

2. Lock on the lid. Bring to high pressure; cook for 12 minutes. Let the pressure come down naturally. Carefully remove the lid, tilting it away from you.

3. Transfer to a bowl or platter and add salt and pepper to taste before serving.

12 minutes high pressure, natural release

1 tablespoon cumin seeds

1 teaspoon mustard seeds

½ teaspoon ground turmeric

1 cup mung beans, soaked and drained

½ cup long-grain brown rice, such as basmati, soaked overnight and drained

1½ cups vegetable stock or water

Salt and freshly ground black pepper

MAIN COURSES

1 cup diced onion

2 to 3 cloves garlic, minced

½ cup diced celery

¼ cup diced red bell pepper

1 teaspoon minced chile pepper, such as jalapeño, optional

1 tablespoon dried oregano

2 teaspoons chili powder or paprika

1 cup small red beans (not adzuki or kidney), soaked and drained

1 cup Thai long-grain red rice

2 cups vegetable stock

Salt and freshly ground black pepper

Splash of hot sauce, optional

Chopped fresh flat-leaf parsley, for garnish

Red Rice and Beans

This is a playful take on the traditional Southern red beans and rice. You can use whatever type of red rice you like or want to try: Bhutanese, Thai, Wehani, or even French or Italian. The red rice varies in size and texture, but all add beautiful color to a dish. The key is to cook the rice for the appropriate amount of time. The instructions below are for Thai long-grain red. If using a different rice, see the Rice Cooking At-a-Glance on page 53 for amounts and cooking times.

SERVES 4 TO 6

1. Heat a stovetop pressure cooker over medium heat or set an electric cooker to sauté. Add the onion and dry sauté for 2 minutes. Add the garlic, celery, bell pepper, chile pepper, oregano, and chili powder and sauté 1 minute longer. Add the drained beans, red rice, and stock.

2. Lock on the lid. Bring to high pressure; cook for 12 minutes. Let the pressure come down naturally. Remove the lid carefully by tilting it away from you.

3. Add salt and pepper to taste, and a splash of hot sauce if desired. Transfer to a dish and garnish with parsley.

Sassy Sesame Tofu

WITH SWEET POTATO, CARROTS, AND SUGAR SNAP PEAS

Photo, page I-11

This crowd-pleasing recipe is a simple and delicious way to prepare tofu, which gets firmer under pressure and absorbs the flavors of the cooking liquid. It cooks very quickly. It's best to cook the sugar snap peas on low pressure for just a minute so they don't become mushy. The sweet and spicy sauce at the end makes it even more special. Serve this over any type of rice or other grain.

SERVES 4

1. Heat a stovetop pressure cooker over medium heat or set an electric cooker to sauté; add the sesame oil. Add the onion, carrot, and sweet potato and sauté for 2 minutes. Add the garlic and 1 tablespoon of the sesame seeds and sauté another minute. Add the tofu, tamari, vinegar, and stock.

2. Lock the lid on the cooker. Bring to high pressure; cook for 3 minutes. Quick release the pressure. Carefully remove the lid, tilting it away from you.

3. Add the peas and lock the lid back on. Bring to low pressure; cook for 1 minute. (If you do not have a low pressure option, lock the lid on and let sit for 2 to 3 minutes.) Quick release the pressure. Remove the lid, carefully tilting it away from you.

4. Stir in the pepper sauce and tahini, if using. Garnish with the remaining 1 tablespoon sesame seeds and the chopped scallion and serve.

Variations: Use broccoli florets or 1-inch pieces of green or wax beans instead of the peas. Cook at low pressure for 2 minutes with a quick release.

3 minutes high pressure, quick release; 1 minute low pressure, quick release

2 teaspoons toasted sesame oil

1 medium yellow, white, or sweet onion, sliced from top to bottom to equal about 2 cups

1 carrot, peeled and cut on the diagonal into ½-inch pieces

1 cup diced peeled sweet potato

3 cloves garlic, minced

2 tablespoons sesame seeds

1 pound extra firm tofu, cut into 1-inch cubes

1 to 2 tablespoons tamari

1 tablespoon rice vinegar

⅓ cup vegetable stock

2 cups sugar snap or snow peas, cut in half

2 tablespoons Sweet and Spicy Red Pepper Sauce (page 283) or sriracha

2 tablespoons tahini, optional, for a richer dish

2 tablespoons chopped scallion, for garnish

Dough

1⅓ cups vital wheat gluten

¼ cup chickpea flour (besan)

¼ cup nutritional yeast

1 teaspoon garlic powder

1 teaspoon dried parsley flakes, optional

½ teaspoon onion powder

½ teaspoon salt

1¼ cups vegetable stock

Broth

2 cups water

3 tablespoons tamari or soy sauce

3-inch piece of kombu

3 to 4 slices fresh ginger, optional

Chicken-Style Seitan

Seitan is the answer for those looking for a meat stand-in. However, people with a gluten intolerance—you know who you are—should run from the stuff. This chicken-y seitan works well in recipes that aren't too strongly flavored as it is rather mild. Using a pressure cooker cuts the cooking time by more than half.

MAKES 2 LARGE LOAVES OR ROLLS, ABOUT 12 OUNCES EACH

1. To make the dough: Combine all the ingredients except the stock in a large bowl. Stir in the stock with a fork and mix well for 1 to 2 minutes. Remove the dough from the bowl and knead for 1 minute. Let rest for 5 minutes.

2. While the dough is resting, make the broth: Combine all the ingredients in the pressure cooker.

3. Knead the dough, which ought to be very stiff, 5 to 10 times. Let rest another 10 to 15 minutes.

4. Divide the dough into 2 pieces, forming each into a log or roll. Add the logs to the broth in the pressure cooker, side by side if possible. (Some people like to wrap them in cheesecloth, but I have not found that necessary.)

5. Lock the lid on the cooker. Bring to high pressure; cook for 20 minutes. Let the pressure come down naturally. When the pressure has released, let the seitan sit in the cooker until cool.

6. Transfer to a bowl or container. Store, in useable sized pieces, in the broth in which it was cooked. The seitan can be stored in the broth (remove the kombu) for at least a week, or frozen whole or in pieces for up to 2 months.

Beef-Style Seitan

Seitan, essentially wheat gluten, is a savory chameleon, taking on the flavor of whatever you add when making it, and then getting infused with whatever liquid it cooks in. The basic recipe here is the same as for Chicken-Style Seitan (page 212), but flavorings in both the dough and the stock are different. And feel free to vary the flavorings other ways; if it doesn't work out perfectly, you can always grind it up to use in another dish or top it with a sauce to enhance its flavor.

It is much less expensive to make your own seitan than to buy it. You can buy chickpea flour, or make your own by grinding dried chickpeas in a high-speed blender.

MAKES 2 LARGE LOAVES OR ROLLS, ABOUT 12 OUNCES EACH

1. To make the dough: Combine all the ingredients except the stock in a large bowl. Stir in the stock with a fork and mix well for 1 to 2 minutes. Remove the dough from the bowl and knead for 1 minute. Let rest for 5 minutes.

2. While the dough is resting, make the broth: Combine all the ingredients in the pressure cooker.

3. Knead the dough, which ought to be very stiff, 5 to 10 times. Let rest for another 10 to 15 minutes.

4. Divide the dough into 2 pieces and form each into a log or roll. Add the logs to the broth in the pressure cooker, side by side if possible. (Some people like to wrap them in cheesecloth, but I have not found that necessary.)

5. Lock the lid on the cooker. Bring to high pressure; cook for 20 minutes. Let the pressure come down naturally. When the pressure has released, let the seitan sit in the cooker until cool.

6. Transfer to a bowl or container. Store, in useable sized pieces, in the broth in which it was cooked (remove the kombu), including the rehydrated tomatoes. It will last in the refrigerator for at least a week; frozen whole or in pieces, it will keep for 2 months or longer.

Dough

1⅓ cups vital wheat gluten

¼ cup chickpea flour (besan)

¼ cup nutritional yeast

2 teaspoons paprika or mild chili powder

2 teaspoons Italian seasoning, store-bought or homemade (page 41)

1 teaspoon garlic powder

½ teaspoon ground fennel seeds

½ teaspoon onion powder

¼ teaspoon cayenne pepper

½ teaspoon salt

1¼ cups vegetable stock

Broth

2 cups water

3 tablespoons tamari or soy sauce

3-inch piece of kombu

6 sun-dried tomato halves

½ cup sliced onion

2 cloves garlic, minced

MAIN COURSES

2 minutes high pressure,
quick release; 1 minute
low pressure,
quick release

1 medium onion, sliced from top to bottom

1 cup sliced crimini or shiitake mushrooms (or a mixture of both)

1 cup red pepper, sliced into thin strips

½ recipe (about 12 ounces) cooked Beef-Style Seitan (page 213) or Chicken-Style Seitan (page 212), sliced

½ cup vegetable stock

1 tablespoon tamari

2 teaspoons sriracha or other hot sauce, optional

2 teaspoons rice vinegar

1 cup sliced baby bok choy or other similar Asian greens, such as tatsoi, or 1 cup broccoli florets

1 teaspoon arrowroot powder, if necessary

1 teaspoon Sucanat or other sweetener, or to taste

½ cup scallions, sliced on the diagonal

½ cup raw cashew pieces, toasted

Say Yes to Seitan with Mushrooms and Cashews

Once you've made a batch of seitan (pages 212 and 213), you might be wondering what to do with it. This recipe uses about half a batch. You can freeze the rest or keep it submerged in liquid for up to 1 week in the refrigerator. The red peppers make this dish more attractive but if they are not in season, feel free to use carrots, sliced diagonally, instead.

SERVES 4

1. Heat a stovetop pressure cooker over medium heat or set an electric cooker to sauté. Add the onion, mushrooms, and bell pepper and dry sauté for 3 minutes. Add the seitan and stock.

2. Lock on the lid. Bring to high pressure; cook for 2 minutes. Quick release. Carefully remove the lid, tilting it away from you.

3. Add the tamari, sriracha, if using, vinegar, and bok choy. Bring to low pressure and cook for 1 minute. (If you don't have a low pressure option, lock on the lid and let sit for 2 minutes.) Release the pressure naturally. Carefully remove the lid.

4. If there is too much liquid in the pot, stir in the arrowroot. Add the sweetener, scallions, and cashews. Stir. Transfer to a dish and serve.

Seitan, Cabbage, and Shiitake Mushroom Stroganoff

This creamy comfort food satisfies any time of year, but especially in the winter. If you don't have fresh shiitake mushrooms, substitute 6 to 10 dried mushrooms. Soak them for at least 30 minutes. Drain and slice. The soy sour cream works well with other dishes, too, such as tacos, chili, soups, and stews.

SERVES 4

1. Heat a stovetop pressure cooker over medium heat or set an electric cooker to sauté; add the oil, if using. Add the onion and dry sauté for 1 minute. Add the garlic and cook another minute. Add the seitan and cook another minute, then add ¼ cup of the broth and the aminos. Add the crimini mushrooms, shiitake mushrooms, and cabbage, then pour the remaining ¼ cup broth over the ingredients.

2. Lock the lid on the pressure cooker. Bring to high pressure; cook for 4 minutes. Quick release the pressure. Remove the lid, tilting it away from you.

3. While the mixture is cooking, make the soy sour cream: Combine the tofu, lemon juice, arrowroot, miso, and sweetener, if using, in a small food processor or a blender. Blend until smooth.

4. Stir the soy sour cream into the hot mushroom mixture. The heat will cook the arrowroot and the sauce should thicken.

5. Season with pepper, garnish with parsley, and serve.

＊ **Note:** Mori-Nu silken tofu comes in 12.3-ounce boxes. You can use half for this recipe and reserve the rest for another creamy dish, such as cooked grains with vegetables. Or double the recipe and use the sour cream on your baked potatoes or in other ways. This will last up to 1 week in the refrigerator. It does not freeze well.

---

4 minutes high pressure, quick release

1 tablespoon oil, optional

2 cups finely chopped onion

3 to 4 cloves garlic, minced

8 to 12 ounces seitan, store-bought or homemade (page 212 or 213), cut into chunks or diced small

½ cup vegetable or mushroom stock, or use the dried mushroom soaking water

1 tablespoon Bragg liquid amino acids, light tamari, or soy sauce

8 ounces crimini mushrooms, sliced

6 to 10 fresh shiitake mushrooms, sliced

2 cups finely sliced green, savoy, or napa cabbage or other greens

Soy Sour Cream

6 ounces Mori-Nu lite silken firm or extra firm tofu

1 tablespoon lemon juice

1 tablespoon arrowroot powder

1 to 2 teaspoons mellow white miso, or miso of your choice

1 teaspoon Sucanat or palm sugar, optional

For Serving

Freshly ground black pepper

¼ cup chopped fresh flat-leaf parsley

1 cup diced onion

½ cup diced carrot

⅓ cup diced celery

½ cup diced turnip or peeled
sweet potato

1 cup French green lentils,
rinsed and picked over

1 teaspoon dried thyme

1 bay leaf

½ teaspoon chopped fresh
rosemary or ¼ teaspoon
dried

1¾ cups vegetable stock

1 to 2 tablespoons browned
rice flour, or other browned
flour (see Note, page 217)

1 tablespoon vegan
Worcestershire sauce

1 to 2 teaspoons tamari, to
taste

1 cup diced fresh or canned
tomatoes

1 tablespoon tomato paste,
optional

1 recipe Garlic Parsley Mashed
Potatoes

Shepherd's Pie

Photo, page I-13

The origin of shepherd's pie was the shepherd using what he, or she, had around to make a dish worth eating. Since we are shepherding in a new way of eating for many people, I have gone beyond the usual commercial meat substitute used for this dish. If you want something a bit more "meaty," try it with cut-up Beef-Style Seitan (page 213) instead of lentils. It changes the recipe quite a bit, so look at the variation below for cooking instructions.

When making this with lentils, you must cook the filling in two steps because cooking lentils with tomatoes for too long tends to toughen lentils. If you want to really change things up, considering using a sweet potato or Japanese white sweet potato mash. Any way that you serve it, it's tasty and filling, even if we aren't outside working as hard as shepherds.

SERVES 4 TO 6

1. Heat a stovetop pressure cooker over medium heat or set an electric cooker to sauté. Add the onion, carrot, and celery and dry sauté for 3 minutes. Add the turnip, lentils, thyme, bay leaf, rosemary, and stock.

2. Lock the lid on the cooker. Bring to high pressure; cook for 10 minutes. Let the pressure come down naturally. Remove the lid carefully, tilting it away from you.

3. Add 1 tablespoon of the browned flour, or 2 tablespoons if the filling seems thin, plus the Worcestershire sauce, tamari, tomatoes, and tomato paste, if using. Stir. Cook on the stove top, stirring to prevent burning; or lock the lid in place and let sit for 3 minutes. Quick release any built-up pressure.

4. Discard the bay leaf. Transfer the filling to a casserole dish or 4 or more ramekins. Top with the mashed potatoes. Run under the broiler to brown, or at least heat, the potatoes.

   Shepherd's Pie with Seitan: Reduce the stock to 1 cup. Add ½ batch, or 3 cups, chopped seitan instead of the lentils and cook at pressure for 3 minutes. Do a quick release. Continue with Step 3.

Garlic Parsley Mashed Potatoes

Pressure cooking potatoes means that making real mashed potatoes takes just minutes. Make them as lumpy or smooth as you like.

SERVES 4 TO 6

1. Add the potato pieces to a pressure cooker along with the stock and garlic.

2. Lock on the lid. Bring to high pressure. Cook for 4 minutes. Quick release the pressure. Remove the lid, carefully tilting it away from you.

3. Mash the potatoes with a potato masher or a hand blender, not an immersion blender. Depending upon the consistency you want, add all the milk or use less. Add the parsley, salt to taste, and margarine, if desired. Stir to combine. Serve hot.

Browning Flour

This simple technique allows you to flavor and thicken stews and fillings without making a traditional roux. To brown flour, add the flour to a dry skillet over medium-high heat. Let the flour sit until you smell it toasting or see the edges getting darker. When that occurs, start stirring. You will see the flour continue to darken. Stop the process when the flour smells toasty and turns brown—not quite chestnut—but don't let it burn. Transfer immediately to a bowl. You can make more than you need. Label and refrigerate. Use within a month.

4 minutes high pressure, quick release

- 4 medium Yukon Gold, yellow Finn, or russet potatoes, peeled, if desired, cut into 2-inch pieces

- 1 cup vegetable or allium stock (for homemade, see pages 157 and 161)

- 6 cloves garlic, peeled and cut in half

- ½ cup soy or other nondairy milk

- ½ cup minced flat-leaf parsley

  Salt

  Vegan margarine, optional

1 cup diced onion

½ cup grated carrot

½ red bell pepper, cored, seeded, and diced to equal ½ to ¾ cup

½ cup finely diced crimini or shiitake mushrooms, optional

3 cloves garlic, minced

½ teaspoon smoked paprika

1 teaspoon mild chili powder or paprika

½ cup grated beet, optional

1 medium apple, grated or finely chopped to equal 1 cup

1 cup dried mung beans

½ cup steel-cut oats

¼ cup finely chopped sun-dried tomatoes

2½ cups vegetable stock

3 tablespoons tomato paste

1 cup diced canned or fresh tomatoes, or 1 cup tomato sauce if you want less texture

1 tablespoon vegan Worcestershire sauce

½ to 1 teaspoon hot chili powder or chipotle powder, to taste, optional

2 teaspoons tamari, optional

Sloppy Jills

I asked people on my mailing list what recipes they'd like to see in this book. They requested sloppy joes. Although I did not grow up eating joes, I certainly understand the *sloppiness* of the iconic sandwich, so here's my best vegan take—the Sloppy Jill. If you don't like mushrooms you can omit them. (I love them.) The mung beans, steel-cut oats, and mushrooms stand in for meat, with the oats adding creaminess and the beans giving it texture. The grated beet, if using, adds color, and the apple adds sweetness and more texture. The sun-dried tomatoes add umami. Sloppy it is. If you don't want to make sandwiches, this is just as good over grains or pasta or in tacos.

SERVES 4 TO 6

1. Heat a stovetop pressure cooker over medium heat or set an electric cooker to sauté. Add the onion, carrot, bell pepper, and mushrooms, if using and dry sauté for 2 minutes. Add the garlic, smoked paprika, chili powder, beet, if using, and half the apple and cook another minute. Add the beans, oats, sun-dried tomatoes, and vegetable stock.

2. Lock on the lid. Bring to high pressure; cook for 6 minutes. Let the pressure come down naturally. Remove the lid, carefully tilting it away from you.

3. Add the remaining apple, tomato paste, diced tomatoes, Worcestershire, chili powder, and tamari, if using. Stir well. Lock the lid on the cooker and let sit for 5 minutes. Remove the lid carefully, tilting it away from you.

4. Serve traditionally on buns or as the "center of your plate" with vegetables on the side.

Sloppy Jills with Adzuki Beans: These have a sweet, nutty taste. Use adzuki beans instead of mung beans and check to see if they are done after 6 minutes.

Soba Noodles in Broth with Shiitakes, Edamame, and Spinach

Soba noodles are made with buckwheat, which is very nourishing. This soupy stew also contains mushrooms, ginger, and garlic, which boost your immune system. Buy organic mushrooms, if you can find them.

SERVES 4

1. Heat a stovetop pressure cooker over medium heat or set an electric cooker to sauté. Add the onion, mushrooms, and carrot and dry sauté for 2 to 3 minutes. Add the garlic and ginger and cook another 30 seconds, stirring to avoid sticking. Add the stock, soba noodles, edamame, and tamari to taste. Make sure that the stock covers the noodles. If not, add water to cover.

2. Lock on the lid. Bring to low pressure; cook for 2 minutes. (If you don't have a low pressure option, bring to high pressure and cook for 1 to 1½ minutes.) Quick release the pressure. Remove the lid carefully, tilting it away from you.

3. Add the spinach and stir. Add the vinegar and chili oil and stir again. Transfer to a large bowl, garnish with sesame seeds and scallions, and serve.

2 minutes low pressure, quick release

½ medium onion (cut from top to bottom), sliced

5 ounces or more shiitake mushrooms, stems removed (save them to make stock), sliced

1 carrot, julienned

2 cloves garlic, minced

1 teaspoon minced fresh ginger

3 cups mushroom stock or vegetable stock (for homemade, see pages 160 and 157)

5 to 6 ounces soba noodles

½ to 1 cup frozen (not thawed) edamame

1 to 2 tablespoons tamari or soy sauce

2 cups or more chopped fresh spinach

2 teaspoons rice or ume vinegar

Drizzle of chili oil or toasted sesame oil

2 teaspoons toasted sesame seeds, for garnish

¼ cup sliced scallions, white and green, for garnish

¼ cup vegetable stock, plus
more if needed

1 tablespoon mirin, or
1 additional tablespoon
stock

8 ounces tempeh, cut into
12 strips

1 teaspoon toasted sesame oil,
optional

2 teaspoons sesame seeds

1 large clove garlic, minced

1 teaspoon minced fresh
ginger

1 tablespoon tamari

Sesame Tempeh Sticks

Tempeh typically benefits from steaming, but the heat of the pressure cooker makes that unnecessary. In any case, tempeh is always better when it's marinated for a short time, as it is in this recipe, which can easily be doubled.

SERVES 2 TO 3 (DEPENDING UPON HOW MUCH YOU LIKE TEMPEH)

1. Combine the stock and mirin in a flat dish. Add the tempeh strips and let marinate for at least 15 minutes, turning once. Do not marinate for longer than 1 hour. If all the liquid is absorbed, add another ¼ cup stock.

2. Heat a stovetop pressure cooker over medium heat or set an electric cooker to sauté; add the sesame oil, if using. Add the sesame seeds, garlic, and ginger and cook for 30 seconds. Add the tempeh with its marinade. Drizzle the tamari on top of the tempeh. Do not stir.

3. Lock the lid on the cooker. Bring to high pressure; cook for 5 minutes. Quick release the pressure. Remove the lid carefully, tilting it away from you.

4. Transfer the tempeh to a serving dish. Drizzle with the sesame seed sauce and serve.

Jerk Tempeh Sticks: Omit the mirin. Marinate the tempeh in ¼ cup stock mixed with 1 tablespoon orange juice, 1 tablespoon lime juice, and 1 tablespoon Jerk Seasoning (page 42) for 15 to 30 minutes. In the sauté stage, omit the sesame seeds, add 2 tablespoons chopped onion, and use 2 cloves minced garlic and 2 teaspoons grated ginger, and if you choose to use oil to sauté, use a neutral oil instead of sesame oil. Tamari is optional. Use the same cooking directions, adding the marinade when cooking. Before serving, season with salt to taste and garnish with 3 tablespoons chopped scallion.

Orange Tempeh Sticks: Instead of the stock and mirin, marinate the tempeh in ½ teaspoon grated orange zest, ¼ cup orange juice, 1 tablespoon rice vinegar, 1 teaspoon grated ginger, and 2 teaspoons tamari. Omit the sesame oil, sesame seeds, garlic, ginger, and tamari. Skip the sauté step and add everything to the pressure cooker with 2 tablespoons vegetable stock. Bring to high pressure and cook 5 minutes. Quick release the pressure. Add sriracha or hot sauce, if desired. Garnish with more grated orange zest and chopped cilantro.

Cooking Pasta in Your Pressure Cooker

Using the pressure cooker to cook pasta is not the best use for this remarkable piece of equipment, yet there are many (maybe you) who want to do so. Although you want the results to be a culinary success, I cannot guarantee this, as I have cooked pasta in a pressure cooker without "perfect" results many more times than I ended up with an edible, or tasty, result.

Here are the keys to successfully cook pasta, beyond the soba or rice noodles found in this chapter.

- Tubular and heartier shapes hold up better than spaghetti or thin pasta. The rule of thumb is to cook the pasta for half the recommended time at low pressure. If your pasta would cook in 8 minutes on the stove, cook it at low pressure for 4 minutes, then do a quick release. (If you don't have low pressure, cook for half the recommended time minus 1 minute at high pressure.)

- It's possible to use gluten-free pasta but it is much trickier to do. Err on the side of less time, rather than more.

- Be sure to add enough water or stock to cover the pasta. For 1 pound of pasta, this will usually be at least 3 cups of liquid. You must determine this by looking at what's in the pot.

- If you are using tomato sauce, put it on top of other ingredients, as tomato products tend to burn with the high heat required to reach pressure.

- If your pasta requires additional cooking once you have released the pressure, simmer over medium heat or use the sauté function in your electric cooker until the pasta is cooked through. It's better to have undercooked, rather than overcooked, pasta.

- Keep track of your successes and failures so that you can repeat, or avoid, them respectively.

Spicy One-Pot Rice Noodle Bowl

WITH MUSHROOMS, EGGPLANT, AND SUMMER SQUASH

After shopping at the farmers' market on a summer day when I had skipped breakfast, all I could think about was what I would cook when I got home. My husband is not a fan of eggplant or mushrooms—or summer squash, for that matter—so what did I make, knowing that he was gone for the day? This tasty dish. There are far too many ways to vary this noodle for me to even start listing them, but let me begin: Use different vegetables.

SERVES 2 TO 4

1. Heat a stovetop pressure cooker over medium heat or set an electric cooker to sauté. Add the onion, garlic, ginger, peppers, and mushrooms and dry sauté for 3 minutes. Add the eggplant, squash, noodles, and stock. If there are any rice noodles sticking out, add more stock to cover them with liquid.

2. Lock on the lid. Bring to low pressure; cook for 3 minutes. (If you don't have a low pressure option, bring to high pressure and cook for 2 minutes.) Quick release the pressure. Carefully remove the lid, tilting it away from you.

3. Stir in the peanut butter, tamari, and chili paste, adding more liquid if the dish looks dry. Transfer to a dish or serving bowl, drizzle with lime juice, if using, and stir. Garnish with the diced tomato, cilantro, and peanuts.

3 minutes low pressure, quick release

½ cup sliced onion

2 to 3 cloves garlic, minced

1 teaspoon grated fresh ginger

¼ cup diced red or yellow bell peppers

1½ cups assorted sliced mushrooms, including crimini and shiitake, stems removed

1 cup diced eggplant (peeled if desired)

1½ cups finely diced summer squash

4 to 6 ounces thin rice noodles

1 cup vegetable stock, plus more if needed

2 tablespoons peanut butter

1 tablespoon tamari

2 to 3 teaspoons chili paste with garlic, or sriracha

Squeeze of lime, optional

½ cup diced fresh tomato, for garnish

2 tablespoons chopped cilantro, for garnish

2 tablespoons chopped peanuts, for garnish

MAIN COURSES

223

Spice Mix

4 teaspoons ground cumin

1 teaspoon ground cinnamon

1 teaspoon ground turmeric

1 teaspoon ground coriander seed

½ teaspoon ground ginger

¼ teaspoon cayenne pepper, or to taste

¼ to ½ teaspoon freshly ground black pepper

½ teaspoon salt

Marinade and Tempeh

½ cup vegetable stock

1 to 2 teaspoons Bragg liquid aminos

4 cloves garlic, minced to equal just over 1 tablespoon

½ teaspoon grated fresh ginger

8 ounces tempeh, diced

Tagine

1 large onion, chopped

Pinch of saffron, optional

2 medium carrots

2 medium sweet potatoes, peeled and cut into 2-inch dice cups

½ cup diced pitted prunes

224

Tempeh Tagine with Carrots and Sweet Potatoes

This stew is sweet and tangy with Moroccan spices. If you don't have saffron, don't worry. It adds a nice touch but it's not necessary. Don't let the long list of ingredients scare you, but don't plan to make this on a weeknight as it will take a bit longer than usual. It's such a pretty and interesting dish that it warrants serving to guests. Serve with the Harissa-Glazed Carrots with Small Green Olives (page 126) and Basic Mmmm . . . Millet (page 66) on the side.

SERVES 4 TO 6

1. Make the spice mix: Mix together all the spice ingredients in a small bowl.

2. Marinate the tempeh: Add 2 teaspoons of the spice mixture to a container large enough to hold the tempeh. Add the stock, aminos, garlic, and ginger. Stir. Add the tempeh and toss to coat. Let marinate for at least 30 minutes.

3. Make the tagine: When you are ready to cook the tempeh, heat a stovetop pressure cooker over medium heat or set an electric cooker to sauté. Add the onion and dry sauté for 2 to 3 minutes. Add the tempeh with its marinade and saffron, if using, and cook for another 3 minutes. Add the remaining spice mixture and cook 1 minute longer. Add the carrots, sweet potatoes, prunes, apricots, bay leaves, and stock.

4. Lock on the lid. Bring to high pressure; cook for 3 minutes. Quick release the pressure. Remove the lid, carefully tilting it away from you.

5. Add the tomatoes and bell pepper, if using. Lock on the lid and let sit for 3 minutes. Carefully remove the lid.

6. Remove and discard the bay leaves. Stir the contents and add the lemon juice. Transfer to a bowl or platter and sprinkle with the parsley.

Chickpea Tagine with Carrots and Sweet Potatoes: Not a big tempeh fan? Make the tagine with chickpeas. Soak 1 cup dried chickpeas for 8 to 12 hours. Drain. Instead of marinating, combine ½ cup stock with 2 teaspoons spice mixture and add to the pressure cooker with the drained chickpeas. (Omit the aminos, and set aside the marinade's garlic and ginger.) Lock on the lid, bring to high pressure, and cook for 12 minutes. Let the pressure come down naturally. Remove the lid carefully.

Add the remaining spice mix, reserved garlic and ginger, the onion, saffron, carrots, sweet potatoes, prunes, apricots, bay leaves, and stock. Do not stir. Lock on the lid, bring back to high pressure, and cook for 3 more minutes. Quick release the pressure. Add the tomatoes and bell pepper, lock on the lid, and let sit for 3 minutes.

Remove the lid. Discard the bay leaves and stir the contents, adding the lemon juice. Transfer to a bowl or platter and sprinkle with the parsley.

½ cup chopped dried apricots

2 bay leaves

1¼ cups vegetable stock

1 (15-ounce) can diced tomatoes, or 1½ cups diced fresh tomatoes

½ cup diced red bell pepper, if in season

Juice of 1 lemon

2 to 3 tablespoons chopped fresh flat-leaf parsley or cilantro, for garnish

1 cup chopped onion

3 cloves garlic, minced

1 small chile pepper, such as jalapeño or serrano, minced

1 New Mexico, Anaheim, or poblano chile, diced

8 ounces tempeh, cut into small chunks

1 tablespoon tamari

2¼ cups chopped tomatillos

1 cup Kamut, soaked (overnight or all day, for at least 8 hours) and drained

1 cup vegetable stock

1 cup fresh corn cut from cob, or frozen (not thawed) corn

Lime wedges, for serving

Chunks of avocado, for serving

Chopped cilantro, for serving

Tempeh and Tomatillo Stew

I like to think of this as chili verde thanks to the tomatillos and garnishes of avocado, lime, and cilantro, although the addition of a grain makes it more like a stew. You can substitute other whole grains if you like, but you must adjust the cooking time accordingly (see Grain Cooking At-a-Glance, page 51). Any whole brown grains are best when they have been soaked overnight. If you have any nondairy yogurt around, a dollop would be a wonderful addition.

SERVES 4 TO 6

1. Heat a stovetop pressure cooker over medium heat or set an electric cooker to sauté. Add the onion and dry sauté for 1 to 2 minutes, adding some of the stock if necessary to prevent sticking. Add the garlic and all the chiles and cook another minute. Add the tempeh and tamari and cook 1 minute longer. Add 1¼ cups of the tomatillos, the Kamut, and stock.

2. Lock on the lid. Bring to high pressure; cook for 15 minutes. Let the pressure drop naturally. If there is still pressure after 15 minutes, do a careful quick release. Remove the lid carefully, tilting it away from you.

3. Add the corn. Close the lid and let sit for 2 minutes. Carefully remove the lid. Stir, adding the remaining 1 cup tomatillos.

4. Transfer to a serving dish and serve with lime wedges, avocado, and cilantro.

Vegetable Chickpea Pie

This vegetable pie is creamy and cheesy tasting. It is easy to put together, as long as you have chickpea flour. Don't have any? Use a high-speed blender (not the food processor) to finely grind whole dried chickpeas until they look like flour or fine powder. Vary the vegetables, according to what's in season. And feel free to change the seasonings to suit your menu. The sun-dried tomatoes add umami flavor.

SERVES 4 TO 6

1. Spray the inside of a 1½- or 2-quart casserole dish that will fit inside your pressure cooker with cooking spray. Add 1½ cups water to the pressure cooker. Add a trivet or rack to elevate the dish above the water (see page 14). Create a helper handle (see page 15) to enable you to remove the casserole, and set on the trivet.

2. Drain the sun-dried tomatoes and reserve the soaking water. Dice the tomatoes.

3. Add the onion, squash, herbs, sun-dried tomatoes, and bell pepper (in that order) to the bottom of the casserole dish.

4. In a large bowl, combine the chickpea flour, arrowroot, baking powder, nutritional yeast, seasoning, paprika, salt, and pepper.

5. In a small bowl, combine the tomato soaking water with enough stock to equal 1½ cups, then add the garlic and olive oil, if using.

6. Mix the liquid ingredients into the dry ingredients. Whisk well. The batter ought to be like pancake batter. Pour the batter over the vegetables in the casserole.

7. Lower the dish into the pressure cooker and cover the dish. Lock on the lid. Bring to high pressure; cook for 25 minutes. Let the pressure come down naturally. Carefully remove the lid, and then remove the casserole from the pressure cooker.

8. Let cool on a rack for a few minutes. Turn out of the container onto a serving plate. Slice and serve.

Vegetable cooking spray

¼ cup sun-dried tomatoes, soaked in ½ cup boiling water for 20 to 30 minutes until soft

1 cup finely diced red onion

½ cup diced zucchini or other summer squash or vegetables

2 tablespoons chopped fresh basil or other green herb

½ cup finely diced red bell pepper

1¼ cups chickpea flour (besan)

2 tablespoons arrowroot or potato starch

½ teaspoon baking powder

3 tablespoons nutritional yeast

2 teaspoons all-purpose seasoning; or 1 teaspoon dried thyme plus ½ teaspoon dried sage plus ½ teaspoon sweet paprika

½ teaspoon smoked paprika or chipotle powder

½ teaspoon salt

Pinch of freshly ground black pepper

About 1¼ cups vegetable stock

4 cloves garlic, minced

1 tablespoon olive oil, optional

MAIN COURSES

227

2 cups finely chopped onion

2 cups cubed butternut or other winter squash (roughly 2-inch pieces)

1 cup adzuki beans, soaked and drained

½ cup diced peeled daikon radish

¼ cup finely chopped sun-dried tomatoes

1 teaspoon coriander seeds

½ to 1 teaspoon chipotle powder

1¼ cups vegetable stock

Salt and freshly ground black pepper

Drizzle of rice vinegar

Winter Squash and Adzuki Bean Stew

There is nothing like the combination of beans and squash, which is why they make up two-thirds of the Three Sisters so beloved by Native Americans. They, of course, did not use adzuki beans, which hail from Japan and are a natural companion for winter squash.

With a few simple additions, this turns into Adzuki Squash Burgers (page 233). Make a double batch if you want to serve it as a stew and then later make into burgers.

SERVES 4 TO 6

1. Heat a stovetop pressure cooker over medium heat or set an electric cooker to sauté. Add the onion and dry sauté for 2 to 3 minutes. Add the squash, beans, daikon, sun-dried tomatoes, coriander, chipotle powder to taste, and stock.

2. Lock on the lid. Bring to high pressure; cook for 4 minutes. Let the pressure come down naturally. Carefully remove the lid, tilting it away from you.

3. Season the stew with salt and pepper to taste. Drizzle with vinegar before serving.

Winter Squash, Millet, and Greens One-Pot

Here is a flexible one-pot dish of beans, greens, and grains made even heartier with winter squash. You can easily make this into soup by adding more stock and some canned diced tomatoes. Customize it further by varying the spice mix—using Italian seasoning, garam masala, harissa, or any blend that strikes your fancy (see Chapter 3 for recipes). If you prefer sweet potato to winter squash, substitute it in the same quantity. If you like smoky flavors like I do, add a little smoked salt to boost the flavor of this dish.

SERVES 4 TO 6

1. Heat a stovetop pressure cooker over medium heat or set an electric cooker to sauté; add the oil, if using. Add the leek and cook for 1 to 2 minutes. Add the cumin, oregano, and paprika and cook 1 more minute. Add the beans, millet, squash, stock, and kombu.

2. Lock on the lid. Bring to high pressure; cook for 10 minutes. Let the pressure come down naturally. Remove the lid, carefully tilting it away from you.

3. Add the greens; do not stir. Lock the lid back on and let sit for 5 minutes. Release any built-up pressure and remove the lid, carefully tilting it away from you.

4. Using tongs, remove the kombu (discard or use in another dish). Add salt and pepper to taste. Add the smoked salt and hot sauce, if desired.

1 to 2 teaspoons olive oil, optional

½ cup chopped leek or onion

2 teaspoons ground cumin

1 teaspoon dried oregano

½ to 1 teaspoon smoked paprika

1 cup dried kidney, black, or pinto beans, soaked and drained

½ cup millet, rinsed

1 cup chopped peeled winter squash, such as butternut or acorn

1½ cups vegetable stock

1 (3-inch) piece of kombu

2 cups finely sliced greens, such as kale or collards

Salt and freshly ground black pepper

Pinch of smoked salt, optional

Hot sauce, optional

MAIN COURSES

NINE

Burgers, Patties, *and* Savory Cakes

Now is the time to put all the bean and grain pressure cooking you've mastered to good use by making a variety of burgers, patties, and savory cakes. If you don't typically make your own vegan burgers, you will be amazed at how easy to make and how tasty homemade patties can be. In fact, once you begin, I bet you'll quickly want to try more flavor combinations—and there are plenty here to inspire.

I live for the 3 Rs: reduce, reuse, and recycle. That's mostly what this chapter is about, as many of the recipes use already cooked beans and grains that you have on hand. (In fact, should you end up with any overcooked bean or grain dishes, burgers, patties, or loaves can be the new incarnation.) Others have a base recipe or additional ingredients that are pressure cooked.

On my burger-making adventures I don't hesitate to use what's in the refrigerator or freezer to come up with a new creation. While you might need a little bit of experience with different ingredients to combine them successfully every time, you can often swap in a different bean or grain in a burger mixture to change the texture, or substitute spices and spice blends to adjust the flavor. There are many other swaps that make burger-making work. See The Basics, page 232, for more on this.

I prefer to bake my burgers rather than pan-fry them because I can easily and quickly slide all of them into the oven at once rather than cook in batches. Using a silicone mat on a baking sheet also works, but I prefer unbleached parchment. Cleanup is a breeze.

The convenience of having cooked burgers handy in the fridge or freezer usually inspires me to make another batch. They can be wrapped and refrigerated for a few days. Or cool, wrap in waxed paper or parchment, and slip into a plastic bag or a glass container and store in the freezer for up to 3 months' time.

To reheat burgers, I generally pop them in the regular, or toaster, oven. Some can be pan-fried. Vegan burgers are often tricky to grill, but you are welcome to try. The microwave is a fast way to defrost and heat burgers.

Burgers are the tastiest form of reuse I can imagine, which yields endless creative opportunities. Consider them for daily fare or perhaps serve them to guests, as I did when I began.

The Basics: Bean Burgers, Cakes, or Patties (and Even Loaves)

There are a number of simple steps to making good burgers, cakes, patties, and loaves.

1. Start with any of your favorite beans, and cook until very tender.

2. Add a cooked grain, uncooked rolled oats, polenta, cornmeal or grits, bulgur wheat, steel-cut oats, or bread or cracker crumbs. The stickier the grain, the easier it is to make into patties. If the beans are very moist, like brown lentils, then you will need to add something firmer, such as rolled oats, to absorb the moisture.

3. Add chopped fresh or dried herbs and spices to taste. The flavors often get muted so add a bit more spice than you think that you need. If you use salt, add it to taste.

4. Mix in your choice of aromatics, such as onions (chopped, minced, or grated), minced or grated garlic, minced or grated ginger, minced chiles, chopped sun-dried tomatoes (rehydrated and drained), or chopped dried mushrooms or powdered mushrooms.

5. Add cooked vegetables. This is where you can get creative. Most cooked vegetables will work, as long as they are not too wet (often the case with summer squash). Mushrooms must be well cooked if you want to add them. Potatoes of any type, white or sweet, work well, as does winter squash, cauliflower, broccoli, and eggplant.

6. Add tahini, another nut butter, or chopped or ground nuts or seeds.

7. Bind the entire mixture with ground flax, chia seeds, or psyllium husk. Add 3 tablespoons to ¼ cup water or stock and let sit until gooey, then blend in. If your bean mixture is very moist you can stir the ground seeds right in without liquid and the seeds will absorb liquid and bind the ingredients together, resulting in a firmer end product. Chickpea flour can also be used this way, but it adds its flavor whereas the flavor of the seeds blends right in.

8. To form burgers, patties, or cakes, use wet hands to shape the burger mixture, or pack into a dry ⅓-cup, ½-cup, or larger measuring cup, turn out, and use damp hands to flatten into patties. You can also pack the mixture into the lid of a wide mouth canning jar lined with plastic wrap; the mixture will come out easily.

9. To bake, place the burgers on a baking sheet lined with parchment sprayed with vegetable spray (or not), or lined with a silicone mat. Bake in a 350° to 400°F oven for 20 to 30 minutes, turning the burgers halfway through cooking. Serve as is, or let cool and freeze, wrapped in waxed paper and sealed in bags, to enjoy at another time. Most burgers will keep in the freezer for at least 3 months but it's unlikely that they will be hanging around that long.

10. To make any of the burger mixtures into loaves, the base mixture needs to be thicker, which you can do by adding more beans and grains, and limiting wet vegetables. Spray a 1- to 2-quart lidded heatproof container that will fit in your pressure cooker with cooking spray, if desired, then pack in the burger mixture—there are also nice 2-cup square and rectangular containers that work well for this. Be aware that you will only be able to pack about 2 to 4 cups of the loaf mixture into most of the dishes. (If you like, turn the rest into firm burgers.) Be sure to cover the dish. Add 1½ cups water to a pressure cooker, along with a trivet or rack. Make a helper handle (see page 15), and put it into the cooker on the rack or trivet. Lower the filled container into the pressure cooker. Lock on the lid. Bring to high pressure and cook for 20 to 25 minutes. Let the pressure come down naturally. Carefully open the cooker, tilting the lid away from you, and lift the dish out using mitts and the helper handle. Or you can bake the loaves in a 350°F oven for 25 to 35 minutes, depending on the size and composition of the loaf.

Adzuki Squash Burgers

The combination of adzuki beans and squash works just as well in this soft-textured burger as it does in the original recipe for the stew. Here it's rounded out with greens and oats and a hint of chipotle powder to make a sweet and savory burger that satisfies. If you like smoky heat, feel free to double the amount of chipotle powder.

MAKES 6 TO 8 BURGERS

1. Heat the oven to 375°F. Line a baking sheet with parchment paper and spray with cooking spray if desired; or line the sheet with a silicone baking mat.

2. Combine all ingredients, starting with ½ cup "baby" oats, in a large bowl and mash a bit while mixing. Let stand for at least 10 minutes. If the mixture still feels wet, add the remaining "baby" oats, two tablespoons at a time until you have a firm mixture that holds together.

3. With wet hands, form the mixture into 6 or 8 burgers and place on the prepared baking sheet. Bake for 15 minutes. Turn and bake another 15 minutes, until firm and crisp.

4. Let sit for 5 minutes. Serve hot or wrap to store or freeze.

Vegetable cooking spray, optional

Winter Squash and Adzuki Bean Stew (page 228)

½ cup firmly packed, finely chopped kale or collard leaves (stems removed)

½ cup steel-cut oats

½ to 1 cup "baby" or regular oats, but not quick oats

2 tablespoons rice vinegar

¼ teaspoon chipotle powder or chili powder

The Way the Burger Crumbles

Of course we all want our food to turn out perfectly, looking like the photos seen in cookbooks and blogs, but that doesn't always happen. Like life, cooking has its ups and downs.

Don't despair if your burgers fall apart; the crumbles have a place in your life, in your kitchen, and on your plate. Use them in tacos and on salads. Or make lettuce wraps. They can be mixed into tomato sauce and served on pasta or your favorite whole grain. They are still quite versatile, even when they can't be contained inside a bun.

Some people take the burger crumbles and re-form them, packing them into mini-muffin tins and baking them. You might decide to mix them with other ingredients and form a loaf or not-meatballs. The ideas for what to do with your burger crumbles are limited only by your imagination.

Vegetable cooking spray,
optional

1 tablespoon grapeseed or
other neutral oil, optional

1 cup coarsely chopped onion

½ cup chopped celery

3 cloves garlic, minced

½ cup quinoa, rinsed

1 cup dried black beans,
soaked and drained

1¼ cups vegetable stock

1 large bay leaf

2 tablespoons Italian
seasoning, store-bought or
homemade (page 41)

1 teaspoon dried oregano
leaves, or 1 tablespoon fresh
oregano

¼ cup packed fresh flat-leaf
parsley

2 tablespoons lemon juice

2 tablespoons tomato paste

½ cup sunflower seeds

¼ cup nutritional yeast

3 tablespoons ground flax
seeds

Pinch of cayenne pepper

Black Bean and Quinoa Burgers

When I first started making burgers regularly, this was my go-to burger combo because I usually had cooked black beans and quinoa on hand. I later discovered that quinoa and black beans can easily be cooked together, which makes these burgers even more convenient.

MAKES 8 TO 10 BURGERS

1. Heat the oven to 350°F. Line a baking sheet with parchment paper and spray with cooking spray, if desired; or line the sheet with a silicone baking mat.

2. Heat a stovetop pressure cooker over medium heat or set an electric cooker to sauté; add the oil, if using. Add the onion, celery, and garlic and cook for 2 minutes. Add the quinoa and cook for a minute or two, until the quinoa gets toasty. Add the beans, stock, bay leaf, Italian seasoning, and oregano and stir well.

3. Lock the lid on the cooker. Bring to high pressure; cook for 7 minutes. Let the pressure come down naturally. Carefully remove the lid, tilting it away from you.

4. Taste the mixture to be sure that the beans are cooked through. If they are not, lock on the lid, bring back to pressure, and cook for 1 minute; then let the pressure come down naturally. Or lock on the lid and let sit for 5 minutes.

5. Transfer the bean mixture to a large bowl and let sit until cool enough to handle. Remove and discard the bay leaf.

6. Add half the mixture to the food processor along with the parsley, lemon juice, tomato paste, and sunflower seeds. Pulse a few times. Return the processed mixture to the bowl with the remaining bean mixture, and add the nutritional yeast, ground flax, and cayenne. Stir and let sit for at least 5 minutes.

7. Using wet hands, shape the mixture into 8 to 10 burgers. Place on the prepared baking sheet. Bake for 15 minutes. Turn and bake another 10 minutes, until the burgers are crisp. Let sit for a few minutes before serving, or let them cool and freeze for up to 3 months.

Cauliflower and Chickpea Burgers

Cauliflower has finally gained status as an everyday vegetable. Use the orange "cheddar" variety, if you can find it, although white works well, too. Two-minute pressure-cooked cauliflower gets soft enough to add moisture to the tasty gluten-free burger. Until now, I found most chickpea burgers too dry, but not this one. The chile pepper is optional. For me, the spice is essential. But I have always been known to be a "hot head."

MAKES 6 BURGERS

1. Heat the oven to 400 °F. Line a baking sheet with parchment paper and spray with cooking spray, if desired; or line the sheet with a silicone baking mat.

2. Heat a stovetop pressure cooker over medium heat or set an electric cooker to sauté; spray with cooking spray, if desired. Add the onion and cook for 2 minutes, adding some of the water if the onion starts to stick. Add half the garlic, the bell pepper, and chile pepper, if using and cook another minute. Add the remaining water and cauliflower.

3. Lock the lid on the pressure cooker. Bring to high pressure; cook for 2 minutes. Quick release the pressure. Carefully remove the lid, tilting it away from you.

4. Transfer the cooked mixture to a large bowl. Add the chickpeas, cornmeal, chia seeds, tahini, mustard, lemon juice, cumin, and cilantro and stir well.

5. Add half the chickpea mixture to a food processor and pulse 10 times, until well combined but not completely smooth.

6. Using a fork or potato masher, mash the remaining chickpea mixture in the bowl. Transfer the processed mixture back to the bowl and combine well. Let sit for at least 5 minutes.

7. Scoop out and form into 6 burgers. Place on the prepared baking sheet. Bake for 30 minutes, turning the burgers once, until golden brown. Let sit for a few minutes to cool before serving. Store in the refrigerator for up to 3 days or in the freezer for up to 3 months.

Vegetable cooking spray, optional

1 cup minced red onion

4 cloves garlic, minced

½ cup diced red bell pepper

1 tablespoon minced chile, such as jalapeño or serrano, optional

½ cup water or vegetable stock

1½ cups chopped cauliflower florets (about ½ medium head)

2 cups well-cooked chickpeas (see Bean Cooking At-a-Glance, page 95)

½ cup medium-grind cornmeal or polenta

2 tablespoons ground chia seeds

2 tablespoons tahini

2 tablespoons prepared mustard

2 tablespoons lemon juice

1 tablespoon ground cumin

¼ cup chopped cilantro

*2 minutes high pressure,
quick release*

1 cup diced onion

1½ cups diced shiitake
mushrooms (stems removed)

3 cloves garlic, minced

1 tablespoon tamari

2 tablespoons water or
vegetable stock

2 cups cooked hull-less barley

2 tablespoons nutritional yeast

2 tablespoons chopped sun-
dried tomatoes

2 tablespoons ground chia
seeds

2 tablespoons vegan
Worcestershire sauce

3 tablespoons chopped
walnuts or other nuts

3 tablespoons chopped fresh
flat-leaf parsley

½ cup chickpea flour (besan)

½ teaspoon freshly ground
black pepper

Barley, Shiitake, and Walnut Burgers

Make these tasty burgers when you have leftover barley, which will be the case if you make the Gingery Barley Salad (page 60). Or you can cook hull-less barley according to the directions in Grain Cooking At-a-Glance, page 51.

MAKES 6 MEDIUM-SIZED BURGERS

1. Heat the oven to 400°F. Line a baking sheet with parchment and spray with vegetable cooking spray, if desired; or line the sheet with a silicone baking mat.

2. Heat a stovetop pressure cooker over medium heat or set an electric cooker to sauté. Add the onion and mushrooms and dry sauté for 1 to 2 minutes, adding some of the water if necessary to prevent sticking. Add two-thirds of the garlic, the tamari, and remaining water.

3. Lock the lid on the pressure cooker. Bring to high pressure; cook for 2 minutes. Quick release the pressure. Carefully remove the lid, tilting it away from you. Let the contents cool for a few minutes.

4. Combine the remaining garlic, the barley, nutritional yeast, sun-dried tomatoes, chia seeds, Worcestershire, walnuts, and parsley in a food processor and pulse a few times, until just combined.

5. Add the sautéed onion and mushroom mixture to the food processor and pulse a few more times, until the mixture is well combined but still has visible barley grains. Transfer to a bowl and stir in the chickpea flour and pepper. Let sit for 5 to 10 minutes to firm up.

6. Using wet hands or a measuring cup, form the mixture into 6 medium-sized burgers. Transfer to the prepared baking sheet. Bake for 15 minutes. Turn and bake 15 minutes longer, until crisp on the outside.

7. Serve hot, let cool to grill later, or freeze for up to 3 months.

Walnut, Mushroom, and Lentil Burgers

If the earthy flavors of mushrooms, walnuts, and lentils wow you as they do me, you'll find that what these burgers lack in looks is made up for in taste.

MAKES 6 BURGERS

1. To make the base: Heat a stovetop pressure cooker over medium heat or set an electric cooker to sauté. Add the onion and dry sauté for 1 minute. Add the crimini and shiitake mushrooms and cook another minute. Add the lentils, quinoa, and stock.

2. Lock the lid on the cooker. Bring to high pressure; cook for 10 minutes. Let the pressure come down naturally. Carefully remove the lid, tilting it away from you. Transfer the mixture to a large bowl and let sit until cool enough to handle.

3. Heat the oven to 400°F. Line a baking sheet with parchment paper and spray with cooking spray if desired; or use a silicone baking mat.

4. While the base mixture is cooking, process ½ cup of the walnuts in a food processor until well chopped but still chunky. Transfer to a small bowl and set aside.

5. Add the garlic to the food processor and process until minced. Add half of the burger base along with the remaining ¼ cup walnuts, the crimini and shiitake mushrooms, onion, parsley, miso, and vinegar. Process for about 20 seconds, until the mixture is smooth. Add the chia seeds and black pepper and pulse a few times. The mixture will be sticky.

6. Mash the remaining burger base with a fork or a potato masher until broken down a bit. Add the processed burger mix and the reserved chopped walnuts. Mix everything thoroughly.

7. Using a scoop or measuring cup, measure ¾ cup of the mixture. With wet hands, form into a patty and put on the prepared baking sheet. Repeat with the remaining mixture to make 6 burgers.

8. Bake for 15 minutes. Turn the burgers and bake another 15 minutes, until brown and crispy on the outside. Let them sit for a few minutes before serving or storing in the refrigerator for up to 5 days or for up to 3 months in the freezer.

10 minutes high pressure, natural release

Burger Base

½ cup diced red onion

2 ounces crimini mushrooms, sliced

2 ounces shiitake mushrooms, stems removed, sliced

⅔ cup French green lentils, rinsed and picked over

⅓ cup quinoa, rinsed

1½ cups vegetable stock or water

Additions

Vegetable cooking spray, optional

¾ cup walnuts

2 cloves garlic, peeled

2 ounces crimini mushrooms, sliced

2 ounces shiitake mushrooms, stems removed and sliced

½ cup diced red onion

½ cup packed fresh flat-leaf parsley or baby arugula

1 tablespoon white or other miso

1 tablespoon red wine or other vinegar

2 tablespoons ground chia or flax seeds

½ teaspoon black pepper

BURGERS

237

Quinoa, Squash, and Apple Cakes

WITH WINE AND CASHEW-CREAM SAUCE

Vegetable cooking spray or 2 tablespoons oil, optional

1 cup shredded summer squash (about ½ medium)

1 medium to large Pink Pearl or other not-too-sweet apple, grated*

½ cup grated onion

2 cups cooked quinoa (see Grain Cooking At-a-Glance, page 51), cooled

1 teaspoon grated fresh ginger

1 small jalapeño chile pepper, seeds removed (or not), chopped

½ teaspoon salt

1 to 2 teaspoons curry powder

Freshly ground black pepper

Wine and Cashew-Cream Sauce (recipe follows)

These sweet and savory cakes are delicious on their own or with the sauce. I concocted this recipe to serve to a group of two hundred people at a fancy late summer wine event. They were a big hit, as each cake provides a few tasty bites. If you prefer to make them larger you can, but increase the cooking time to a total of 25 to 30 minutes. If you like them spicy, add some jalapeño to the quinoa/squash mixture.

MAKES 24 (2-INCH) CAKES

1. Heat the oven to 400°F. Line a baking sheet with parchment paper and spray with cooking spray, if desired; brush the oil onto the parchment; or leave the parchment bare. Combine the grated squash, apple, and onion in a large bowl. Set aside.

2. Combine the quinoa, ginger, jalapeño, if using, salt, and curry powder to taste in a food processor fitted with the standard chopping blade. Process until the quinoa is still a bit crunchy, about 10 seconds.

3. Add the quinoa mixture to the squash mixture in the bowl, add black pepper to taste, and stir. Let the mixture sit for a few minutes.

4. With wet hands, form the mixture into 24 cakes. Put the cakes on the prepared baking sheet. If you sprayed or oiled the sheet, spray or oil the tops of the cakes once you put them down.

5. Bake for 15 minutes. Turn the cakes and bake another 5 minutes, until crispy. The cakes tend to firm up when allowed to sit for at least 5 minutes. Serve warm or hot, drizzled with sauce.

*You can quickly grate the squash, apple, and onion with the shredding blade of the food processor; grate each separately and measure out what you need.

Wine and Cashew-Cream Sauce

This is an easy sauce to make and can be flavored many different ways—with curry, smoked paprika, or Italian herbs—or served just as it is. It also tastes great drizzled on cooked vegetables or grains, or even as a pasta topping. To grind cashews, place in a coffee grinder or blender and blend until powdered.

MAKES ABOUT 1½ CUPS

1. Combine the milk, water, and nutritional yeast in a 1-quart or larger saucepan. Bring to a boil over medium high heat, being careful not to let it boil over. Add the salt and pepper to taste.

2. Whisk in the ground cashews. Continue to cook, whisking, for a minute, until the mixture thickens. Stir in the wine. You can use the sauce at this point, or cook it for 1 to 2 minutes to evaporate the alcohol. Taste and adjust the seasonings. If the mixture seems too thick, add more water, wine, or milk.

½ cup soy or other nondairy milk

1 cup water

¼ cup nutritional yeast

½ teaspoon salt

Freshly ground black pepper

½ cup finely ground cashews or cashew meal

½ cup white wine

Brown Rice and Lentils

2 cups brown basmati rice,
soaked overnight in 3 cups
water

3¼ cups vegetable stock or
water

¾ cup French green lentils,
rinsed and picked over

Patties

Vegetable cooking spray,
optional

½ large leek, chopped to equal
at least 1 cup

¼ cup cilantro or fresh flat-leaf
parsley

1 stalk green garlic or 2 cloves
garlic, chopped

1½ cups cooked black beans
(see Bean Cooking At-a-
Glance, page 95)

1½ cups cooked winter squash

2 tablespoons ground cumin

3 tablespoons shelled hemp
seeds or sunflower seeds

½ teaspoon salt, optional

1 to 2 tablespoons oil, optional

Green Garlic–Cilantro Sauce
(recipe follows)

Rice, Bean, and Squash Pat-a-Cakes
WITH GREEN GARLIC-CILANTRO SAUCE

There are a number of steps to making these burgers, but it's worth it as
you end up with cakes or burgers with complex texture and flavor. Don't let
making this overwhelm you. If you don't want to bother cooking the rice and
lentils together, use any type of plain cooked brown rice instead and mix with
already cooked lentils, or just use 5 cups of cooked brown rice.

MAKES 30 SMALL CAKES OR 12 LARGE BURGERS

1. To make the rice and lentils: Drain the rice. Add rice, stock, and
   lentils to the pressure cooker.

2. Lock on the lid. Bring to high pressure; cook for 15 minutes. Let the
   pressure come down naturally. Remove the lid carefully, tilting it
   away from you. Let the mixture cool a bit. (You should have about
   6 cups rice and lentils, more than the 5 cups you need for the
   recipe—save the extra for another use.)

3. To make the patties: Preheat the oven to 350°F. Line a baking
   sheet with parchment paper and spray with cooking spray, if
   desired; or line the sheet with a silicone baking mat.

4. Combine the leek, cilantro, and garlic in a food processor and pulse
   until finely chopped. Add 4 cups of the rice and lentils, the beans,
   squash, and cumin. Pulse until the mixture comes together into a
   mass.

5. Transfer to a bowl. Add another cup of the rice and lentils, the
   hemp seeds, and salt, if using, and stir well. Scoop the burger
   mixture out with wet hands or a ¼-cup scoop to make 30 small
   patties; or use about ⅔-cup portions to make 12 larger patties.
   Brush the tops of the patties with oil, if using, and place oil-side
   down on the prepared baking sheet.

6. Bake for 15 minutes or until golden brown on the bottom. Turn
   the patties over carefully. Bake another 10 to 15 minutes, until
   the patties are browned on both sides. Serve with the sauce. The
   burgers will keep for 3 days in the refrigerator. Freeze any extra
   burgers for up to 3 months.

Green Garlic–Cilantro Sauce

This is a zippy and versatile sauce that enhances the flavor of the rice and bean burgers, but you'll probably also find other ways to use it. Green garlic is the immature bulb of garlic that looks like a leek or scallion but has mild garlicky flavor. The entire stalk is edible. If you love cilantro, as I do, you'll want to make a double batch. You can freeze this for up to 3 months.

MAKES ABOUT ⅓ CUP

Combine the garlic and cilantro in the bowl of a mini food processor or a blender and process until chopped. Add the sunflower seeds and process again. Add the citrus juices to taste, and blend until the mixture starts getting smooth. Add water or stock to make a creamy sauce. Taste and adjust seasoning.

1 stalk green garlic or 2 cloves garlic, coarsely chopped

½ cup packed cilantro, mostly leaves

3 tablespoons sunflower seeds

1 to 2 tablespoons lime juice

1 to 2 tablespoons orange juice

Water or vegetable stock, as needed

Mung Beans

1½ cups mung beans, soaked
and drained

2½ cups water

Millet and Amaranth

¾ cup millet

¼ cup amaranth

2 cups vegetable stock or
water

For Moroccan Patties

Vegetable cooking spray,
optional

1 cup cooked mung beans
(above)

1 cup cooked millet and
amaranth (above)

2 teaspoons berbere spice
blend, store-bought or
homemade (page 36)

1½ tablespoons psyllium husks

2 tablespoons lemon juice

1 cup grated sweet potato
(about ⅓ of a large sweet
potato)

¼ cup chopped cilantro

¼ cup currants

¼ cup sliced almonds, lightly
chopped

Salt and freshly ground black
pepper

Mung and Millet Burgers, Two Ways

Here is a great example of how varying a few seasonings can completely change a recipe. It's hard to believe these two burgers are essentially the same recipe, but they both use the same basic mixture of cooked mung beans and millet mixed with amaranth.

The recipe makes 3 cups each of beans, millet, and amaranth—enough to make 3 batches of either of the versions below.

MAKES 3 CUPS BEANS AND 3 CUPS MILLET AND AMARANTH

1. To make the beans: Add the beans and water to the pressure cooker. Lock on the lid. Bring to high pressure; cook for 8 minutes. Let the pressure come down naturally, then let the pot rest undisturbed for 10 minutes. Carefully remove the lid, turning it away from you. Transfer the beans to a bowl.

2. To make the millet and amaranth: Combine the millet, amaranth, and stock in the pressure cooker. Lock on the lid. Bring to high pressure; cook for 10 minutes. Let the pressure come down naturally. Carefully remove the lid, tilting it away from you. Use this base to make 3 batches of either of the following recipes; freeze the remainder for up to 3 months.

MOROCCAN MUNG AND MILLET PATTIES

These burgers are flavorful and full of texture with just a hint of spice from the berbere. The currants and sweet potato balance the tang of the spice and lemon juice.

MAKES 10 SMALL PATTIES

1. Heat the oven to 375°F. Line a baking sheet with parchment paper and spray with cooking spray, if desired; or line the sheet with a silicone baking mat.

2. Combine ¾ cup of the mung beans and the millet and amaranth mixture in a food processor. Add the berbere and process with a few pulses. Add the psyllium husks and lemon juice and pulse briefly once more.

3. Transfer to a bowl and add the remaining ¼ cup mung beans, the grated sweet potato, cilantro, currants, almonds, and salt and pepper to taste. Stir well to combine. Let sit for 5 minutes. Form the mixture into 10 small patties. Place on the prepared baking sheet. Bake for 15 minutes. Turn the patties and bake another 10 minutes, until golden brown.

4. Let cool for a few minutes, then serve; or wrap for the refrigerator or freezer.

SESAME MUNG AND MILLET BURGERS WITH PEAS

These Asian-style burgers have an incredible depth of flavor and also look great with the flecks of black sesame and the bright green peas.

MAKES 6 LARGE BURGERS

1. Heat the oven to 375°F. Line a baking sheet with parchment paper and spray with cooking spray if desired; or line the sheet with a silicone baking mat.

2. Add the ginger, garlic, and scallions to a food processor and pulse a few times. Add ¾ cup mung beans and 1 cup cooked millet and amaranth to the processor. Pulse a few times. Add the vinegar, chia seeds, and sesame oil. Pulse 2 more times.

3. Transfer the mixture to a bowl with the grated sweet potato, the remaining mung beans, and remaining millet. Mix together while adding the sesame seeds and green peas.

4. Let sit for 5 minutes and then form into 6 patties with wet hands. Place on prepared baking sheet.

5. Bake for 15 minutes, then turn them over. Bake for another 15 minutes. Let set for a few minutes and serve hot, or wrap for storing in the refrigerator or freezer

For Sesame Burgers

Vegetable cooking spray, optional

1-inch piece ginger root, peeled and minced

3 cloves garlic, roughly chopped

2 scallions, sliced

1 cup cooked mung beans (above)

1½ cups cooked millet and amaranth (above)

2 teaspoons unseasoned rice vinegar

2 tablespoons ground chia seeds

2 teaspoons hot or regular toasted sesame oil

1 cup grated sweet potato

1 tablespoon black sesame seeds

½ frozen green peas, thawed

1 cup minced onion

2 teaspoons grated fresh ginger

1 cup minced mushrooms, such as shiitake (stems removed) or crimini

1 cup red lentils, rinsed and picked over

1½ sweet potatoes, peeled and cut into large pieces (1 medium)

2¼ cups vegetable stock

Vegetable cooking spray, optional

¼ cup hemp seeds

¼ cup finely chopped fresh flat-leaf parsley

¼ cup finely chopped cilantro

1 tablespoon curry powder

1 cup "baby" or quick oats

1 to 4 tablespoons brown rice flour, if needed

Red Lentil, Sweet Potato, and Hemp Burgers

Photo, page I-10

When I first made these burgers, in a class I was teaching, everyone loved the flavor, but also that they were packed with nutrition. I have to agree that they are mighty tasty, and they are easy to make for a quick weeknight meal. If you do not like curry, season instead with a tablespoon of Salt-Free Spicy Mix (page 45), store bought all-purpose seasoning, or your favorite blend; smoked paprika and cumin would work as well.

MAKES 8 TO 10 BURGERS

1. Heat a stovetop pressure cooker over medium heat or set an electric cooker to sauté. Add the onion, ginger, and mushrooms and dry sauté for 2 to 3 minutes. Add the lentils, sweet potatoes, and stock.

2. Lock on the lid. Bring to high pressure; cook for 6 minutes. Let the pressure come down naturally. Carefully remove the lid, tilting it away from you. Transfer the lentil mixture to a large bowl and let stand until cool enough to handle, at least 15 minutes.

3. Heat the oven to 375°F. Line a baking sheet with parchment paper and spray with cooking spray, if desired; or line the sheet with a silicone baking mat.

4. When the lentil mixture is cool, mash it with a potato masher or a fork. Stir in the hemp seeds, parsley, cilantro, and curry powder. Stir in the oats. The mixture should come together and form a thick paste; if it is too wet, add brown rice flour by the tablespoon, as necessary.

5. With wet hands, form into 8 to 10 patties and place on the prepared baking sheet. Bake for 10 minutes. Turn the burgers and bake for another 10 minutes, until they are firm and brown.

6. Let cool for a few minutes. Serve immediately, refrigerate, or freeze for up to 3 months.

Herbed Lentil Burgers

I love the enticing flavor and firm texture of these burgers. If you want to make them gluten-free, use steel-cut oats instead of bulgur. They taste great on a bun with mustard, onion, lettuce, and tomato, and are equally as good cut into pieces and sprinkled on a salad or as a topping for cooked grains and vegetables.

MAKES 8 GOOD-SIZED BURGERS

1. Put the garlic and onion in a food processor and pulse 3 to 5 times in short bursts. Add the carrot, 1 cup of the lentils, the tomatoes, tamari, parsley, thyme, and sage and pulse with 5 to 7 short bursts, until the mixture comes together. Add the tahini and pulse 2 to 3 more times. Transfer to a bowl and stir in the remaining lentils and bulgur. Let sit for at least 10 minutes.

2. Heat the oven to 375°F. Line a baking sheet with parchment paper and spray with cooking spray, if desired, or line the sheet with a silicone mat.

3. Stir the nutritional yeast and chia seeds into the lentil mixture and let sit another 10 minutes, until the mixture is firm.

4. Using a ⅓- or ½-cup measure, scoop out the mixture. Using wet hands, shape into burgers. Place on the prepared baking sheet. Bake for 15 minutes. Turn the burgers over and bake another 10 to 15 minutes, until golden brown and crisp.

5. Let cool for a few minutes and then serve, refrigerate, or freeze for up to 3 months.

2 cloves garlic, minced

½ cup diced onion

1 cup grated carrot (from 1 large)

1½ cups cooked lentils (see Bean Cooking At-a-Glance, page 95)

½ cup chopped fresh tomato or diced canned tomatoes, drained

1½ tablespoons tamari

3 tablespoons chopped fresh flat-leaf parsley

1 teaspoon dried thyme, or 1 tablespoon fresh thyme leaves

¾ teaspoon dried sage

3 tablespoons tahini

½ cup dried bulgur

Vegetable cooking spray, optional

3 tablespoons nutritional yeast

2 tablespoons ground chia seeds

¾ cup black rice

¼ cup brown rice

1½ cups water or vegetable stock

1 cup kidney beans, soaked and drained

4 cloves garlic, minced

1 tablespoon plus 2 teaspoons curry powder

1 cup water

Vegetable cooking spray, optional

½ cup sliced scallions

1 medium plum tomato; or ¼ cup diced canned tomato, drained

1 tablespoon lemon juice

½ cup hemp seeds

1 cup packed stemmed kale leaves

1 tablespoon mustard seeds

½ teaspoon salt

Rajma Curry Burgers

Rajma *is what kidney beans* are called in India. These burgers are seasoned with traditional Indian spices and bound with two kinds of rice to add color and flavor interest. You can add a small, chopped chile pepper for more heat.

MAKES 6 TO 8 BURGERS

1. Combine the black rice, brown rice, and 1½ cups water or stock in a pressure cooker. Lock on the lid. Bring to high pressure; cook for 20 minutes. Let the pressure come down naturally. Carefully remove the lid, tilting it away from you. Transfer the rice mixture to a bowl and set aside.

2. Combine the beans, half the minced garlic, 1 tablespoon of the curry powder, and 1 cup water in the pressure cooker. Bring to high pressure; cook for 7 minutes. Let the pressure come down naturally. Remove the lid, carefully tilting it away from you. Transfer the beans to a large bowl.

3. Heat the oven to 375°F. Line a baking sheet with parchment paper and spray with cooking spray, or line the sheet with a silicone mat.

4. Combine 1 cup of the rice mixture, half of the beans, the remaining garlic, the scallions, tomato, lemon juice, hemp seeds, and kale in a food processor. Process for 5 to 10 pulses, until the mixture is blended but still chunky.

5. Add ½ cup of the remaining rice to the remaining beans in the large bowl. (Set aside any remaining rice for another use.) Mash with a fork or a potato masher.

6. Transfer the rice and bean mixture from the food processor to the bowl with the mashed rice and beans. Add the remaining 2 teaspoons curry powder, the mustard seeds, and salt and mix well. Let the mixture sit for a few minutes.

7. Using wet hands, shape the mixture into 6 to 8 patties and place on the prepared baking sheet. Bake for 15 minutes. Turn burgers and bake on the second side until crisp and brown, another 10 to 15 minutes. Serve or wrap and refrigerate for up to 3 days or freeze for up to 3 months.

Smoky Double-Corn Pinto Burgers

If you like things hot, use the chipotle chili powder; if you prefer a milder burger, use sweet (not hot) smoked Spanish paprika (pimenton). These come together quickly and easily. I love that they contain two types of corn, one for crunch and texture and the other for its natural freshness and sweetness; choose organic corn, in any format, when you can as it limits your exposure to GMOs (genetically modified ingredients).

MAKES 6 TO 8 BURGERS

1. Heat the oven to 400°F. Line a baking sheet with parchment paper and spray with cooking spray, if desired; or line the sheet with a silicone baking mat.

2. Combine 1 cup of the beans, the onion, garlic, bell pepper, chile, if using, cilantro, chili powder, cumin, and chipotle powder in a food processor. Pulse 5 times and then add the polenta and pulse 2 more times until the mixture comes together but is not paste.

3. Mash the remaining 1 cup beans in a large bowl with a fork or a potato masher until just broken up. Stir in the corn. Add the bean mixture from the food processor and mix well. Let the mixture sit for 5 minutes. This mixture might seem loose but will firm up in the oven.

4. Using wet hands, form the mixture into 6 to 8 burgers and place on the prepared baking sheet. Bake for 15 minutes, then turn the burgers over. Bake another 15 minutes, until the burgers are brown and crisp. Let cool for a few minutes and serve, refrigerate, or freeze.

   Variation: For a more highly seasoned and salsa-flavored burger, add ¼ cup of your favorite tomato-based salsa, 2 tablespoons ground chia seeds, and 2 additional tablespoons polenta to the beans that you blend in the food processor. Mix with the mashed beans and corn, and let sit for 5 minutes before shaping into burgers.

Vegetable cooking spray, optional

2 cups well-cooked pinto beans (see Bean Cooking At-a-Glance, page 95)

1 cup chopped onion

4 cloves garlic

½ cup chopped red bell pepper

1 small hot chile, such as jalapeño or serrano; or 1 tablespoon hot sauce, optional

¼ cup chopped cilantro

1 tablespoon mild chili powder

2 teaspoons ground cumin

1 to 2 teaspoons chipotle chili powder or sweet smoked paprika

6 tablespoons coarse ground polenta, cornmeal, or corn grits

½ cup fresh or frozen (not thawed) corn

Spiced Jumpin' John Burgers

Vegetable cooking spray, optional

1 medium carrot, peeled and cut into 4 pieces

1 medium stalk celery, cut into 4 pieces

½ medium onion, cut into 4 pieces

2 cups cooked black-eyed peas (see Bean Cooking At-a-Glance, page 95)

1½ cups cooked brown rice (see Rice Cooking At-a-Glance, page 53)

1 cup packed kale or collard leaves, thick stems removed

½ cup canned, or fresh, diced tomatoes, drained

¼ cup fresh flat-leaf parsley

1 tablespoon red wine vinegar

1 to 2 tablespoons mild chili powder, to taste

1 to 2 teaspoons smoked paprika, to taste

Salt, to taste

These burgers were inspired by my favorite New Year's dish, a variation on the Southern black-eyed pea and rice dish Hoppin' John—which I call Jumpin' John because my version is meat-free, so I thought it should have a different name. If you love black-eyed peas, this burger will light up your taste buds. You can turn up the heat by using chipotle powder instead of the smoked paprika, and using canned diced tomatoes with green chiles instead of regular. This burger uses no binder but holds together very well. If you are concerned about this, you can stir in 2 tablespoons ground chia or flax seeds.

MAKES 6 TO 8 BURGERS

1. Heat the oven to 400°F. Line a baking sheet with parchment paper and spray with cooking spray, if desired; or line the sheet with a silicone baking mat.

2. Combine the carrot, celery, and onion in a food processor and pulse quickly 5 times. Add 1½ cups of the black-eyed peas and 1 cup of the rice. Pulse 5 times to blend. Add the kale, tomatoes, parsley, vinegar, and chili powder and paprika. Pulse until well blended but still chunky, 5 to 7 times more.

3. Transfer the mixture to a large bowl. Add the remaining ½ cup black-eyed peas and ½ cup rice and stir until well mixed.

4. Using wet hands, or a spoon and a measuring cup, measure about ¾ cup into a 1-cup measure. Pop the mixture out, form into a burger, and put on the prepared baking sheet. Repeat with the remaining mixture to make 6 to 8 burgers. Sprinkle the burgers with salt, if desired.

5. Bake 15 minutes. Turn burgers and bake another 15 minutes, until crisp and firm. Let sit for 5 minutes and serve. Refrigerate the burgers for up to 3 days, or wrap and freeze for up to 3 months.

Sunny Thai Split Pea Patties

These easy-to-make, easy-to-digest, flavorful patties have a tropical flair. They are best served without a bun so that you can pick up the flavor nuances. Either fruit chutney or tropical salsa would be a perfect complement.

MAKES 8 PATTIES

1. Combine the split peas and 2 cups water or stock in a pressure cooker. Lock on the lid. Bring to high pressure; cook for 10 minutes. Let the pressure come down naturally. Remove the lid carefully, tilting it away from you. Stir in the red curry paste while the peas are still warm. Let cool and transfer to a food processor. Rinse and dry the pressure cooker.

2. Combine the millet, coconut milk, 1 cup water, and coconut flakes in the pressure cooker. Lock on the lid. Bring to high pressure; cook for 10 minutes. Let the pressure come down naturally. Carefully remove the lid and transfer the mixture to a bowl.

3. Heat the oven to 375°F. Line a baking sheet with parchment paper and spray with cooking spray, if desired; or line the sheet with a silicone baking mat.

4. Measure out 1½ cups of the millet mixture and add to the food processor with the split peas. Measure 1 cup millet and add to a large bowl. (Set aside any remaining millet for another use.)

5. Add the scallions, cilantro, lime juice, chia seeds, peanut butter, and salt, if using, to the food processor with the millet and peas. Process until almost smooth, pulsing 7 to 10 times.

6. Mix the processed mixture with the reserved millet and stir to combine. Let sit for a few minutes. Then form into 8 patties and put on the prepared baking sheet.

7. Bake for 15 minutes on one side. Turn over and bake the other side for 10 to 15 minutes, until crispy. Serve hot. Refrigerate for up to 5 days, or freeze for up to 3 months.

10 minutes high pressure, natural release; 10 minutes high pressure, natural release

1 cup yellow split peas

2 cups water or vegetable stock

3 tablespoons Thai red curry paste

1 cup millet

1 cup coconut milk or coconut water

1 cup water

2 tablespoons unsweetened coconut flakes

Vegetable cooking spray, optional

½ cup chopped scallions

½ cup packed cilantro

¼ cup fresh squeezed lime juice

¼ cup ground chia seeds

3 tablespoons peanut butter

½ teaspoon salt, optional

25 minutes high pressure, natural release; 2 minutes high pressure, quick release

¾ cup wild rice

¼ cup short-grain brown rice

2¼ cups water or mushroom stock

Vegetable cooking spray, optional

1 teaspoon grapeseed or other neutral oil

½ cup chopped leek, white part only

1 cup sliced crimini or shiitake mushrooms (remove stems from shiitakes)

1 small sweet potato, peeled and diced small to equal 1 to 1½ cups

⅓ cup water

2 tablespoons fresh flat-leaf parsley

½ teaspoon minced fresh sage leaves

½ teaspoon salt

⅛ teaspoon freshly ground black pepper

Sweet Potato Relish (recipe follows)

Wild Rice– Mushroom Cakes

I first served these as a great little appetizer at a wine event. Few people knew exactly what was in the savory bites but they came back for second and third servings because they are textured, savory, sweet, and earthy all at once. The sweet potato relish is optional but adds some helpful color and pizzazz.

MAKES 20 TO 25 SMALL CAKES

1. Combine the wild rice, brown rice, and water or stock in a pressure cooker. Lock on the lid. Bring to high pressure; cook for 25 minutes. Let the pressure come down naturally. Remove the lid, carefully tilting it away from you. Transfer the rice mixture to a bowl and let cool.

2. Heat the oven to 425°F. Line a baking sheet with parchment paper and spray with cooking spray, if desired; or line the sheet with a silicone baking mat.

3. While rice is cooking, heat the oil in a medium sauté pan over medium heat. Add the leek and mushrooms and sauté for about 10 minutes, until the mushrooms release their liquid and are dry.

4. Add the sweet potato and the ⅓ cup water to the pressure cooker. Lock on the lid. Bring to high pressure; cook for 2 minutes. Quick release the pressure. Remove the lid, tilting it away from you. Check that the sweet potato is cooked through by inserting a knife into a few pieces. If not thoroughly cooked, bring back to pressure for 1 more minute and quick release. Transfer the sweet potato to a small bowl.

5. In a food processor, combine 3 cups of the cooked rice mixture, ½ cup of the cooked sweet potato, and the sautéed mushrooms and leek, along with the parsley, sage, salt, and pepper. (Set aside the remaining sweet potato for the relish; reserve any remaining rice for another use.) Process in short bursts until the ingredients are combined and sticking together.

6. With wet hands, form the sweet potato-rice mixture into patties and transfer to the prepared baking sheet. Bake for 15 minutes. Turn cakes and bake 5 minutes, until crispy. Serve with the Sweet Potato Relish. Store in the refrigerator for up to 5 days, or in the freezer for up to 3 months.

SWEET POTATO RELISH

Combine all ingredients and let sit for a few minutes. Serve on the side or on top of the wild mushroom cakes.

1 cup cooked diced sweet potato (or whatever remains after making the patties)

2 tablespoons balsamic vinegar

3 tablespoons chopped fresh flat-leaf parsley

TEN

Toppers: Sauces, Fillings,

and More

When you follow a whole foods, plant-based diet, the joy is in eating "real" food. But many simply cooked beans and grains are, well, kind of plain looking and not quite as flavorful as they could be, and that is where sauces and toppings come into play. They are the perfect way to enhance the flavor of grains, beans, and vegetables—or serve them in sandwiches, over pasta, or as a dip for bread. And they can be a great way to add more protein and other important nutrients to your meal. These are not the thin, runny sauces that you might find elsewhere, and they often add great flavor as well as substance. Some of these can easily be turned into fillings for corn or flour tortillas, enchiladas, or fajitas or added to plain ingredients to make savory pies. These flavorful enhancers are easy to make and incredibly tasty when they come out of the pressure cooker. You get long-cooked flavor in just a short time. Many can be frozen, which saves time later.

The uses for the recipes in this chapter are many. I hope that they will pique your interest.

4 minutes high pressure,
quick release; 2 minutes
high pressure,
quick release

½ cup allium stock or vegetable stock (see pages 157 and 161)

2 teaspoons tamari

1 clove garlic, minced

1 small hot chile, such as jalapeño or serrano, minced, optional

1 teaspoon crushed or ground coriander seeds

8 ounces tempeh, minced, diced, or crumbled

Vegetable cooking spray, optional

1 cup diced onion

3 cups fresh or frozen corn kernels (2 large or 3 small ears)

5 plum tomatoes, peeled and chopped to equal ¾ cup; or ½ pint cherry tomatoes, chopped; or ¾ cup diced canned tomatoes

1 tablespoon arrowroot powder, if needed

Salt and freshly ground black pepper

Chunky Corn and Tempeh Sauce

Somewhere in between a stew and a relish, this hearty topper is chock full of corn, tomatoes, and tempeh. It turns any bowl of grains and vegetables into a complete meal. Or serve it over "baked" regular or sweet potatoes (see page 121). Leave out the chile if you don't care for heat. Make it when corn is freshest or use frozen corn instead. Store for to 5 days in the refrigerator or freeze for up to 1 month.

MAKES 4 CUPS

1. Combine the stock, tamari, garlic, chile, if using, and coriander in a medium dish. Stir in the tempeh and marinate for at least 15 minutes, or up to 1 hour.

2. Heat a stovetop pressure cooker over medium heat or set an electric cooker to sauté. Spray with cooking spray, if using. Add the onion and cook for 1 minute. Add the tempeh with its marinade.

3. Lock on the lid. Bring to high pressure; cook for 4 minutes. Quick release the pressure. Remove the lid, carefully tilting it away from you.

4. Add the corn and tomatoes. Lock the lid back on the cooker. Bring to high pressure and cook for 2 minutes. Quick release the pressure. Remove the lid, carefully tilting it away from you.

5. If the sauce looks too runny, add the arrowroot powder and stir well. Add salt and pepper to taste.

Creamy Summer Squash and Mushroom Sauce

This easy vegan mushroom cream sauce is very rich, so you only need a little bit. It freezes well so make a big batch and freeze in the amounts that you will want to use later: ¼ to ½ cup. Serve over vegetables, grains, beans, baked potatoes, or other favorite foods. You can even combine it with other cooked mushrooms or vegetables and turn it into a pot pie filling.

MAKES 2 TO 3 CUPS

1. Heat a stovetop pressure cooker over medium heat or set an electric cooker to sauté. Add the onion and dry sauté for 2 minutes. Add the garlic, mushrooms, and milk.

2. Lock on the lid. Bring to high pressure; cook for 2 minutes. Quick release the pressure. Remove the lid, carefully tilting it away from you.

3. Add the squash and ground cashews, plus the dried basil, if using (add fresh basil later). Lock on the lid. Bring to high pressure and cook for 1 more minute. Quick release. Remove the lid carefully, tilting it away from you.

4. Stir the mixture, adding the fresh basil and salt, if desired.

2 minutes high pressure, quick release; 1 minute high pressure, quick release

1 cup finely chopped onion

2 cloves garlic, minced

1 cup diced crimini mushrooms (4 to 6 medium)

1 cup almond or other nondairy milk (but not soy)

1½ cups diced summer squash (1 to 2 medium)

½ cup raw cashews, ground in a coffee or spice grinder until powdered

2 tablespoons minced fresh basil, or 2 teaspoons dried basil

½ teaspoon salt, optional

Creamy Beany Sauce for Daily Meals

1½ to 2 cups cooked beans of your choice

¼ cup diced onion

2 cloves garlic, peeled

1 to 2 tablespoons tomato paste, optional

2 teaspoons grated lemon zest

½ cup vegetable stock

¼ cup rice vinegar or lemon juice

1 tablespoon maple syrup; or 1 or 2 soft pitted dates

1 tablespoon mellow white miso

When you want a new way to use beans, make this hearty, versatile sauce for topping salads, cooked potatoes, grains, and vegetables. If you make it a bit thicker, you can use it as a dip or as a spread for wraps. The fun part is that you can customize the seasonings to your liking: Add minced ginger, curry powder, Italian seasoning, all-purpose seasoning, nutritional yeast, or even part of a jalapeño, if you desire. Or try fresh herbs such as flat-leaf parsley, basil, or cilantro when blending. The choices are endless once you've mastered the basic recipe.

Added bonus: This is a great way to use very soft beans that may have cooked a little longer than you wanted. Or use any leftover beans you have, or raid your freezer and combine small amounts of various beans to equal 1½ cups. And keep in mind that the type of bean often affects the flavor. Some beans, such as Anasazi, pinto, or black, cry out for cumin and smoked paprika; garbanzo beans pair well with extra garlic and a touch of cumin and cayenne.

MAKES JUST OVER 1½ CUPS

1. Combine all the ingredients in a high-speed blender or food processor and blend until smooth (use more beans if you want to serve this as a spread).

2. Use within 3 to 5 days or freeze in ½- or 1-cup portions. It will last in the freezer for up to 3 months.

Gingery Spinach, Scallion, and Sesame Sauce

Photo, page I-8

Using both cooked and raw scallions punches up the flavor of this bright, versatile sauce. Try it tossed with soba noodles or Asian rice noodles, or over black or brown rice. If you don't care for ginger, leave it out and add another seasoning, such as 1 teaspoon of curry powder or garam masala. One medium scallion yields about 2 to 3 tablespoons finely chopped.

MAKES ABOUT 3 CUPS

1. Heat a stovetop pressure cooker over medium heat or set an electric cooker to sauté. Add the sesame seeds and dry sauté for 1 minute. Add 1½ cups of the scallions and the ginger and dry sauté another minute, adding the stock as soon as the mixture starts to stick. Stir well. Add the milk.

2. Lock the lid on the cooker. Bring to high pressure; cook for 1 minute. Quick release the pressure. Remove the lid, carefully tilting it away from you.

3. Add the frozen spinach; do not stir. Lock the lid on the cooker. Bring to high pressure and cook for 1 more minute. Quick release the pressure. Remove the lid, tilting it away from you.

4. Transfer the contents of the cooker to a blender or food processor, always taking precaution with hot liquids. Add the remaining 1 cup scallions, the lemon zest and juice, tahini, and tamari. Blend until smooth. Add salt and pepper to taste.

5. The sauce will keep for up to 5 days in the refrigerator and can be frozen for up to 1 month.

1 minute high pressure, quick release; 1 minute high pressure, quick release

1 teaspoon sesame seeds

2½ cups finely chopped scallions, about 2 bunches of 6 scallions each

1 tablespoon grated fresh ginger

½ cup vegetable stock or water

1 cup unsweetened nondairy milk

2 cups (about 5 ounces) frozen chopped spinach

1 teaspoon grated lemon zest

2 tablespoons fresh lemon juice

3 tablespoons tahini

1 to 2 teaspoons tamari, to taste

Salt and freshly ground black pepper

TOPPERS

1 cup diced leek, white part only

1 stalk celery, diced to equal about ¼ cup

1 small to medium celery root (also called celeriac), peeled and diced to equal 2 cups

1 to 1½ cups vegetable stock

½ cup unsweetened nondairy milk

2 tablespoons Dijon mustard

1 to 3 tablespoons chopped peeled horseradish root, to taste

Salt and freshly ground black pepper

Horseradish Cream Sauce
WITH CELERY ROOT

Essentially a thick, creamy puree, this horseradish-spiked sauce has a nice bite, tempered by celery root. It's great over potatoes, mixed in with grains, or served over cooked root vegetables such as carrots, turnips, parsnips, or rutabaga. Thin it with nondairy milk or stock if you want a more pourable sauce. Add enough stock and you will have made a horseradish and celery root soup, which you could serve hot or cold, garnished with parsley.

MAKES ABOUT 3 CUPS

1. Heat a stovetop pressure cooker over medium heat or set an electric cooker to sauté. Add the leek and dry sauté for 2 minutes. Add the celery and dry sauté for another minute. Add the celery root and 1 cup of the stock.

2. Lock on the lid. Bring to high pressure; cook for 5 minutes. Let the pressure come down naturally. Remove the lid, carefully tilting it away from you.

3. Transfer the contents to a blender or food processor. Add the milk, mustard, and horseradish and process until smooth, adding the remaining ½ cup stock, if needed, to reach the desired consistency. Add salt and pepper to taste. Refrigerate for up to 1 week or freeze for up to 2 months.

Lentil Tomato Sauce

This hearty sauce is wonderful tossed with pasta, raw zucchini noodles, quinoa, or any of your favorite grains. Or serve it over plain cooked vegetables. I also like to wrap it in a tortilla or use it as a taco filling with a shot of hot sauce.

MAKES 4 CUPS

1. Heat a stovetop pressure cooker over medium heat or set an electric cooker to sauté. Add the onion and mushrooms and dry sauté for 2 minutes. Add the carrot and garlic and dry sauté another 30 seconds, adding a bit of the stock if the vegetables start to stick. Add the lentils, half the parsley, half the basil, the bay leaf, and stock.

2. Lock on the lid. Bring to high pressure; cook for 10 minutes. Let the pressure come down naturally. Remove the lid, carefully tilting it away from you.

3. Add the tomatoes. Lock on the lid, bring to high pressure again, and cook for 4 minutes. Let the pressure come down naturally. Remove the lid, carefully tilting it away from you.

4. Add the remaining parsley and basil. If you have a stovetop cooker, simmer over medium heat for 5 to 7 minutes, until the sauce is reduced and the thickness that you like. If you have an electric cooker, use the sauté function to cook to desired thickness. Remove the bay leaf and add salt and pepper to taste. Refrigerate for 3 days or freeze for up to 3 months.

Lemony Lentil Tomato Sauce: Add 1 teaspoon grated lemon zest and 1 tablespoon lemon juice at the end of cooking.

Mexican-Style Lentil Tomato Sauce: Add 2 teaspoons ground cumin when dry sautéing the onion and mushrooms and use cilantro instead of basil. If you'd like a spicy sauce, add a pinch of cayenne pepper, chipotle powder, or crushed red pepper when seasoning, or add a chopped jalapeño or serrano pepper when cooking the onion.

---

10 minutes high pressure, natural release; 4 minutes high pressure, natural release

1 cup finely chopped onion

½ cup finely minced crimini mushrooms

½ cup finely chopped carrot

4 cloves garlic, minced

½ cup green or brown (not French) lentils, rinsed and picked over

¼ cup chopped fresh flat-leaf parsley

¼ cup chopped fresh basil

1 bay leaf

1 cup vegetable stock

3 cups diced fresh or canned tomatoes

Salt and freshly ground black pepper

1 tablespoon oil

1 cup diced onion

1 cup diced crimini, oyster, shiitake, or white mushrooms

4 cloves garlic, minced

2 teaspoons minced fresh chile

2 teaspoons ground toasted cumin

¼ teaspoon cayenne pepper

2 teaspoons mild or hot chili powder, or to taste

1 cup brown or green lentils, rinsed and picked over

1¾ cups vegetable stock

3 cups finely sliced kale, stemmed

Salt

Hot sauce

Chopped cilantro or parsley, for garnish

Mushroom, Lentil, and Kale Filling

I am a fungophile, a mushroom lover. Cooking them under pressure firms them up, which can be a great way to win over people who find them slimy. This would be a nice filling for soft tacos or enchiladas. Add some rice and you have a filling for burritos. Or just serve it on top of rice or your favorite grain, or as a side dish with a variety of foods. Splash with hot sauce and add chopped cilantro, if you are a fan, as I am.

SERVES 4

1. Heat a stovetop pressure cooker over medium heat or set an electric cooker to sauté; add the oil. Add the onion and mushrooms and sauté for 2 to 3 minutes. Add the garlic, chile, if using, and spices and sauté another minute. Add the lentils and stock.

2. Lock the lid on the cooker. Bring to high pressure; cook for 5 minutes. Let the pressure come down naturally. Remove the lid, carefully tilting it away from you.

3. Add the kale. Lock on the lid, bring back to high pressure, and cook for 1 minute. Let sit for 2 minutes and then quick release the pressure. Remove the lid, carefully tilting it away from you.

4. If you like your kale more cooked, lock the lid back on the cooker and let sit another few minutes. To serve, add salt and hot sauce to taste and garnish with chopped herbs.

Portobello Fajita Filling

I used to make fajitas with seitan when I ate wheat. These days I use mushrooms, tofu, or tempeh to make an easy filling for corn tortillas (or use flour tortillas if you prefer). If you want to substitute tofu or tempeh, use 8 ounces instead of the 2 portabello mushrooms. This is also a tasty topping for brown rice or any other cooked grain. Serve with sliced avocado, soy sour cream (page 215), and your favorite salsa or hot sauce.

SERVES 4 TO 6

1. Combine the lime juice, minced garlic, 2 teaspoons mild or hot chili powder, cumin, cilantro, and stock in a blender or mini food processor and blend well.

2. Transfer the marinade to a large flat dish and add the mushroom slices. Let marinate for at least 10 minutes. Remove the mushrooms from the marinade. Set the marinade aside.

3. Heat a stovetop pressure cooker over medium heat or set an electric cooker to sauté. Add the mushrooms and onion and cook for 3 minutes. Add the bell peppers, chiles, and sliced garlic and cook for 2 more minutes. Add the marinade.

4. Lock on the lid. Bring to high pressure; cook for 2 minutes. Quick release the pressure. Remove the lid, carefully tilting it away from you.

5. Add the tomatoes, 1 tablespoon mild chili powder, Mexican seasoning, and cayenne. Close the lid and let sit for 3 minutes.

6. Add salt to taste. Transfer the mushroom mixture to a platter. Store refrigerated for up to 3 days. Garnish with lime wedges and cilantro before serving.

- 2 tablespoons lime juice
- 2 cloves garlic, minced
- 2 teaspoons mild or hot chili powder, to taste
- 1 teaspoon ground toasted cumin
- 3 tablespoons chopped cilantro
- 2 tablespoons vegetable stock
- 2 medium portobello mushrooms, sliced
- 1 large onion, cut into ¼-inch slices
- 3 red bell peppers, cored, seeded, and sliced
- 1 jalapeño chile, minced
- 1 Anaheim or poblano chile, sliced
- 4 cloves garlic, sliced
- 3 medium plum tomatoes, diced; or ⅔ cup diced canned tomatoes
- 1 tablespoon mild chili powder
- 2 teaspoons Mexican seasoning, store-bought or homemade (page 43)
- Pinch of cayenne pepper
- Salt
- Lime wedges and chopped cilantro, for garnish

TOPPERS

261

5 minutes high pressure, quick release

1 cup chopped onion

3 cloves garlic, minced

2 cups diced peeled winter squash

1 cup vegetable stock

2 tablespoons chickpea flour

1 (15-ounce) can fire roasted tomatoes with chilies, or Ro*Tel tomatoes

½ cup almond or cashew meal, or dry almonds or cashews ground into fine powder

½ cup unsweetened nondairy milk

¼ cup nutritional yeast

1 to 2 tablespoons mellow white miso

1 tablespoon apple cider vinegar

1 teaspoon turmeric

1 teaspoon paprika

1 teaspoon mustard powder

¼ to ½ teaspoon hot chili or chipotle powder, to taste, optional

Salt and freshly ground black pepper

Hot sauce, optional

Queso Sauce

This spicy, cheesy sauce should be a standard in your repertoire. Use it as a topping for nachos, to jazz up rice and vegetables, or as a topping for any savory dish that needs zip. It freezes well, too, for up to 3 months.

MAKES AT LEAST 3 CUPS

1. Heat a stovetop pressure cooker over medium heat or set an electric cooker to sauté. Add the onion and garlic and dry sauté for 2 minutes. Add the squash and stock and sprinkle the chickpea flour over the top.

2. Lock on the lid. Bring to high pressure; cook for 5 minutes. Quick release the pressure. Remove the lid, carefully tilting it away from you.

3. Transfer the cooked squash mixture to a blender or food processor. Let cool for at least 10 minutes. Add the tomatoes, almond meal, milk, nutritional yeast, miso, vinegar, turmeric, paprika, mustard, and chili powder, if using. Blend or process until smooth.

4. Taste and add salt and pepper and a dash of hot sauce if you prefer a hotter sauce.

Nut-Free Queso Sauce: If you prefer a sauce without nuts, omit the almond meal and sprinkle ½ cup rolled oats on top of the squash before adding the stock to the cooker. This will thicken up the sauce nicely.

Raita

Until I made my own soy yogurt in my electric pressure cooker, I was not a vegan yogurt fan. I found that most of them, even the plain varieties, were too sweet and thick for me. Making my own soy yogurt (page 266) changed that, since I could control the sweetness and consistency. Now, I use my own soy yogurt to make raita, the Indian yogurt-based accompaniment to curries and other dishes. It can also be served on its own as a cucumber salad.

MAKES 1½ CUPS (CAN EASILY BE DOUBLED)

Combine the yogurt, cucumber, onion, coriander, cumin, and mustard seeds in a small bowl and season with salt to taste. Cover and refrigerate for at least 30 minutes. Store in the refrigerator for up to 2 days.

Variations: Add 2 tablespoons chopped fresh mint or cilantro and a pinch of cayenne pepper. Or add ½ cup chopped fresh tomato and a bit of hot chili pepper.

1 cup soy or other nondairy yogurt, homemade (see page 266) or store-bought

½ cup diced seeded peeled cucumber

3 tablespoons diced red onion

½ teaspoon ground coriander

½ teaspoon ground toasted cumin

¼ teaspoon black mustard seeds, toasted

Salt

1 medium sweet potato, peeled and chopped to equal 1½ to 2 cups

1½ to 2 cups chopped onion

1 small cauliflower, cut into florets to equal 1 to 1½ cups

3 medium carrots, peeled and chopped to equal 2 cups

4 small turnips, quartered to equal 1 cup

6 cloves garlic, cut in half

2 medium beets, peeled and cut into chunks

1½ cups vegetable stock

1 to 2 tablespoons your favorite herb and/or spice blend (see pages 36 to 45)

Red Beauty Vegetable Sauce

The veggie-packed blended sauce is wonderful over pasta, grains, or cooked broccoli, carrots, winter squash, or diced sweet potato, and can be used as a sauce to make tomato- (and nightshade-) free lasagna or layered vegetable dish. Season it with your favorite herbs and spices, according to how you will be using it.

Or jazz it up with mustard, grated horseradish root, fresh herbs, nut or seed butter, or nutritional yeast. You can also turn it into soup by adding stock, a splash of lemon juice, and chopped fresh herbs such as cilantro or parsley.

MAKES 4 CUPS

1. Combine the sweet potato, onion, cauliflower, carrots, turnips, garlic, beets, and stock in the pressure cooker. Lock on the lid. Bring to high pressure; cook for 10 minutes. Let the pressure come down naturally. Remove the lid, carefully tilting it away from you.

2. Stir in the herb or spice blend. In batches, transfer to a blender or food processor and process until smooth. Store in the refrigerator for up to 5 days or freeze for 2 months.

Red Beauty Sauce with Potatoes and Bell Peppers (not nightshade-free): Use Yukon Gold potatoes instead of the sweet potatoes, and 3 cups chopped red bell pepper instead of the beets. Then add 1 tomato or ½ cup diced tomatoes when blending. Season with Italian seasoning or herbs de Provence.

Salsa di Pomodoro e Melanzane

(TOMATO AND EGGPLANT SAUCE)

This Italian sauce feeds my love for in-season eggplant and tomatoes and gives me even more reason to use the pressure cooker for fresh vegetables in the summertime. If you like, add other vegetables, but beware that summer squash exudes a lot of liquid. I would add it to the hot sauce at the end if I were using it. Serve hot, over pasta or whole grains, or as a topping for toasted bread.

MAKES 3 TO 4 CUPS

1. Heat a stovetop pressure cooker over medium heat or set an electric cooker to sauté; add 1 tablespoon of the oil. Add the onion and sauté for 2 to 3 minutes, until it begins to soften. Add half the garlic, all the eggplant, and the salt and sauté another minute. Add the stock.

2. Lock the lid on the cooker. Bring to high pressure; cook for 1½ minutes if using a stovetop cooker, or 1 minute in an electric cooker. Quick release the pressure. Remove the lid carefully, tilting it away from you.

3. Add the tomatoes; do **not** stir. Lock on the lid. Bring back to high pressure. Cook for 1½ minutes in a stovetop cooker, 1 minute in an electric cooker. Quick release the pressure. Carefully remove the lid.

4. Stir in the remaining garlic, the herbs, additional 1 to 3 tablespoons oil, and capers, if using. Taste and season with salt and pepper.

1 or 1½ minutes high pressure, quick release; 1 or 1½ minutes high pressure, quick release

2 to 4 tablespoons olive oil, to taste

1 cup diced onion

6 cloves garlic, minced

2 cups diced peeled (if tough) eggplant

½ teaspoon salt

¼ cup vegetable stock

3 cups diced ripe tomatoes

2 to 3 tablespoons chopped fresh flat-leaf parsley, to taste

2 to 3 tablespoons chopped fresh basil, to taste

1 to 2 tablespoons chopped capers or cured olives, to taste, optional

Freshly ground black pepper

1 packet vegan yogurt starter,
or 1 probiotic capsule, or
1 tablespoon commercial
vegan yogurt with active
cultures

1 (32-ounce) box plain (not
enriched or fortified) organic
soy milk (just beans and
water), at room temperature

Soy Yogurt

Once you make your own, your idea of vegan yogurt will be forever altered.
At least that's what happened for me: I learned that homemade nondairy
yogurt is more affordable, convenient, and tastier than store-bought.

The process is easy. Unfortunately you will have to start with commercial
soy milk, because making your own soy milk in the pressure cooker renders it
too pasteurized to then turn into yogurt.

Once you have your yogurt, enjoy it as is or use it to make a variety of
wonderful sauces; see my suggestions below.

MAKES 1 QUART

1. Add the yogurt starter, probiotic, or yogurt to the milk. Shake well
   in the box or pour into a quart glass jar and shake well. If in the
   box, transfer to a quart jar, or smaller jars if desired. No need to
   seal the jars.

2. If you have an electric pressure cooker with a yogurt setting, this
   step is easy. Set the yogurt setting for 8 to 10 hours and add the
   jar(s). Lock on the lid, close the vent, and do not check until the
   time is up.

3. If you don't have a pressure cooker with a yogurt setting, do not
   despair. Find a place that is between 100° and 110°F, but no hotter.
   This can be your oven with the light on, the pilot light on, or set
   at 100°F if your oven goes that low. You can set a rack on top of
   4 closed jars of boiling water in a Styrofoam or other kind of
   cooler, and put the jar(s) on the rack, then cover the cooler. Or
   even set it outdoors (on a porch, perhaps), if the temperature is
   close to 100°F. You can also use a yogurt maker.

4. It takes 8 to 12 hours for your soy milk to become cultured and turn
   into yogurt. Sometimes it will separate into curds and whey. You
   can pour off and drink the whey and keep the curds.

5. For Greek-style yogurt or yogurt cheese, strain the yogurt in a fine strainer or cheesecloth-lined colander for 8 hours or more. The drained liquid contains active "good" bacteria (cultures), so don't toss it: drink it in smoothies, straight, or use in recipes that call for buttermilk-type flavors.

6. Refrigerate the yogurt after making and use within a week.

YOGURT SAUCES

Here are some suggestions for flavoring combinations to add to your yogurt to make it saucy for savory dishes:

• Fresh chopped dill and chives

• Scallion and black pepper

• Fresh grated horseradish with Dijon mustard

• Garlic and parsley

• Raita, page 263

• Cilantro and curry

• Lemon zest and cumin powder

• Mango and chutney

You get the idea: Stir in your favorite spices and veggies and it's sauce.

2 minutes high pressure,
quick release; 1 minute
high pressure,
quick release

1 cup diced onion

3 cloves garlic, minced

1 teaspoon minced fresh
ginger

1 cup diced shiitake
mushrooms (stems removed)

½ cup sliced crimini mushrooms

1 cup diced Yukon Gold
potatoes (peeled or not)

1¼ cups mushroom stock (to
make your own, see page
160)

2 cups (about 5 ounces) frozen
chopped spinach

1 tablespoon mellow white
miso or 1 tablespoon tamari,
optional

½ teaspoon salt, optional

⅛ teaspoon freshly ground
black pepper

Shiitake Spinach Sauce

Here is a bright green sauce with great umami flavor, which can be varied almost any way to suit your tastes. If you want to make it richer, substitute coconut milk for some of the mushroom stock. To thicken it further, add ¼ to ½ cup cooked white beans before blending. To add sweetness, substitute diced sweet potatoes or winter squash for the Yukon Gold potatoes. Serve over cooked vegetables such as broccoli or cauliflower, or mix the vegetables with the sauce and pasta or cooked grains, or use as a dip or spread. To kick up the spice, add a minced clove of garlic, ½ teaspoon minced ginger, or a pinch of cayenne or other hot pepper after the sauce is blended. Or add a spice blend, such as 2 to 3 teaspoons curry powder, before cooking. Consider the mushrooms and spinach your food canvas to paint.

MAKES ABOUT 3 CUPS

1. Heat a stovetop pressure cooker over medium heat or set an electric cooker to sauté. Add the onion and dry sauté for 2 minutes. Add the garlic and ginger and cook 1 minute. Add the mushrooms and cook 1 more minute. Add the potatoes and stock and scrape the bottom of the cooker to remove any food that has stuck.

2. Lock the lid on the pressure cooker. Bring to high pressure; cook for 2 minutes. Quick release the pressure. Remove the lid, carefully tilting it away from you.

3. Add the spinach. Do not stir. Put the lid back on the cooker. Bring back to high pressure and cook for 1 minute longer. Quick release the pressure. Remove the lid carefully, tilting it away from you.

4. Blend the ingredients with a handheld immersion blender, or in a blender or a food processor, adding the miso, if using, the salt, if using, and the pepper. Add more stock if you want a thinner sauce. Refrigerate up to 3 days or freeze for up to 1 month.

Spicy Tomatillo Sauce

This brightly flavored sauce has a lot of flavor and plenty of heat. Of course, you can also make it not-so-spicy and it will still taste great. The sauce makes a wonderful accompaniment for any kind of beans, grains, vegetables, loaves, and burgers, or your favorite tacos, enchiladas, or tamales. If you use red bell pepper, it turns out a pretty peach color. Otherwise, it will be green.

MAKES 2½ CUPS

1. Heat a stovetop pressure cooker over medium heat or set an electric cooker to sauté. Add the onion and dry sauté for 2 minutes. Add the garlic, bell pepper, and chiles and cook another minute. Add the tomatillos and stock.

2. Lock the lid on the cooker. Bring to high pressure; cook for 3 minutes. Quick release the pressure. Remove the lid, carefully tilting it away from you.

3. Pour the mixture into a blender. Let cool for at least 10 minutes. Add the avocado, lime juice, and cilantro. Process until smooth. Add salt to taste. Store in the refrigerator for up to 5 days.

3 minutes high pressure, quick release

2 cups chopped onion

4 cloves garlic, minced

1 red or green bell pepper, cored, seeded, and chopped

1 poblano or Anaheim chile pepper, chopped

1 hot chile pepper, such as jalapeño or serrano, minced (seeded to decrease the heat, if you like)

½ pound tomatillos, cut in halves or quarters

¼ cup vegetable stock

1 medium avocado, chopped

1 to 2 tablespoons lime juice, to taste

½ cup packed cilantro leaves

Salt

TOPPERS

ELEVEN

Appetizers

The pressure cooker is amazing when it comes to cooking the ingredients needed to make tasty dips, spreads, relishes, and other dishes for starting a meal or serving at a party. Any bean can quickly become a dip. Many vegetables can be thoroughly cooked in minutes to blend into a spread. I offer recipes that you can use over and over and that will, I hope, inspire you to come up with your own.

1 cup dried cannellini beans, soaked and drained

¾ cup vegetable stock

3 cloves garlic, peeled

1 (1-inch) piece peeled fresh ginger

1 to 2 tablespoons peanut butter, to taste

1½ teaspoons rice vinegar

1 tablespoon mellow white or any other miso

1 tablespoon or more cilantro leaves

1 tablespoon Sucanat or coconut palm sugar; or 1 small pitted date

1 scallion, sliced

Asian Bean Dip

This dip has the zip of Asian seasonings mixed with creamy cannellini beans. Serve with vegetables or use as a spread for rice crackers or a filling for wraps.

You can also make it with any types of cooked beans that you have. (If you are using your pressure cooker as often as I do, you most likely have several.) Just use 2 to 2½ cups cooked beans and start at Step 2. Freeze any extra beans and label them so you will have a start on the next batch of dip.

MAKES ABOUT 2½ CUPS

1. Combine the beans, stock, and 1 clove garlic in the pressure cooker. Lock on the lid. Bring to high pressure; cook for 8 minutes. Let the pressure come down naturally. Carefully open the cooker, tilting the lid away from you. Drain the beans into a colander set over a bowl and set aside the drained beans and their cooking liquid.

2. Add the remaining garlic and the ginger to the food processor and process until finely chopped.

3. Add the beans to the food processor along with the peanut butter, vinegar, miso, and 3 tablespoons of the bean-cooking liquid. Add more bean liquid to reach the desired consistency.

4. Process until slightly chunky. Add the cilantro, sweetener, and scallion and process briefly, until combined. Taste and adjust the seasonings to your liking by adding more vinegar, miso, or sugar. Refrigerate for up to 3 days or freeze for up to 1 month.

Baba Ganoush

This dip feeds my tahini habit. Eggplant and the pressure cooker are made
for one another, and making baba ganoush has never been so fast and easy.
It won't have the smokiness that you can get when grilling the eggplant, but
add a touch of smoked salt or a few drops of liquid smoke (or even ¼ to ½
teaspoon smoked paprika or chipotle powder) instead.

Serve with vegetables, crackers, or toasted bread, or use as a spread in
wraps or on sandwiches. You can also freeze it for when eggplant is not in
season.

MAKES 2 CUPS

1. Heat a stovetop pressure cooker over medium heat or set an
   electric cooker to sauté. Add most of the garlic and dry sauté for
   30 seconds, adding a tablespoon of the stock if the garlic starts to
   stick. Add the eggplant and stock.

2. Lock the lid. Bring to high pressure; cook for 2 minutes. Quick
   release the pressure. Carefully open the cooker, tilting the lid away
   from you. Check to be sure that the eggplant is cooked through. If
   it's not, bring back to pressure for 1 more minute and quick release.

3. Transfer the cooked eggplant to a blender or food processor. Add
   the remaining garlic, lemon juice, tahini, and parsley. Pulse until
   almost smooth. Taste and add salt, if desired. Chill or serve at room
   temperature. Store for up to 5 days in the refrigerate or freeze for
   up to 1 month.

4 cloves garlic, minced

1½ to 2 pounds eggplant, peeled
and diced

¼ cup vegetable stock

1 to 2 tablespoons lemon juice,
to taste

2 to 3 tablespoons tahini, to
taste

2 tablespoons chopped fresh
flat-leaf parsley

Smoked or regular salt,
optional

1 tablespoon sesame seeds

1 teaspoon ground toasted cumin

1 teaspoon grated fresh ginger

4 to 5 medium carrots, peeled and cut into 1-inch pieces (3 to 4 cups)

½ cup vegetable stock or water

2 tablespoons tahini

1 to 2 teaspoons rice vinegar, to taste

1 teaspoon ground ginger

¼ to ½ teaspoon salt

Freshly ground black pepper

Carrot Sesame Spread

This recipe was inspired by one that I saw on fortheloveoffood.org, the website of fellow registered dietitian Eileen Behan. I love the whole idea of a dip made from well-seasoned carrots enriched with a double hit of sesame, and I knew that it would easily adapt to the pressure cooker. The spread can be used on bread instead of butter or mayo, or as a dip. You can even thin it with some nondairy milk or yogurt and use it as a sauce. It's simple to make, with a pretty light orange color and great flavor. If you want to spice it up, stir in a shot of Sriracha or other hot sauce.

MAKES 2½ CUPS

1. Heat a stovetop pressure cooker over medium heat or set an electric cooker to sauté. Add the sesame seeds and dry sauté for 2 minutes, until they smell toasty. Add the cumin and grated ginger, then stir. Add the carrots and stock.

2. Lock on the lid. Bring to high pressure; cook for 5 minutes. Let the pressure come down naturally. Carefully open the cooker, tilting the lid away from you.

3. Transfer the contents to a blender, carefully scraping in all the sesame seeds. Add the tahini, rice vinegar, ground ginger, and salt to taste. Blend for 1 to 2 minutes, until the mixture is smooth.

4. Refrigerate for at least 1 hour before serving. The spread will keep in the refrigerator for up to 3 days or in the freezer for up to 1 month.

Eggplant "Caviar"

My grandmother used to make a dip like this: chunky, garlicky, with a salty kick that might resemble caviar to some but not to me. Still, I like it better than the fish eggs. Someone in the family has Nana's original recipe, but it's not me. This is my closest guess, although hers was better. Maybe she added more love. She didn't use a pressure cooker, but doing so speeds up the process and almost instantly infuses the eggplant with wonderful flavors.

Serve as a dip with crackers and vegetables, use as a wrap filling, or stuff into pita bread with other vegetables.

MAKES 1½ TO 2 CUPS

1. Toss the eggplant with the balsamic vinegar in a bowl. Let sit for a minute. Add to the pressure cooker with three-fourths of the garlic and the stock.

2. Lock on the lid. Bring to high pressure; cook for 2 minutes. Quick release the pressure. Carefully open the cooker, tilting the lid away from you.

3. Transfer the contents to a bowl. Add the remaining garlic, the tomatoes, parsley, capers, sugar or date (with its water), olive oil, if using, and salt and pepper to taste. Stir well. Taste and adjust the seasonings. The flavor should be a bit sweet and sour. Let sit for an hour at room temperature to allow the flavors to meld.

4. Before serving, taste again and adjust flavors, adding more vinegar or sweetener to taste. This will last for a few days in the refrigerator, if you can keep from eating all of it.

* Note: If you prefer a smoother dip, put all the ingredients in the food processor and blend to a puree.

2 minutes high pressure, quick release

2 pounds eggplant, peeled and cut into 1-inch cubes

3 tablespoons balsamic vinegar

8 cloves garlic, minced

¼ cup vegetable stock

¼ cup finely chopped tomatoes, fresh or canned

2 tablespoons chopped fresh flat-leaf parsley

2 tablespoons capers

1 teaspoon (or more) Sucanat or sugar; or 1 date soaked in 3 tablespoons water for 30 minutes

2 tablespoons olive oil, optional

Salt and freshly ground black pepper

APPETIZERS

275

2 cloves garlic, peeled

1½ to 2 cups Chickpeas and
Garlic for Hummus (page
107) or plain cooked
chickpeas (page 95), liquid
reserved

2 tablespoons tahini

2 tablespoons fresh lemon
juice

1 dash cayenne pepper

1 tablespoon reduced-sodium
tamari or Bragg liquid aminos

2 tablespoons water or more
as needed

½ teaspoon ground cumin,
optional

Hummus

A vegan cookbook would be incomplete without a recipe for hummus. It's easy to make and easy to adapt, and why buy it when you can flavor it any way you like at home? Best of all, a pressure cooker makes it easy to start from dried chickpeas, which vastly improves the flavor.

You can use plain-cooked chickpeas, but for the best flavor start with Chickpeas and Garlic for Hummus, which has underlying notes of cooked garlic and cumin.

Hummus makes a great dip and can easily be turned into salad dressing. (At least that's what one of my students told me. I prefer to dollop it directly on my salad, then drizzle with vinegar.) Hummus is great served with warmed pita bread triangles or raw vegetables. I'll put it in pita bread with salad for a sandwich or use it as a base in a vegetable-stuffed wrap.

MAKES 1¾ CUPS

1. Process the garlic in a food processor for about 15 seconds, until well chopped.

2. Add the remaining ingredients, blending to the desired consistency. If it seems too thick, add some bean-cooking liquid, water, or lemon juice. Taste and adjust the seasonings.

3. The hummus will keep in the refrigerator for up to 5 days. It can also be frozen for up to 3 months, but I doubt it will be around that long.

Roasted Red Pepper Hummus: Add ½ cup roasted red pepper when blending.

Kale, Chard, and Dandelion Spread

I tasted this chunky spread at a potluck and found the flavor enticing: a little bitter, but very green-tasting and fresh. I was given the briefest recipe and came up with this as my version. It might not be the same but I won't know unless Sue serves her tasty treat again, and I bring mine, too. Serve as a side dish, on top of cooked grains, or as a spread for crostini or crackers.

SERVES 4

1. Heat a stovetop pressure cooker over medium heat, or set an electric pressure cooker to sauté; add 1 tablespoon of the oil, if using. Add half of the garlic and cook for 1 minute.

2. Add the greens and stock. Lock on the lid, bring to high pressure, and cook for 5 minutes. Quick release the pressure. Remove the lid, carefully tilting it away from you.

3. Transfer the greens to a food processor and add the remaining garlic, the scallions, lemon zest and juice, and 1 to 2 tablespoons olive oil, if using.

4. Process, pulsing until finely chopped but not totally pureed. Add salt and pepper to taste. Serve hot, warm, or at room temperature.

5 minutes high pressure, quick release

2 to 3 tablespoons olive oil, optional

6 cloves garlic, minced

1 medium bunch kale, leaves stripped from stems, thinly sliced

1 small bunch dandelion greens, cut into thin strips (2 cups)

1 small bunch Swiss chard (about 6 leaves), stems and leaves finely chopped

½ cup vegetable stock

½ cup chopped scallions

1 teaspoon grated lemon zest

3 tablespoons lemon juice

Salt and freshly ground black pepper

1 cup white beans, soaked and
drained

½ cup chopped red bell pepper
or drained roasted red
peppers

¾ cup vegetable stock

½ teaspoon dried sage

1¾ teaspoons dried thyme

1 tablespoon lemon juice

1 tablespoon olive oil, optional

½ teaspoon salt

½ teaspoon freshly ground
black pepper

Chopped fresh flat-leaf
parsley, for garnish

Red Pepper and White Bean Dip

Photo, page I-1

I have been serving this pretty dip for years. It's one of the few that I make that works well for those who avoid onions and garlic, because the sweetness of the red pepper makes up for the lack of alliums. It's simple to make and easy to eat. Spread on crostini (toasted bread slices) or crackers, or serve with vegetables. See the sauce variation below.

MAKES AT LEAST 2 CUPS

1. Combine the beans, red pepper, stock, sage, and 1½ teaspoons of the thyme in a pressure cooker. Lock on the lid. Bring to high pressure; cook for 8 minutes. Let the pressure come down naturally. Carefully open the cooker, tilting the lid away from you.

2. Transfer the cooked beans to a blender or food processor and let them cool for at least 10 minutes.

3. Add the remaining ¼ teaspoon thyme, the lemon juice, olive oil, if using, salt, and pepper to the blender or processor. Process until smooth.

4. Serve garnish with parsley. This will keep refrigerated for 3 days, or frozen for up to 1 month.

Cheezey Red Pepper Sauce: Add 1 teaspoon minced garlic, 3 tablespoons nutritional yeast, 2 tablespoons cashew meal or flour, 2 to 3 tablespoons nondairy milk, and 1 tablespoon lemon juice when blending. If the mixture seems too thick, add more milk. If it seems too thin, add more cashew meal or nutritional yeast.

Apple Chutney

You can serve this chutney on top of tofu, tempeh, or vegetables, or alongside your favorite curry or cooked beans. Adjust the seasonings for your taste: hot, sweet, sour, and bitter. You can also make it with other fall fruit, listed below.

MAKES 1 TO 2 PINTS

1. Combine all the ingredients, except the salt, in a pressure cooker. Lock on the lid. Bring to high pressure; cook for 5 minutes. Let the pressure come down naturally. Carefully open the cooker, tilting the lid away from you.

2. Let cool, add salt, if desired, then taste and adjust the seasonings. You can freeze or can the chutney to have on hand for another time.

4 Gravenstein or other tart sweet apples (or a combination of quince (peeled), pear, and apples), sliced to equal about 3 cups

2 cups diced onion

1 chile (or to taste), such as jalapeño or serrano, minced

1 cup raisins or currants

¾ to 1 cup apple cider vinegar, to taste

½ cup brown sugar, or to taste

1 to 2 teaspoons grated fresh ginger, to taste

1 tablespoon mustard seeds

½ to 1 teaspoon salt, to taste

APPETIZERS

279

1 pound white or crimini mushrooms, ends trimmed but left whole

1 cup water

1 cup red or white wine or other vinegar

6 to 12 cloves garlic, minced

½ teaspoon salt

Marinated Mushrooms

Photo, page I-1

If you don't already love marinated mushrooms, make them using the pressure cooker, as the heat firms them up and infuses them with flavor nicely and quickly. These are better than what you buy at the store because they have a cleaner, fresher taste, and you can make them just how you like them. Buy loose mushrooms, if possible, and choose those of similar size that are very fresh and firm. Generally I choose larger mushrooms for eating, but in this case small to medium-sized mushrooms work best.

After making the mushrooms and packing into jars, you can process them in a boiling water bath, using all canning precautions, to keep on hand for when people pop by or to give as gifts. Otherwise, store in the refrigerator for up to 2 weeks.

MAKES 1 (16-OUNCE) OR 2 (8-OUNCE) JARS

1. Combine the mushrooms, water, vinegar, half the garlic, the salt, and any optional flavorings (see Note) in the pressure cooker. Bring to high pressure; cook for 5 minutes. Let the pressure come down naturally. Remove the lid carefully, tilting it away from you.

2. Transfer the mushrooms and cooking liquid to 1 or 2 jars, adding the remaining garlic, and any other optional ingredients. If you have more than 16 ounces, use another jar for the extra.

✱ **Note:** Optional ingredients to add either before cooking or afterward: 2 slices lemon peel, 1 teaspoon coriander seeds, 1 dried chile pepper, 1 teaspoon black peppercorns, or ¼ to ½ teaspoon of your favorite dried herbs, such as rosemary or thyme.

Black Bean, Corn, and Tomatillo Salsa

Combine freshly cooked black beans with corn and tomatillos for a pretty salsa that tastes great, too. Serve with chips, use to top grilled or baked tofu or tempeh, add to tacos, or mix into cooked grains. Get the best tomatillos that you can. Make it hot with the jalapeños, or don't—it's up to you.

MAKES ABOUT 3 CUPS

1. Combine the beans, kombu, and stock in a pressure cooker. Lock on the lid. Bring to high pressure; cook for 6 minutes. Let the pressure come down naturally. Carefully open the cooker, tilting the lid away from you.

2. Taste to be sure the beans are cooked through. If not, bring back to pressure and cook for 2 minutes longer, then let the pressure release naturally. Release any remaining pressure after 10 minutes. Carefully remove the lid.

3. Remove the kombu (discard or use elsewhere). Add the corn, stir, and lock on the lid. Let sit for another 3 minutes. Remove the lid carefully.

4. Transfer the beans and corn to a medium bowl, draining any cooking liquid. Put the bowl in the refrigerator for at least 30 minutes.

5. Add the tomatillos, onion, garlic, cilantro, lime juice, cumin, and jalapeño, if using, and stir. Add the avocado, if using, and stir carefully so it remains intact. Taste and adjust the seasoning if necessary, adding salt and pepper, more lime juice, or cilantro.

6. Cover the salsa and let it rest for at least 30 minutes in order for the flavors to meld and the beans to soak up the flavors. Store in the refrigerator for up to 3 days.

---

6 minutes high pressure, natural release

1 cup dried black beans, soaked and drained

1 (3-inch) piece kombu

½ to ⅔ cup vegetable stock or water

1 cup fresh or frozen corn, thawed (or not)

2 cups chopped tomatillos (about 1 pound)

½ cup chopped onion

2 to 3 cloves garlic, minced

½ cup chopped cilantro

Juice of 1 small lime

1 to 2 teaspoons ground toasted cumin, to taste

1 jalapeño, seeded and minced, optional

½ cup chopped avocado, optional

Salt and freshly ground black pepper

2 cups chopped onion

1 tablespoon mustard seeds

2 teaspoons grated fresh ginger

1 tablespoon vegetable stock or water, if needed

1 small summer squash, diced small

4 Gravenstein or other tart, sweet apples, diced (2 to 3 cups)

2 tablespoons lemon juice or apple cider vinegar

1 to 2 tablespoons agave nectar or maple syrup, to taste

About ½ teaspoon salt

Apple and Squash Relish

Gravenstein apples grow where I live in northern California. You may not be able to find them, so buy any tart, sweet apples you can find, such as Pink Lady, Fuji, or Granny Smith—you ought to be able to find something that will work. You can serve this sweet, chunky, and tart relish on top of cooked or grilled tofu, tempeh, veggie burgers, or vegetables. If you have the grill going, you can easily grill the onions (cut into thick slices), then chop them and add to the relish. Feel free to adjust the recipe to include any other herbs, spices, or vegetables you like.

MAKES 1 TO 1½ CUPS

1. Heat a stovetop pressure cooker over medium heat or set an electric cooker to sauté. Add the onion and dry sauté for 1 minute. Add the mustard seeds and ginger and sauté another 30 seconds, adding the stock or water if anything begins to stick. Turn off sauté if using an electric cooker. Add the squash, apples, and lemon juice.

2. Lock on the lid. Bring to high pressure; cook for 1 minute for a firm texture, or 2 minutes if you'd like it mushier. Quick release the pressure. Carefully open the cooker, tilting the lid away from you.

3. Transfer the mixture to a medium bowl. Taste and adjust the seasonings, adding more lemon if needed, and sweetener and salt to taste. The relish will last in the refrigerator for at least 1 week. It can also be canned or frozen.

✴ **Note:** If you like heat, add a chopped chile, such as a jalapeño or serrano, when sautéing the onion.

Sweet and Spicy Red Pepper Sauce

This sauce was inspired by the Sweet and Spicy Pepper Jam from the Jimtown Store in Healdsburg, California. Their jam is less saucy, but this is just as tasty. You do not have to make this spicy if you don't care for the heat: Seed the chile to tone down the heat, or eliminate it altogether. Drizzle the sauce over vegetables to serve as an appetizer, or serve over cooked grains and beans. After tasting it, you will likely find other uses for it.

MAKES ABOUT 1 CUP

1. Combine the bell peppers, chile pepper, if using, water, and 2 tablespoons of the vinegar in a pressure cooker. Lock on the lid. Bring to high pressure; cook for 5 minutes. Let the pressure come down naturally. Carefully open the cooker, tilting the lid away from you.

2. Add 1 tablespoon of the sweetener and stir. Transfer to a blender and let cool for 10 minutes, then blend until smooth. Pour back into the pressure cooker, or any other pot or pan, and cook over medium heat or on sauté for 5 to 10 minutes, until the mixture thickens. Add the remaining 1 teaspoon vinegar, remaining 1 teaspoon sweetener, and season with salt and cayenne, if desired. The sauce will last up to 1 month in the refrigerator.

5 minutes high pressure, natural release

3 medium red bell peppers, cored, seeded, and diced small

1 hot chile of your choice, seeds and ribs removed (or not), optional

½ cup water or vegetable stock

2 tablespoons plus 1 teaspoon white vinegar

1 tablespoon plus 1 teaspoon coconut palm or date sugar, or other sugar

Pinch of salt, optional

Pinch of cayenne pepper, optional

TWELVE

Desserts

The pressure cooker can easily be used to make desserts, from simple fruit-based numbers to "real" cakes. I don't eat a lot of sugary foods, but once in a while something sweet at the end of a meal is a nice treat. My go-to desserts are based on seasonal fruit, although I have branched out recently, much to my husband's delight, by making puddings, cakes, and *cheezecakes* in the pressure cooker. They turn out very well and most can be frozen for those times when you want dessert but don't want to make it. I think that you will be pleased with the results.

Topping

¼ cup almonds

1 cup "baby" or quick oats

¼ cup coconut palm sugar, Sucanat, or regular sugar

1 teaspoon ground cardamom

Fruit

3 medium apples, cored and thinly sliced (3 to 3½ cups)

1 cup frozen (not thawed) berries of any type

¼ cup coconut palm sugar, Sucanat, or regular sugar

1 teaspoon ground cinnamon

½ teaspoon grated nutmeg

¼ teaspoon ground cardamom

¼ cup water

1 to 2 teaspoons lemon juice, to taste

1½ tablespoons arrowroot powder

Apple Berry Crisp or Not-So-Crisp

This dessert can be made two different ways: with the more typical crispy oat topping or with the oats stirred in—which I first did by mistake. The oats throughout lack crispness, but with almonds they add an appealing texture.

Enjoy as is or serve with vegan vanilla ice cream, or sweeten nondairy yogurt and drizzle that on top.

SERVES 4

1. To make the topping: Put the almonds in a blender or food processor and chop coarsely, or do the same with a knife. Dry sauté the almonds and oats in a skillet over medium-high heat for 3 to 5 minutes, until toasted; transfer to a small bowl. Stir in the sugar and cardamom and set aside.

2. To prepare the fruit: Combine the apples and berries in a large bowl and add the sugar, cinnamon, nutmeg, and cardamom. Toss with the apples to coat. Add the water and lemon juice, and then the arrowroot. Stir to combine. Transfer the fruit mixture to a 1½- to 2-quart casserole that fits into the pressure cooker.

3. Sprinkle the oat topping over the apple mixture. (Or alternately, mix the topping into the apples and berries.) Cover the dish.

4. Add 1½ cups water to the pressure cooker. Add a trivet or rack to elevate the dish above the water (see page 14). Create a set of helper handles (see page 15). Place the handles on top of the rack. Set the casserole dish onto the trivet in the cooker.

5. Lock on the lid. Bring to high pressure; cook for 25 minutes. Let the pressure come down naturally. Carefully open the cooker, tilting the lid away from you. Using the helper handle, carefully take the casserole dish out of the cooker. Remove the cover from the dish and let cool for a few minutes before serving.

Variation: For a moister topping, combine 3 tablespoons almond butter and 3 tablespoons maple syrup with the toasted oats rather than the almonds and sugar. After removing the cover, broil for 3 to 5 minutes to crisp the topping.

Apple Raisin Walnut Cake

I'm not sure whether to call this a bread, cake, or pudding—in any case, it turns out moist and delicious. It's best to wrap it up and put it in the refrigerator after it cools, or wrap in waxed paper and put in the freezer. Then, any time you feel like eating dessert, just take a piece out. It's better than any store-bought cake because it's made from real ingredients. The cake is gluten-free; you can probably make it with gluten-containing flour, but it's so good as is, why bother?

MAKES 1 CAKE, 8 TO 10 PIECES

1. Spray a 1½- to 2-quart casserole dish or glass container that fits into your pressure cooker with cooking spray and set aside.

2. Combine the flours, flour mix, sugars, baking soda, baking powder, cinnamon, ginger, and cardamom, if using, in a large bowl. Add the lemon zest, walnuts, and raisins and stir well. Stir in the apples.

3. Combine the ground flax and juice in a medium bowl and stir well. Let sit for 5 minutes. Stir in the applesauce and vinegar.

4. Add the wet ingredients to the dry ingredients and stir until well-combined. Pour into the prepared dish.

5. Add ¾ cup water to the pressure cooker. Add a trivet or rack to elevate the dish above the water (see page 14). Create a set of helper handles (see page 15) to enable you to remove the dish, and set them on the trivet. Place the dish on the trivet and cover with foil or put on a lid.

6. Lock on the lid. Bring to high pressure; cook for 35 minutes. Let the pressure come down naturally. Carefully open the cooker, tilting the lid away from you.

7. Remove the dish and set on a cooling rack. Remove the cover carefully so any accumulated moisture does not drip onto the cake. Let cool for at least 20 minutes. The cake will continue to firm up as it cools.

Vegetable cooking spray

½ cup teff or buckwheat flour

1 cup gluten-free all-purpose baking flour

¼ cup Sucanat, coconut palm, or brown sugar

⅓ cup organic sugar

1 teaspoon baking soda

½ teaspoon baking powder

1 teaspoon ground cinnamon

½ teaspoon ground ginger

¼ teaspoon ground cardamom, optional

½ teaspoon grated lemon zest

¾ cup chopped walnuts or pecans

½ cup raisins

2 cups sliced peeled sweet-tart apples, such as Fuji, Jonathan, or Rome

3 tablespoons ground flax seeds

½ cup apple juice or water

¾ cup applesauce

2 teaspoons white vinegar or lemon juice

DESSERTS

287

Vegetable cooking spray

1 cup gluten-free all-purpose baking flour

⅓ cup almond flour

1 teaspoon baking powder

1 teaspoon baking soda

¼ teaspoon salt

6 tablespoons cocoa powder

½ cup coconut palm sugar

¼ cup Sucanat

3 tablespoons golden or brown flax seeds, ground

½ cup plus 3 tablespoons water

½ cup applesauce

1 tablespoon white vinegar

1 teaspoon vanilla extract

⅓ cup chocolate chips; or your favorite chocolate bar, chopped

Moist Chocolate Cake

This is the cake that I served at my son's birthday parties because I wanted a dessert that looked familiar to the other children. The ones who liked chocolate always ate it with gusto. Since it's gluten-free, if you are a little overzealous with the batter, it's not likely to get tough. If you want to make it richer, add 2 tablespoons of a neutral oil such as sunflower, untoasted pure sesame, or canola, or melted coconut oil, but I find it unnecessary to do so. Leftovers can be wrapped well and frozen for up to 3 months.

MAKES 1 CAKE, 12 PIECES

1. Spray a 1½- to 2-quart casserole that fits into your pressure cooker with cooking spray.

2. In a large bowl, combine the flour mix, almond flour, baking powder, baking soda, salt, and cocoa and stir well.

3. In a medium bowl, combine the sugar, Sucanat, flax, water, applesauce, vinegar, and vanilla. Let sit for 5 minutes, until the flax seeds get a little sticky.

4. Quickly stir together the wet ingredients with the dry ingredients, along with the chocolate chips, until just combined. Pour the batter into the prepared dish. Cover the dish.

5. Add 1 cup water to the pressure cooker. Add a trivet or rack to elevate the dish above the water (see page 14). Create a set of helper handles (see page 15) to enable you to remove the casserole. Lower the dish into the cooker, using a helper handle.

6. Lock on the lid. Bring to high pressure; cook for 22 minutes. Let the pressure come down naturally. Carefully open the cooker, tilting the lid away from you. Carefully remove the baking dish, using the foil handle, if necessary, and uncover.

7. Let cool on a rack for at least 30 minutes and then put a plate over the baking dish. Invert the dish and turn out the cake. Turn the cake back over so the top side is up. Let cool and serve.

Pear Almond Upside-Down Cake

Photo, page I-4

The key to making this lovely cake in the pressure cooker is to have a foil helper handle available and to use the right size vessel. I use a 1½-quart glass storage bowl or round casserole dish.

MAKES 1 (8-INCH) CAKE, 8 TO 12 PIECES

1. Spray a 1½- to 2-quart glass dish or other vessel that fits into your pressure cooker with cooking spray. Sprinkle with the coconut sugar and shake the dish to coat evenly. Arrange the pear slices in the dish in a swirl pattern from the inside out. Sprinkle the toasted almonds on top of the pear.

2. In a large bowl, combine the flour mix, almond flour, sugar, baking powder, baking soda, arrowroot, and salt and mix well. Add the lemon zest to the dry ingredients and mix well.

3. In a medium bowl, whisk together the milk, flax, and lemon juice. Let stand for at least 5 minutes, until the mixture thickens.

4. Stir the wet mixture into the dry mixture by quickly folding it in. The batter will seem a bit sticky, and that's OK. Pour the batter over the pears and almonds. Cover the baking dish with a lid or foil.

5. Put 1 cup water into your pressure cooker. Add a trivet or rack to elevate the dish above the water (see page 14). Create a set of helper handles (see page 15) and set them on the trivet. Add the covered baking dish.

6. Lock on the lid. Bring to high pressure; cook for 22 minutes. Let the pressure come down naturally. Carefully open the cooker, tilting the lid away from you. Carefully remove the baking dish, using the helper handle, and uncover.

7. Let cool for at least 30 minutes and then put a plate over the baking dish. Invert and turn out the cake. Let cool and serve.

Cranberry Upside-Down Cake: Mix ½ teaspoon allspice into the coconut sugar for the bottom of the dish. Use 1 cup fresh cranberries instead of the pear. Use the nut of your choice. Proceed with the recipe.

---

22 minutes high pressure, natural release

Vegetable cooking spray

2 tablespoons coconut sugar, brown sugar, or Sucanat

1 large firm ripe pear, cut into thin slices

¼ cup sliced or slivered almonds, toasted

1 cup gluten-free all-purpose baking flour

½ cup almond flour

¼ cup granulated organic sugar

1 teaspoon baking powder

½ teaspoon baking soda

1 tablespoon arrowroot powder

¼ teaspoon salt

1 teaspoon grated lemon zest

1 cup vanilla almond or other nondairy milk (if you don't have vanilla flavored, add 1 teaspoon vanilla extract)

3 tablespoons golden flax seeds, ground in a spice grinder or blender

1 tablespoon lemon juice

DESSERTS

289

20 minutes high pressure, natural release

Crust

1 cup quick oats

½ cup walnuts

½ cup chopped dates, soaked in ¼ cup water for 15 to 30 minutes, drained, but reserve soaking liquid

Filling

1 cup cashews, soaked in 1 cup water for 2 to 4 hours

½ cup coconut flour

¼ cup coconut palm sugar

½ cup vanilla nondairy milk

1 to 2 teaspoons grated lemon zest

2 tablespoons lemon juice

1 teaspoon vanilla extract

1 tablespoon arrowroot powder

½ cup fresh raspberries, blueberries, or strawberries; or 6 figs, sliced; or other fruit to top the cheezecake

Straightforward Cashew Lemon Cheezecake

I am not a dairy cheesecake fan, but I love vegan *cheezecake* as it's usually not cloyingly sweet or overly fatty. This comes together rather easily but seems like a very special dessert. It can be served with a variety of fruit toppings, depending upon what's in season. The star is the filling, although the crust is mighty tasty, too. You do, however, need to remember to soak the cashews for at least 2 hours in advance.

To get the best results, you need to use a high-speed blender. You can also make this in a regular blender or food processor, but know that you won't get the creamy result that is intended (it will still taste darned good). You will need a 6-, 7-, or 8-inch springform pan that fits inside your pressure cooker. If you don't want to make an oat crust, use your favorite raw crust.

MAKES 1 CAKE, 8 TO 12 SLICES

1. Add 1½ cups water to your pressure cooker and add a rack elevated above the water (see page 14). Create a set of helper handles (see page 15) to enable you to remove the pan.

2. To make the crust: Combine the crust ingredients in a mini food processor and process briefly until the mixture comes together. If it seems too dry, add a tablespoon at a time of the date soaking liquid until you have a cohesive "dough." It should be firm but not gooey. Press into the bottom and a little way up the sides of a springform pan that will fit in your pressure cooker.

3. To make the filling: Drain the cashews, reserving the soaking water. Add the cashews and half the soaking water to a high-speed blender or food processor and process until smooth. Add more water, if necessary. Add the coconut flour, palm sugar, milk, lemon zest, lemon juice, and vanilla to the blender or processor. Blend well. Add the arrowroot and blend again.

4. Pour the filling into the crust, smoothing out the top. Cover the pan with foil or a cover. Lower the pan into the pressure cooker, using the helper handle, if necessary.

5. Lock on the lid. Bring to high pressure; cook for 20 minutes. Let the pressure come down naturally. Carefully open the cooker, tilting the lid away from you.

6. Using the helper handle, carefully take the pan out of the cooker. Remove the cover carefully so any accumulated moisture does not drip onto the cake. Set the pan on a rack to cool. Place the fruit on top of the cheezecake. Let cool for at least 30 minutes, then refrigerate for at least 1 hour before removing the outer part of the pan and serving.

Filling

1 cup sunflower seeds, soaked in 1 cup water for at least 2 or up to 8 hours

1 cup cashew meal, or you can grind cashews into a fine meal

1 tablespoon soy yogurt

1 cup canned or firm fresh-cooked pumpkin or other firm winter squash, such as kabocha

½ cup coconut palm sugar

¼ cup coconut flour

1 tablespoon arrowroot powder

2 teaspoons pumpkin pie spice, store-bought or homemade (page 44)

1 teaspoon grated fresh ginger

Crust

1 cup quick or "baby" oats

½ cup chopped pecans or walnuts

½ cup chopped dates, soaked in ½ cup water

1 to 2 teaspoons ground ginger

292

Pumpkin Ginger Cheezecake

WITH PUMPKIN CASHEW TOPPING

This fermented cheezecake with a gingery crust is worth the time it takes to make. If you are a traditional cheesecake lover, your vegan cheesecake yearning will be fulfilled with the creamy, tangy flavor and "just right" texture, which can be best achieved only with a high-speed blender. You have to culture the base at least 8 hours or overnight, but then you're ready to proceed. Use canned or fresh-cooked drained pumpkin or other squash (kabocha is especially wonderful). If you can find vegan gingersnaps, use them, processed with a little water, instead of the pecan/oat crust. If you want to use dates for sweetening the filling, feel free, although I did not test it that way.

Freeze any remaining cheezecake in single-slice portions by wrapping them well in waxed paper or parchment and storing them in a freezer bag. Take them out and allow them to briefly defrost when life calls for dessert.

MAKES 1 CAKE, 16 TO 18 THIN SLICES

1. To make the filling: Drain the sunflower seeds, reserving the soaking water, and add to a high-speed blender. Add ½ cup of the soaking water and blend for at least 1 minute. If it seems too stiff, like thick paste and not thick cream, add another ½ cup soaking water and blend again. Add the cashew meal and blend until smooth. If the mixture seems too thick, add 1 tablespoon or so of nondairy milk until the mixture blends well and is firm, yet creamy. Pour this mixture into a container with a cover. Stir in the yogurt. Cover and let sit at room temperature for at least 8 hours or overnight.

2. Open the container. The mixture should smell sour. Taste to see if it is. (Even if it isn't sour, it will still be good to use but the goal is to have a fermented cheeze.) Transfer to the blender and add the pumpkin, sugar, flour, arrowroot, pumpkin pie spice, and ginger. Blend until smooth. Set the filling aside.

3. To make the crust: Combine all the ingredients in a food processor and pulse until just combined. Press this mixture onto the bottom and up the sides of a 7- or 8-inch springform pan that fits into your pressure cooker.

4. Pour the filling into the pan with the crust. Smooth out the top.

5. Add 1 cup water to the pressure cooker. Add a trivet or rack to elevate the dish above the water (see page 14). Create a set of helper handles (see page 15). Using the helper handles, lower the pan carefully into the cooker. Cover the pan with foil or a cover.

6. Lock on the lid. Bring to high pressure; cook for 25 minutes. Let the pressure come down naturally.

7. While the cake is cooking, make the topping: Blend the topping ingredients in a mini food processor or blender until smooth. Cover and refrigerate to chill.

8. When the pressure has released, carefully open the cooker, tilting the lid away from you. Using the helper handles, carefully take the pan out of the cooker. Set the pan on a rack and remove the cover carefully so any accumulated moisture does not drip onto the cake. Let cool for at least 1 hour. Chill for at least 3 hours.

9. Remove the outer part of the pan and put the cake on a nice plate. Spread the topping on top or serve on the side.

✱ **Note:** You can use the cultured seed and nut cheeze (the mixture prepared through Step 1) in other ways, such as making creamy cultured sauces by blending in flavored stock, vegetables, and herbs. You can also turn it into soft cheeze to spread on bread by adding garlic, chopped onion, herbs, sun-dried tomatoes, or your favorite seasoning or herb blend. It will last for up to 5 days in the refrigerator or up to 2 months in the freezer.

Topping

½ cup canned or firm fresh-cooked pumpkin or other firm winter squash, such as kabocha

½ cup cashew meal

2 to 3 tablespoons maple syrup

1 teaspoon pumpkin pie spice, store-bought or homemade (page 44)

1 or 2 minutes high pressure, running water release or quick release in bursts

6 medium to large freestone peaches, pits removed, partially peeled if you like, and cut in half through the equator (not up and down)

1 cup red wine

1 cinnamon stick

2 whole cloves

2 to 3 whole peppercorns

3 to 4 pieces of organic orange or lemon peel, inner white pith removed

1 piece fresh ginger, about the size of a quarter

¼ to ½ cup organic sugar, Sucanat, or coconut palm sugar

Peaches Poached in Red Wine

Poaching in red wine is a great way to cook any fruit. It's an easy process and produces peaches with a wonderful deep, winey flavor. Look for just ripe, but not overripe, peaches. They look best when partially peeled, halfway up the peach or in strips, but if that seems like too much work, cut them in half and leave them as is. If you are also able to get nectarines or apricots, add them to the peaches.

When pears are in season, pick not-quite-ripe ones and give them the same treatment, but peel them halfway up the fruit, top or bottom, slice lengthwise, and cook for up to 4 minutes at pressure.

Serve the poached fruit as is or with chopped almonds on top; drizzle with soy yogurt mixed with vanilla extract and cinnamon; or slice or chop and use the fruit as a topping for your favorite frozen dessert.

_____

SERVES 4 TO 6

1. Add the peaches to a pressure cooker, then the wine, cinnamon stick, cloves, peppercorns, citrus peel, and ginger. Lock on the lid. Bring to high pressure; cook for 2 minutes if using a stovetop cooker, 1 minute for an electric cooker.

2. If using a stovetop cooker, release the pressure by carefully running water over the cooker but not near the vent valve, or by turning the release valve slowly back and forth to immediately release pressure. If using an electric cooker, release the pressure by turning the pressure valve in short bursts. Once the pressure has dropped, remove the lid, tilting it away from you.

3. With a slotted spoon, carefully transfer the hot peaches from the liquid to a bowl and set aside. Add the sweetener of your choice, to taste, to the liquid and stir well. Simmer over medium heat or on sauté until the wine mixture is reduced by half. Pour the liquid through a strainer over the peaches, being careful as it is very hot.

4. Taste and add more sweetener, if necessary. Stir to combine. Pour the liquid over the peaches. Cool in the refrigerator. Store in the refrigerator for up to 1 week.

Cinnamon Applesauce

I guess I hadn't completely read my instruction manual when I first decided to make quick applesauce in the pressure cooker. The manual warns against doing so because apples foam when cooked and there is a chance that the pressure vent can get clogged, but as it turned out, I had no problem.

Once you know how easy it is to make applesauce, you'll likely never buy it from the store again. The most convenient method is to add the apples cut in halves or quarters or simply cored, cook them, and then run them through the food mill. Cooking the apples with the skin on adds more flavor and sometimes a beautiful pink tinge to the sauce. Can your applesauce using the proper canning procedures, or freeze it so that you can use it all year.

4 pounds or more apples of your choice, such as Empire, Pink Lady, or Macintosh, washed and quartered

½ cup water

2 cinnamon sticks

Ground cinnamon

MAKES 2 QUARTS (OR 4 PINTS) OR MORE, DEPENDING UPON THE SIZE OF YOUR COOKER

1. Add the apples, water, and cinnamon sticks to the pressure cooker. Be sure to fill the cooker only half full as the apples will foam when they cook.

2. Lock on the lid. Bring to high pressure; cook for 5 minutes. Quick release the pressure. Remove the lid, carefully tilting it away from you.

3. Let the apples cool until they are no longer piping hot. With long tongs, carefully remove and discard the cinnamon sticks.

4. In batches, run the cooked apples through a food mill into a bowl to remove the skin, seeds, and core, if there is any left. Use a coarse blade if you like your sauce chunkier, a fine blade if you like your applesauce smooth. Sprinkle in ground cinnamon to taste.

5. Transfer to pint or quart jars or freezer containers. Store in the refrigerator for up to 1 week, or freeze for up to 3 months.

✽ **Note:** You shouldn't need any sweetener unless your apples are very tart. If so, add ¼ to ½ cup sugar or other sweetener after you have processed the apples.

DESSERTS

¼ cup water

1¼ cups diced rhubarb (about
3 stalks)

3 cups sliced strawberries
(about 1½ baskets)

½ cup chopped date pieces
with oat coating or chopped
dates

Strawberry Rhubarb Sauce

My mother loved strawberries paired with rhubarb, so I was exposed to the combination at a young age, mostly as a pie filling. But you don't need to bake a pie to enjoy this thick sauce, which is not too sweet and not too tart. Serve it over vegan ice cream (coconut vanilla is especially good), or spooned over soy yogurt (see page 266), or eat as is. Or fill a simple no-bake pie made with a date-nut crust similar to the one used for either of the cheezecakes (see page 290 or 292).

If your berries are tart, you may want to use up to double the amount of dates, to taste. The oat flour that coats the date pieces helps thicken the sauce. This is a wonderful sauce to make in double batches. Freeze half to defrost in the dead of winter and add color and sweetness to the end of any meal.

MAKES 2 CUPS

1. Put the water in a pressure cooker. Add the rhubarb, then the berries and then the date pieces. Do not stir.

2. Lock on the lid. Bring to high pressure; cook for 2½ minutes. Quick release the pressure. Carefully open the cooker, tilting the lid away from you.

3. Stir well. Serve warm or let cool. Store in the refrigerator for up to 5 days or in the freezer for up to 3 months.

Triple-Ginger Pear Sauce

This simple sauce highlights the contrast between spicy ginger and sweet pears. Each type of ginger adds its own flavor to the sauce. If you like star anise, add one or two. If you find the sauce a bit too sweet, add the lemon juice to tone it down. Spoon over your favorite frozen dessert, serve as is, or mix into your morning oatmeal for a change of pace.

MAKES 2 CUPS

1. Put the water in a pressure cooker, then add the pears, fresh ginger, candied ginger, ground ginger, and star anise, if using.

2. Lock on the lid. Bring to pressure; cook for 3 minutes. Quick release the pressure. Carefully open the cooker, tilting the lid away from you. Let the mixture sit with the lid off or ajar for 5 minutes to cool.

3. Remove the star anise, if you added it. Transfer the mixture to a blender or food processor and pulse a few times until the sauce is to your liking, from chunky to very smooth.

4. Taste and add lemon juice, if desired. The sauce can be refrigerated for up to 1 week or frozen for up to 3 months.

¼ cup water

3 or 4 firm, ripe pears, cored and chopped

1 teaspoon grated fresh ginger

¼ cup chopped candied ginger

1 teaspoon ground ginger

1 or 2 star anise, optional

1 to 2 teaspoons lemon juice, optional

DESSERTS

3 minutes high pressure,
quick release; 1 minute
high pressure,
quick release

2 quince, peeled and diced

1 cup prunes, pitted if possible

1 cup red or white wine, or
grape or apple juice

2 apples (peeled or not), cored
and diced

2 pears (peeled or not), cored
and cut into chunks

2 cinnamon sticks

Whole cloves, cardamom, or
coriander, optional

Strips of zest from 1 organic
orange

Maple or agave syrup, to
taste

Toasted walnuts, optional

Spiced Fruit Compote
WITH CITRUS AND NUTS

I refer to fall and winter as apple-pear-citrus season. This compote turns these simple ingredients into a delight. Choose firm fruit. If you can't find quince, use Asian pears, or more apples and pears, and cut the pressure cooking time to just 1 minute. The prunes round out the flavor—feel free to substitute other dried fruit, such as raisins or apricots.

Pour the spiced concoction over sliced plain cake or vanilla coconut milk vegan ice cream, or just eat it right out of a bowl.

SERVES 4

1. Put the quince and prunes in the pressure cooker with ¾ cup of the wine. Lock on the lid. Bring to high pressure; cook for 3 minutes. Quick release the pressure. Carefully open the cooker, tilting the lid away from you.

2. Add the apples, pears, cinnamon sticks, the other spices, orange zest, and remaining ¼ cup wine. Lock on the lid. Bring to high pressure and cook for 1 minute longer. Quick release the pressure. Carefully open the cooker.

3. Remove the fruit with a slotted spoon. Simmer the liquid with the spices over medium heat or using the sauté function until reduced by half, 5 to 10 minutes. Pour the liquid through a strainer over the fruit.

4. Taste and add sweetener if needed. Serve topped with toasted walnuts, if desired.

Millet, Amaranth, and Sweet Potato "Pudding"

This recipe was an invention from when I was only able to eat soft foods for a few days. I was hungry, and this came to mind. I had it for breakfast, and the combination of well-cooked grains with soft, creamy sweet potato was so satisfying. I then polled people who said it would be good for dessert. Make it creamier and more pudding-like by adding another cup of almond milk. To make it very rich, add 1 tablespoon almond or pecan butter to each serving and sprinkle with ground cinnamon. No sweetener necessary.

¾ cup millet, rinsed

¼ cup amaranth or teff

1½ cups diced peeled sweet potato (1 small or medium)

1 cup vanilla almond milk

2 cups water

2 cinnamon sticks

2 tablespoons coconut flakes

3 tablespoons raisins

SERVES 4 TO 6

1. Combine all the ingredients in a pressure cooker. Lock on the lid. Bring to high pressure; cook for 10 minutes. Let the pressure come down naturally. Carefully open the cooker, tilting the lid away from you.

2. Transfer to a bowl and remove the cinnamon sticks. Serve warm, or let cool. Drizzle each bowl with up to ¼ cup more almond milk if you like it creamier or add it during the cooking process. Refrigerate for up to 3 days.

22 minutes high pressure, natural release; 5 minutes high pressure, 5 minutes natural release (then quick release)

Pinch of saffron threads

3 tablespoons hot or boiling water

3 cups vanilla nondairy milk, sweetened or unsweetened

1 cup short- or medium-grain brown rice

Pinch of salt

½ cup dried tart cherries

¼ cup amaranth or teff

Your favorite sweetener

3 to 4 tablespoons toasted pistachio nut meats, whole or chopped

Saffron Rice Pudding
WITH DRIED CHERRIES AND PISTACHIOS

Do you love rice pudding but want something just a bit more complex? This is it. The amaranth adds a little texture, and the saffron adds an exotic aroma and beautiful color. If you don't have amaranth or teff, use 1¼ cups rice and cook the pudding at high pressure for 25 minutes with natural release. The dried cherries add intrigue, but if you can't find them or don't like them, substitute raisins. Pistachios add nice color and texture contrast. This makes a simple dessert or a wonderful breakfast for those times when you are tired of steel-cut oats.

SERVES 4 TO 6

1. Combine the saffron with the water in a small bowl and let sit for at least 5 minutes.

2. Pour the milk into a pressure cooker and add the rice, salt, saffron and its soaking water, and ¼ cup of the cherries. Lock on the lid. Bring to high pressure; cook for 20 minutes. Let the pressure come down naturally. Carefully open the cooker, tilting the lid away from you.

3. Add the amaranth and lock the lid back on. Bring to high pressure and cook for 5 minutes. Let the pressure come down naturally for 5 minutes, then quick release any remaining pressure. Carefully remove the lid.

4. Transfer the pudding to a bowl and add the remaining ¼ cup cherries and sweetener to taste. Top with pistachios and serve. Store in the refrigerator for up to 3 days.

Spiced Quinoa Pudding
WITH CRANBERRIES AND RAISINS

This quick, easy-to-make whole grain pudding is sweet from the nondairy milk, dried fruit, warming spices, and the double dose of vanilla. Vanilla beans are expensive, so using one is optional, but I find it enhances the vanilla flavor of this pudding. Enjoy any leftovers for breakfast, if you like.

SERVES 4 TO 6

1. Heat a stovetop pressure cooker over medium heat or set an electric cooker to sauté. Add the quinoa and dry sauté for 1 to 2 minutes to toast it a bit. Turn off sauté if using an electric cooker. Add the milk, raisins, cranberries, cinnamon sticks, and vanilla bean, if using.

2. Lock on the lid. Bring to high pressure; cook for 5 minutes. Let the pressure come down naturally. Carefully open the cooker, tilting the lid away from you.

3. Using tongs, carefully remove the cinnamon sticks and vanilla bean. You can cut the vanilla bean in half and scrape the seeds into the pudding with a knife, or set it aside as described in the note below. Add the ground cinnamon, cardamom, vanilla extract, and salt, if using. Stir and serve warm or let cool. Drizzle with more almond milk, if desired.

∗ Note: You can rinse off the vanilla bean, let it dry, and then use it to flavor sugar, or use it again in another recipe, such as steel-cut oats.

1 cup quinoa, rinsed

2 cups vanilla sweetened almond milk

½ cup raisins

¼ cup dried cranberries

1 to 2 cinnamon sticks

½ vanilla bean, optional

1½ teaspoons ground cinnamon

¼ teaspoon ground cardamom

1 teaspoon vanilla extract

Pinch of salt, optional

DESSERTS

½ cup small pearl (not instant) tapioca

2 cups almond or any nondairy milk

Pinch of salt, optional

¼ cup organic sugar or blonde coconut palm sugar

1 teaspoon vanilla extract

½ teaspoon lemon zest

2 cups fresh berries of your choice, sliced as needed

Fresh mint, for garnish

Tapioca Berry Parfait

Photo, page I-14

Making dessert doesn't get much easier than this. Be sure to use a 6-quart (or larger) cooker as this gets very foamy, which can clog the vent or cause spewing liquid in a smaller pot. Make a double batch if you have enough room; it's that good.

––––––––
SERVES 4

1. Place the tapioca pearls in a fine mesh strainer and rinse under running water for 30 seconds.

2. Add the milk to a pressure cooker. Add the tapioca and salt, if using, and stir. Lock on the lid. Bring to high pressure; cook for 4 minutes. Let the pressure come down naturally. Quick release any remaining pressure after 20 minutes. Open the lid carefully, tilting it away from you.

3. Stir in the sugar, vanilla, and lemon zest.

4. Spoon 2 tablespoons berries into the bottom of 4 pretty bowls or parfait glasses. Add about ¼ cup tapioca, then 3 tablespoons berries. Add another ¼ cup tapioca and top with berries. Garnish with mint.

Variation: If stone fruits are in season, substitute chopped stone fruit for the berries.

Acknowledgments

It almost takes a small village to massage, knead, and shape words and photos, and masterfully turn them into a cookbook. I have deep gratitude for everyone who helped, listed in a random order. If I didn't specifically mention you by name, I am still eternally grateful.

My husband, Rick, has stood by me through it all, providing many much-needed hugs during long days of writing and cooking. He helped smooth my hair after long bouts of hair-pulling.

Barbara Stone, my mostly daily rock, heartfelt friend, and so much more.

Beth Shephard, my agent, assisted throughout this project, listened well when necessary, and gave me good advice plus a few much-needed laughs.

Nicole Steen, my former virtual assistant, made the spreadsheets sparkle. She gracefully coordinated the recipe testing team, which was a project unto itself.

Dana Martin, my former virtual intern, who took on a number of behind-the-scenes critical tasks, including dealing with my website, which was ailing at the time.

My recipe testers, listed in alphabetical order: Sara Bir, Donna Burns, LaJuana Dunn, Sue Ferguson, Roberta Joiner, Martha Josey, Toni Kulma, Sharon McRae, Deborah Plowman, Laurie Reaume, Deborah Schapiro, Zannetta Smith, Warren Stone, Sarah Sturm, Chelsea Stroh, Sigrid Trombley, and Shirley Utz, some of whom went above and beyond what was asked. A few were unstoppable and told me how grateful they were to be doing the testing. To all of them I am deeply indebted and beyond grateful. Without recipes, there is no cookbook.

My editor at Houghton Mifflin Harcourt, Adam Kowit, and his assistant, Molly Aronica, who continued to ask questions, helped refine my writing, and encouraged me to keep going through some tough times. I thank everyone else on the team, too, including copy editor Deri Reed, production editor Jamie Selzer, and designer Alissa Faden.

Photographer Lauren Volo and food stylist Molly Shuster took the words on the page and turned them into highly edible, and beautiful, food. It was a pleasure to see them in action. Illustrator Olivia De Salve Villedieu, who was able to take my simple drawings and mediocre photographs and turn them into useful illustrations.

My friends, who took "extra" food off my hands, and provided support as I sat glued to my computer or stood cooking in the kitchen. My friends Shirley and Wendy got me out of the house for necessary, almost-weekly walks that helped me maintain my sanity and keep my back intact.

I am deeply indebted to my yoga teachers, Clare Venet and Shannan Donovan, without whom I would not have the stamina, compassion, and clarity to complete a project like this.

Social media participation has been invaluable to my learning about what people want, and need, to know about pressure cooking. A number of Facebook Instant Pot groups have been especially supportive of my work. I now consider many to be true friends.

Lorna Sass, who paved the way by writing the first popular modern pressure cooker cookbook, *Cooking Under Pressure*, in 1989. It's been my pleasure to know her and to get her advice and counsel over the years.

The following pressure cooker manufacturers (in alphabetical order) contributed to my already too large pressure cooker collection: B/R/K, Breville, Cuisinart, Fagor, Fissler, Instant Pot, and Magefesa. Due to this, I was able to test the recipes in a number of different types and sizes of pressure cookers.

I'd especially like to thank everyone who has previously purchased my books and read my blog. Thank you for walking the path with me, as we continue to evolve while under pressure.

Resources

There are many companies that have ingredients and equipment that I use and like. There will be companies that introduce products after this book goes to press. These are just some of the companies that currently have the items that appeal to me and make my cooking life easier. I hope that they will do the same for you.

BEANS AND GRAINS

Bob's Red Mill The largest company carrying a wide assortment of beans and grains, and flours, which are available in many stores. They also do mail order.

bobsredmill.com (800) 349-2173

Lotus Foods Importer of an amazing array of organic rice from various parts of the world, but mostly from Asia. They have rice in colors ranging from white to black and brown, green, pink, and red.

lotusfoods.com (866) 972-6879

Purcell Mountain Farms A wide range of rice, as well as a large assortment of lentils and conventional and organic beans. They now also sell spices, dried mushrooms, and mushroom powders.

purcellmountainfarms.com (208) 267-0627

Rancho Gordo Twenty to thirty varieties of heirloom beans, dried posole (hominy), wild rice, amaranth, quinoa, Mexican oregano, and chocolate.

ranchogordo.com (707) 259-1935

Tierra Vegetables A variety of beans grown and sold each year, available by mail order. They also have the most amazing chipotle peppers, smoked on-site. They are local to me in Sonoma County, California.

tierravegetables.com (707) 837-8366

Timeless Food Organic split peas, black chickpeas, six types of lentils, and purple hull-less barley.

timelessfood.com

SPICES

Mountain Rose Herbs Many different bulk organic herbs and spices.

mountainroseherbs.com (800) 879-3337

Tierra Vegetables They have the best chipotles (smoked chiles) and chipotle pepper powder, as well as smoked onion salt and smoked onions and tomatoes.

tierravegetables.com (707) 837-8366

Whole Spice Offers freshly ground spices in varying quantities with wonderful spice blends, if you don't want to make your own.

wholespice.com (707) 778-1750

MISCELLANEOUS FOODS

Goldmine Natural Foods Carries a wide selection of beans, grains, miso, and other macrobiotic and natural food items.

goldminenaturalfoods.com (800) 475-3663

South River Miso Located in Massachusetts, this is my favorite American-made miso. You might be able to find it at your local natural foods store or you can order it in the non-summer months directly from them. They also sell incredible tamari.

southrivermiso.com (413) 369-4057

PRESSURE COOKERS

As I write this, I am pretty sure that another pressure cooker is being released into the marketplace. I have used many different cookers, some of which have appealed to me more than others.

Here is my short list of pressure cooker manufacturers that have products in the marketplace. This list is not all-inclusive:

Fagor America Offers the most well known and generally affordable "modern" pressure cookers in a variety of styles and sizes, ranging from 4-quart to 10-quart, as well as sets of two sizes with one pressure lid and glass lid plus accessories. They also have electric pressure cookers available.

fagoramerica.com/cookware

Fissler These cookers have patented safety valves and large indicator rods. They are heavy, shiny stainless steel, and are beautiful. They come in sizes from 2.7-quart to 10.8-quart, sold individually or in sets.

fisslerstore.com

Kuhn Rikon This Swiss company offers beautiful stainless steel cookers that come in sizes from 2.5 quart to 12 quart.

http://us.kuhnrikon.com

Magefesa Offers many different models with a variety of prices. The "modern" Super Fast cookers are the type that you want. They range in size from 4.2-quart to 8.5-quart and offer two-pot sets.

magefesausa.com

ELECTRIC COOKERS

Breville Offers the 6-quart Fast Slow Cooker, which has a nonstick liner.

brevilleusa.com/the-fast-slow-cooker.html

Cuisinart Offers a 6-quart cooker called the CPC-600, which has low and high settings, with a sauté function and a nonstick interior inner pot.

cuisinart.com

Fagor Offers a 6-quart three-in-one model with a nonstick interior, plus a stainless inner pot as an accessory, and a new LUX seven-in-one model that comes in a 6-quart size and an 8-quart size with a ceramic-coated interior that has a yogurt setting.

fagoramerica.com/cookware

Instant Pot Offers a 5- or 6-quart cooker with one setting (high), or the Duo with low and high settings. Both are multifunctional, and all models have a stainless steel inner pot. The Duo also has a yogurt function.

instantpot.com

Index

Note: Page references in *italics* indicate the page number for recipe photos in the color insert.